Ageing and
Development

ABOUT THE EDITORS

Rob Vos is Director of the Development Policy and Analysis Division at the Department of Economic and Social Affairs of the United Nations, New York, and Affiliated Professor of Finance and Development at the Institute of Social Studies, The Hague.

José Antonio Ocampo is Professor in the Professional Practice of International and Public Affairs at Columbia University, New York. At the time of writing he was Under-Secretary General for Economic and Social Affairs at the United Nations.

Ana Luiza Cortez is Chief of the Secretariat of the Committee for Development Policy at Department of Economic and Social Affairs of the United Nations, New York.

Ageing and Development

Edited by
Rob Vos, José Antonio Ocampo and Ana Luiza Cortez

Zed Books
London and New York

Published in association with the UNITED NATIONS

Ageing and Development was first published in 2008.

Published in association with the United Nations

Published in the Indian Subcontinent, South East Asia (except Malaysia and Singapore) and Africa by
ORIENT LONGMAN PRIVATE LIMITED
Registered Office: 3-6-752 Himayatnagar, Hyderabad 500 029 (A.P.), India
Email: orientswan@gmail.com
Other Offices: Bangalore, Bhopal, Bhubaneshwar, Chennai, Ernakulam, Guwahati, Hyderabad, Jaipur, Kolkata, Lucknow, Mumbai, New Delhi and Patna

Published in the UK, Europe, USA, Canada and Australia by
ZED BOOKS LIMITED
7 Cynthia Street, London N1 9JF, UK and
Room 400, 175 Fifth Avenue, New York, NY 10010, USA
www.zedbooks.co.uk
Distributed in the USA on behalf of Zed Books by
Palgrave Macmillan, a division of St Martin's Press, LLC
175 Fifth Avenue, New York, NY 10010, USA

Published worldwide by the United Nations and distributed worldwide via the UN specialized network of agents
United Nations Publications
2 United Nations Plaza Room DC2-853, New York, NY 10017, USA
https://unp.un.org Email: publications@un.org

United Nations' sales number: E.08.II.A.9
ISBN: 978 81 250 3526 8 Pb (Orient Longman)
ISBN: 978 1 84813 052 4 Hb (Zed Books)
ISBN: 978 1 84813 053 1 Pb (Zed Books)

A catalogue record for this book is available from the British Library
US CIP data is available from the Library of Congress

Cover design by Rogue Four Design
Printed in India by Graphica Printers, Hyderabad 500 013

Contents

EXPLANATORY NOTES

The following symbols have been used in the tables throughout the book:

..	**Two dots** indicate that data are not available or are not separately reported.
–	**A dash** indicates that the amount is nil or negligible.
-	**A hyphen** (-) indicates that the item is not applicable.
-	**A minus sign** (-) indicates deficit or decrease, except as indicated.
.	**A full stop** (.) is used to indicate decimals.
/	**A slash** (/) between years indicates a crop year or financial year, for example, 1990/91.
-	**Use of a hyphen** (-) between years, for example, 1990-1991, signifies the full period involved, including the beginning and end years.

Reference to "dollars" ($) indicates United States dollars, unless otherwise stated.

Reference to "tons" indicates metric tons, unless otherwise stated.

Annual rates of growth or change, unless otherwise stated, refer to annual compound rates.

Details and percentages in tables do not necessarily add to totals, because of rounding.

The following abbreviations have been used:

AARP	formerly, American Association of Retired Persons
BIS	Bank for International Settlements
CASMU	Centro de Asistencia del Sindicato Medico del Uruguay
CCRC	continuing care retirement community
CIS	Commonwealth of Independent States
DB	defined benefit (pension scheme)
DC	defined contribution (pension scheme)
EBRI	Employment Benefit Research Institute
ESCAP	Economic and Social Commission for Asia and the Pacific
ESCWA	Economic and Social Commission for Western Asia
EU	European Union
EURAG	European Federation of Older Persons
FDI	foreign direct investment
FF	fully funded (pension scheme)
FIAPA	International Federation of Senior Citizens Associations

GDP	gross domestic product
GNP	gross national product
GSEs	government-sponsored enterprises
HALE	health-adjusted life expectancy
IAGG	International Association of Gerontology and Geriatrics
ICT	information and communication technologies
IFA	International Federation on Ageing
ILO	International Labour Organization
IMF	International Monetary Fund
NBER	National Bureau of Economic Research (Cambridge, Massachusetts)
NDC	notional defined contribution (pension scheme)
NORC	naturally occurring retirement community
OECD	Organisation for Economic Co-operation and Development
PAYG	pay-as-you-go (pension scheme)
PBGC	Pension Benefit Guaranty Corporation
PPP	purchasing power parity
PRED	Population, Resources, Environment and Development
R&D	research and development
REITs	real estate investment trusts
UN/DESA	Department of Economic and Social Affairs of the United Nations Secretariat
WHO	World Health Organization

COUNTRY GROUPINGS

The designations employed and the presentation of the material in this publication do not imply the expression of any opinion whatsoever on the part of the United Nations Secretariat concerning the legal status of any country, territory, city or area or of its authorities, or concerning the delimitation of its frontiers or boundaries.

The term "country" as used in the text of this report also refers, as appropriate, to territories or areas.

For analytical purposes, the following country groupings and subgroupings have been used:

Developed economies (developed market economies):

European Union, Iceland, Norway, Switzerland, Canada, United States of America, Australia, Japan, New Zealand.

Subgroupings of developed economies:

Europe:

European Union (EU):

Austria, Belgium, Bulgaria, Cyprus, Czech Republic, Denmark, Estonia, Finland, France, Germany, Greece, Hungary, Ireland, Italy, Latvia, Lithuania, Luxembourg, Malta, Netherlands, Poland, Portugal, Romania, Slovakia, Slovenia, Spain, Sweden, United Kingdom of Great Britain and Northern Ireland.

EU-25:

EU excluding Bulgaria and Romania.

EU-15:

EU-12 plus Denmark, Sweden and the United Kingdom of Great Britain and Northern Ireland.

EU-12 (euro area):

Austria, Belgium, Finland, France, Germany, Greece, Ireland, Italy, Luxembourg, Netherlands, Portugal, Spain.

EU-10:

EU-25 minus EU-15.

Other Europe:

Iceland, Norway, Switzerland.

Economies in transition:

South-eastern Europe:

Albania, Bosnia and Herzegovina, Croatia, Montenegro, Romania, Serbia, the former Yugoslav Republic of Macedonia.

Commonwealth of Independent States:

Armenia, Azerbaijan, Belarus, Georgia, Kazakhstan, Kyrgyzstan, Moldova, Russian Federation, Tajikistan, Turkmenistan, Ukraine, Uzbekistan.

Developing economies:

Latin America and the Caribbean, Africa, Asia and the Pacific (excluding Japan, Australia, New Zealand and the member states of CIS in Asia).

Subgroupings of Latin America and the Caribbean:

South America and Mexico:

Argentina, Brazil, Chile, Colombia, Ecuador, Guyana, Mexico, Paraguay, Peru, Uruguay, Venezuela (Bolivarian Republic of).

Central America and the Caribbean:

All other countries in Latin America and the Caribbean.

Subgroupings of Africa:

Northern Africa:

Algeria, Egypt, Libyan Arab Jamahiriya, Morocco, Tunisia.

Sub-Saharan Africa:

All other African countries.

Subgroupings of Asia and the Pacific:

Western Asia:

Bahrain, Iraq, Israel, Jordan, Kuwait, Lebanon, Occupied Palestinian Territory, Oman, Qatar, Saudi Arabia, Syrian Arab Republic, Turkey, United Arab Emirates, Yemen.

East and South Asia:

All other developing economies in Asia and the Pacific (including China, unless stated otherwise). This group is further subdivided into:

South Asia:

Bangladesh, Bhutan, India, Iran (Islamic Republic of), Maldives, Nepal, Pakistan, Sri Lanka.

East Asia and the Pacific:

    East Asia:

        China

        Newly industrialized economies:

            Hong Kong Special Administrative Region of China, Republic of Korea, Singapore, Taiwan Province of China.

        Other East Asia:

            Democratic People's Republic of Korea, Mongolia.

    South-East Asia:

        Brunei Darussalam, Cambodia, Timor-Leste, Indonesia, Lao People's Democratic Republic, Malaysia, Myanmar, Philippines, Singapore, Thailand, Viet Nam.

    Oceania:

        Fiji, Kiribati, Marshall Islands, Micronesia (Federated States of), Papua New Guinea, Samoa, Solomon Islands, Tonga, Tuvalu, Vanuatu.

Least developed economies:

Afghanistan, Angola, Bangladesh, Benin, Bhutan, Burkina Faso, Burundi, Cambodia, Cape Verde, Central African Republic, Chad, Comoros, Democratic Republic of the Congo, Djibouti, Equatorial Guinea, Eritrea, Ethiopia, Gambia, Guinea, Guinea-Bissau, Haiti, Kiribati, Lao People's Democratic Republic, Lesotho, Liberia, Madagascar, Malawi, Maldives, Mali, Mauritania, Mozambique, Myanmar, Nepal, Niger, Rwanda, Samoa, Sao Tome and Principe, Senegal, Sierra Leone, Solomon Islands, Somalia, Sudan, Timor-Leste, Togo, Tuvalu, Uganda, United Republic of Tanzania, Vanuatu, Yemen, Zambia.

World Health Organization country and region classifications:

Africa:

    All African countries except Egypt, Libyan Arab Jamahiriya, Morocco, Somalia, Sudan, Tunisia.

Americas:

    All the countries of Central, Northern and South America and the Caribbean.

Eastern Mediterranean:

    Afghanistan, Bahrain, Djibouti, Egypt, Iran (Islamic Republic of), Iraq, Jordan, Kuwait, Lebanon, Libyan Arab Jamahiriya, Morocco, Oman, Pakistan, Qatar, Saudi Arabia, Somalia, Sudan, Syrian Arab Republic, Tunisia, United Arab Emirates, Yemen.

Europe:

    All of the Commonwealth of Independent States (CIS), Europe (including Turkey), Israel.

South-East Asia:

    Bangladesh, Bhutan, Democratic People's Republic of Korea, India, Indonesia, Maldives, Myanmar, Nepal, Sri Lanka, Thailand, Timor-Leste.

Western Pacific:

    Australia, Brunei Darussalam, Cambodia, China, Hong Kong Special Administrative Region of China, Japan, Lao People's Democratic Republic, Macao Special Administrative Region of China, Malaysia, Mongolia, New Zealand, Papua New Guinea, Philippines, Republic of Korea, Singapore, Viet Nam, and the Pacific islands.

ACKNOWLEDGEMENTS

This book presents a revised version of the *World Economic and Social Survey 2007: Development in an Ageing World* issued by the United Nations Department of Economic and Social Affairs in June 2007. It has been revised and updated by Rob Vos, José Antonio Ocampo and Ana Luiza Cortez, who were also responsible for the coordination and supervision of the original edition of the *Survey*. The following contributed to the original versions of the chapters of the *Survey*: Chapter I was prepared by Rob Vos with inputs from Diana Alarcón; Chapter II was prepared by John Wilmoth and Paulo Saad; Chapter III was prepared from inputs by Diana Alarcón, Peggy Kelly, Alexandre Sidorenko and Robert Venne; Chapter IV was prepared by Ana Cortez, Marva Corley, Piergiuseppe Fortunato, Peggy Kelly and Codrina Rada; Chapter V was prepared by Ana Cortez, Oliver Paddison, Alex Julca and Codrina Rada; and Chapter VI was prepared by Simon Cunningham, and Hiroshi Kawamura with inputs from Alexandre Sidorenko. In various capacities, valuable support to the original Survey was also provided by Jomo K.S., June Chesney, Leah C. Kennedy, Mary Nolan, Phillicia Waite, Michael Brodsky, Valerian Monteiro, Johan Scholvinck, Sergei Zelenev, and Hania Zlotnik.

NOTES ON THE CONTRIBUTORS

Diana Alarcón is a Senior Economic Affairs Officer at the Development Policy and Analysis Division at the Department of Economic and Social Affairs of the United Nations, New York.

Marva Corley is Economic Affairs Officer at the Development Policy and Analysis Division at the Department of Economic and Social Affairs of the United Nations, New York.

Simon Cunningham is a Senior Economic Affairs officer at the Development Policy and Analysis Division at the Department of Economic and Social Affairs of the United Nations, New York.

Piergiuseppe Fortunato is an Associate Economic Affairs Officer at the Development Policy and Analysis Division at the Department of Economic and Social Affairs of the United Nations, New York.

Alex Julca is Economic Affairs Officer at the Development Policy and Analysis Division at the Department of Economic and Social Affairs of the United Nations, New York.

Hiroshi Kawamura is Economic Affairs Officer at the Development Policy and Analysis Division at the Department of Economic and Social Affairs of the United Nations, New York.

Peggy Kelly is Social Affairs Officer at the Division for Social Policy and Development at the Department of Economic and Social Affairs of the United Nations, New York.

Oliver Paddison is Economic Affairs Officer at the Development Policy and Analysis Division at the Department of Economic and Social Affairs of the United Nations, New York.

Codrina Rada is Assistant Professor of Economics at the University of Utah and was at the time of writing an Associate Economic Affairs Officer at the Development Policy and Analysis Division at the Department of Economic and Social Affairs of the United Nations, New York.

Paulo Saad was at the time of writing with the Population Division of the Department of Economic and Social Affairs of the United Nations, New York.

Alexandre Sidorenko is with the Division for Social Policy and Development at the Department of Economic and Social Affairs of the United Nations, New York.

Robert Venne is with the Division for Social Policy and Development at the Department of Economic and Social Affairs of the United Nations, New York.

John Wilmoth is a Professor of Demography at the University of California at Berkeley and at the time of writing he was chief of the mortality section at the Population Division of the Department of Economic and Social Affairs of the United Nations, New York.

PREFACE

Ageing will have a profound impact on societies and will need to occupy an increasing amount of policymakers' attention in the 21st century. In the developed world, but also in many parts of the developing world, the share of older persons in the population is rising rapidly. Ageing is a reflection of success in the process of human development, as it is the result of lower mortality (combined with reduced fertility) and greater longevity. Ageing also provides new opportunities, arising from the active participation of older generations in the economy and society at large. Also, in those countries, primarily in the developing world, that still have a growing youth bulge, there is a window of opportunity for economic development. Population ageing also poses important challenges, especially the financial viability of pension systems, the cost of health care, and the full integration of older people as active agents of societal development.

This book is based on research conducted at the United Nations Department of Economic and Social Affairs for the World Economic and Social Survey 2007. It analyses the challenges and opportunities associated with ageing populations and aims to facilitate discussions in furthering the Madrid International Plan of Action on Ageing (MIPAA), adopted by member states of the United Nations in 2002. The MIPAA focuses on three sets of priorities: older people and development; advancing health and well-being into old age; and ensuring enabling and supportive environments for older persons.

The book underscores the need to fully recognize and better harness the productive and social contributions older persons can bring to societies but in many instances are prevented from doing so. It also emphasizes that the prospect of a shrinking labour force which must support an increasing older population is among the most pressing challenges. Changes in intergenerational relationships may affect the provision of care and income security for older persons, particularly in developing countries where family transfers often play a major role. Thus, societies must also cater for the particular needs of older populations in terms of the requisite health care, assistance in case of disabilities and appropriate living conditions. We argue that these challenges are not insurmountable, but societies everywhere need to put in place the required policies to confront them effectively. To support such adaptations, the international community will need to put population ageing prominently on the international development agenda.

Rob Vos, José Antonio Ocampo and Ana Luiza Cortez
New York, March 2008

Chapter I
Introduction

Ageing will be a dominant theme in the twenty-first century. Population ageing is probably one of the major achievements of modern societies. Major improvements in nutrition, sanitation, medicine, health care, education, knowledge and economic well-being in general have made it possible for people to live longer. Fertility and mortality rates have decreased. These factors are driving up the shares of older people in the total population in the developed world and, even more rapidly, in many developing countries.

In 2005, about 21 per cent of the population in the developed countries was aged 60 years or over. The proportion is projected to rise to 32 per cent in 2050. In the developing countries, only 8 per cent of the population was aged 60 years or over in 2005 but this share is expected to reach nearly 20 per cent by 2050, which means that the number of older persons in the developing countries will almost quadruple between 2005 and 2050. The increase will be much larger than in the developed countries and in the economies in transition and it is expected that by 2050 about 80 per cent of older persons (nearly 1.6 billion people) will live in what are now developing countries.

Population ageing poses important challenges, especially ones related to the financial viability of pension systems, the provision of adequate health and long-term care, and the full integration of older people as active agents of societal development. Ageing will also provide new opportunities, associated with the active participation of older generations in the economy and society at large. In countries with a still growing and younger workforce, primarily those in the developing world, there may be a window of opportunity for accelerated economic development. The *World Economic and Social Survey 2007* analyses these challenges and opportunities.

How old is old?

In demographic analysis, age 60 is typically taken as the dividing line between older and younger cohorts of the population. On the other hand, many people, especially in the developed countries, think of 65 as the cut-off point because it is at this age that many people become eligible for full pension and social security benefits for older persons; but such a cut-off point does not apply everywhere else. Old age, then, cannot be defined exactly because the concept does not have the same meaning in all societies. Nor, with the steady expansion of life expectancy, does it correspond to a specific time span. Often people are considered old not just because they are thought to be nearing the end of their expected lifespan but also because they undergo certain changes in their social roles and activities. Older persons may become grandparents, may work less or may stop working, or they may undertake different activities; and they also tend to be more prone to disease and disabilities than other adults. However, all of these changes evolve over time and are perceived differently across societies.

The average lifespan of human beings, for instance, continues to increase. Around 1900, life expectancy ranged from 45 to 50 years in the industrialized countries of the time and was beginning to increase in other areas as well. One century later, life expectancy stands at about 65 years for the world as a whole and it is expected to increase to 75 years by 2050. In developed countries, life expectancy averages 78 years and will increase to about 85 by 2050; in developing countries, it is expected to increase from 63 to 74 years between 2005 and 2050. It has also been observed, in developed countries at least, that though they live longer, people do not appear to spend more years in poor health over age 60.

Some industrialized countries, taking note of the enlarged lifespan of their population, have changed the retirement age in an effort to reduce the demographic pressure on pension and social security systems. In the United States of America, for example, the age at which a person becomes eligible for full social security benefits will increase gradually until it reaches 67 in 2027. France has made the number of years during which one must contribute to pension schemes dependent on changes in life expectancy. But aside from considerations of the effect of lifespan on the viability of pension systems, there is the fact that longer and healthier lives offer older people the opportunity to "rejuvenate" and increase their contribution to society.

Other countries may not have reached this stage as yet, however. In Africa, for instance, life expectancy averages 49 years, and in several countries in the region the figure is even lower. Moreover, most developing countries do not have well-developed pension systems. Thus, the assumption that people can retire at a certain age with a reasonable pension cannot be applied to large proportions of older people who continue working most of their life. Also, the fact that the number of years spent in poor health over age 60 tends to be higher in many developing countries relative to developed countries limits the contributions that older people can make.

All of these observations suggest that a more fluid concept of "older persons" is needed—one that would change over time (for instance, with life expectancy) and vary across social contexts. Understanding the specific conditions of older people in each country and their contribution to society is essential to identifying appropriate responses to ageing as an inevitable trend.

THE MADRID INTERNATIONAL PLAN OF ACTION ON AGEING

The complex challenges posed by population ageing are fully recognized in the Madrid International Plan of Action on Ageing (United Nations, 2002a) adopted by consensus by the Second World Assembly on Ageing on 12 April 2002. The Madrid Plan of Action aims "to ensure that persons everywhere are able to age with security and dignity and to continue to participate in their societies as citizens with full rights" (para. 10). At the same time, it clearly recognizes that the specific contributions and concerns of older persons must be placed within the context of the advancement of the objectives of the international development agenda, including the Millennium Development Goals.

Ageing as a process of physiologic deterioration that gradually impairs the capacity of people to function socially constitutes a continuum that requires multiple development responses. The Madrid Plan of Action provides the framework for incorporating the discussion of population ageing into the international debate on development and the implementation of national policies designed to respond to the challenge of building societies for all ages. The specific objectives of protecting the rights of older people and promoting their active participation in society, as defined by the Madrid Plan of Action, are based on the principle of equity in the distribution of benefits from growth and development. The three sets of priority directions identified by the Plan of Action—older persons and development; advancing health and well-being into old age; and ensuring enabling and supportive environments for older persons—encompass in detail the specific issues that concern the well-being of older people and the specific actions that would be required to meet their development needs, their health needs and their need to enjoy full participation in society.

AGEING AND DEVELOPMENT

This book analyses the challenges and opportunities associated with ageing populations and aims to facilitate discussions in furthering the Madrid Plan of Action and the broader policy debate on how societies should adapt to ageing populations. The next chapters analyse the challenges for population and migration policies (chapter II), adapting living conditions in ageing societies and empowering older persons (chapter III), economic growth and labour market policies (chapter IV), pension system reforms (chapter V), and the provisioning of adequate health and long-term care for older persons as populations age rapidly (chapter VI).

An ageing world population

The age distribution of the world's population is undergoing a profound transformation. As mortality and fertility have fallen, the age distribution has been shifting gradually to older ages. All regions of the world are experiencing this change. *Chapter II* analyses the major trends and factors underlying the demographic transition across major regions of the world. It shows increased life expectancy and reduced fertility rates as key factors driving the rapid process of population ageing that already has taken place during the twentieth century, and is continuing into the present century. In most developing countries, population ageing is taking place at an accelerated speed. Currently, 63 per cent of the world's older persons live in developing countries and by 2050, 79 per cent of the population aged 60 years or over, amounting to nearly 1.6 billion people, will reside in those countries

Population ageing is perceived as a process that is largely inevitable. Policy interventions intended to encourage childbearing in low-fertility countries are not expected to modify the process of population ageing to any substantial degree. Increases in the number of international migrants might alter the trend towards increases in the numbers of older persons in relation to the working-age population in developed countries. However, as demonstrated by the chapter, only very large—and unachievable—levels of migration could prevent old-age dependency ratios from rising. Changes in the population structure, then, may be inevitable, but they are also well understood and can therefore be anticipated.

Ageing and changing societies

Chapter III discusses how, with population ageing and the modernization of societies (including urbanization), the social environment within which people grow older is changing as well. Family sizes are declining and perceptions of intergenerational support and caring are changing. The fact that older persons increasingly live alone is putting heavier pressures on formal systems of long-term care and income support for older persons. Informal mechanisms (largely based on family support) have come under stress as well. Moreover, the many negative stereotypes of older persons depict them, for example, as imposing cost-related burdens on health and pension systems and as being "inevitably unproductive". These factors increase the risk of elder neglect and abuse. The chapter analyses these challenges in different contexts and suggests ways of dealing with these issues and of empowering older persons so as to increase their participation in society.

Changes in the living arrangements of older people have important policy implications in both developing and developed countries. Developed countries need to expand the supply of formal long-term care for older persons, including institutional living, as well as to develop alternative services to allow older persons to age in their home if they so desire. Developing countries confront even bigger challenges as they still need to provide basic infrastructure (water, sanitation, etc.) and social services to older people in addition to providing increased formal long-term care and developing new forms of informal care.

Guaranteeing and protecting their human rights as defined by the Universal Declaration of Human Rights (General Assembly resolution 217 A (III)) is an important means of reducing the risk of abuse of older persons and of empowering them. Complementary legislation may be needed in some countries to improve the legal framework in order to protect the rights of older persons, prevent abuse and neglect, and bolster their opportunities for participating in all aspects of social life. A better legal framework will not suffice, however. In addition, societies will need to find adequate mechanisms through which to prevent age discrimination in labour markets, ensure intergenerational solidarity through adequate old-age income security systems, and mobilize the resources needed to provide adequate health and long-term care.

Economic consequences of population ageing

Population ageing could, as analysed in *Chapter IV*, become a drag on economic growth unless anticipated declines in the labour force can be arrested or labour productivity increased. As mentioned, international migration is not regarded as a principal remedy, as it is believed that no country would admit the massive numbers of migrants required to stop old-age dependency ratios from rising in low-fertility countries. In those countries, measures providing incentives for increased labour participation of female and older workers may have greater potential. This in turn raises questions how to improve labour-market conditions so as to give greater opportunities to both female and older workers, and in this regard how to counter sex- or age-based discrimination in hiring practices and adapt training programmes to the needs of older workers. It is increased labour productivity growth that may in fact be needed the most if existing welfare levels are to be sustained and negative growth effects from shrinking labour forces averted.

In countries with still growing and relatively young labour forces, there may be a window of opportunity for enhanced growth. However, reaping this demographic dividend may not be easy, especially if there are other structural impediments to economic growth in developing countries (United Nations, 2006; Ocampo and Vos, 2007; and Ocampo, Jomo, and Vos, 2007).

Population ageing could also affect economic growth through changes in consumption and savings patterns. It is often expected that economies with high levels of child or old-age dependency will have a relatively low national saving rate, while economies with large shares of working-age population will have a high savings rate. This might then reduce the availability of global investment finance, since the countries with more advanced population ageing currently generate the bulk of world savings. However, as argued in chapter IV, it is very difficult to predict such developments, because many non-demographic factors have a more important influence on consumption and savings behaviour.

Ensuring old age economic security

It can be said with greater certainty that population ageing will strain systems of old-age income security. As examined in *Chapter V*, reduced labour participation and deteriorating health conditions increase the vulnerability to poverty at older ages. This holds in particular in developing countries where most older persons are not insured against health risks or do not have access to formal systems of old-age income protection. A universal social insurance mechanism providing a minimum pension benefit could overcome the risk of poverty at old age. This proposal may seem like an ambitious goal for many of the developing countries with very little social security coverage to begin with. The analysis of the chapter suggests, however, that basic social pension schemes seem affordable, even in most low-income countries and also after taking into account further population ageing in the next half-century.

Chapter V indicates that pension systems should be tailored to specific country contexts, but built up or reformed based on broad principles of which financial sustainability is but one. Intergenerational solidarity and adequacy of benefits with respect to providing sufficient income security for all should be other guiding principles. In practice, these principles appear to be best approached through national pension systems designed on the basis of multiple layers, the importance of each depending on the needs of different segments of society.

Much of the debate on pension systems, however, concentrates on the financial sustainability of alternative schemes. Measures aiming at strengthening existing systems by changing underlying parameters have been implemented in virtually every pay-as-you-go scheme. These are schemes where contributions paid by the current generation of workers are disbursed as benefits to today's retirees. In particular, measures are increasingly being adopted to raise the effective retirement age. In most countries, delaying retirement and staying longer in the workforce can go a long way towards keeping pay-as-you-go systems viable.

Other countries have focused on changing the design or structurally reforming their pension schemes and moved from pay-as-you-go scheme with defined benefits to a fully funded defined-contribution system. Under the latter, benefits are financed by the principal and return on previously invested contributions. Because of the capitalization of pension contributions, it was believed that the system would stimulate national savings and, through this, overall economic growth.

Despite their contribution to the deepening and development of financial markets, there is no unambiguous evidence that mandatory fully funded schemes have led to higher savings and growth. For one, the fiscal costs associated with the transition from one system to another are high and have negative implications for the public budget. Moreover, inasmuch as benefits depend on the rates of return on pension investments, full income security during old age is not guaranteed. Equally important, these schemes are not immune to the pressures exerted by a rising share of the non-working population.

Overall, however, demographic dynamics may not pose an insoluble problem for old-age pension schemes if growth can be accelerated. In fact, many reforms have overlooked the fact that regardless of the type of financing mechanism, all schemes face a similar sustainability problem as they all imply a claim towards the future output. Under both types of scheme a redistribution of income between the retired and the active populations has to take place. With increasing old-age dependency ratios, maintaining the same level of amount of old-age income security implies that either output growth will have to increase to facilitate this redistribution or greater pension contributions will have to be drawn from the working population.

Health and long-term care into old age

Population ageing will increase the demand for health and long-term care. Changing disease patterns are requiring adaptation in health-care systems. As analysed in *Chapter VI*, the extension of life expectancy around the world is being accompanied by an epidemiological transition implying a shift from a predominance of infectious diseases and high maternal and child mortality to that of non-communicable diseases, especially chronic illnesses. This is posing challenges to health-care systems. For developed countries the main concerns are with maintaining adequate levels and quality of care for an ageing population against a background of overall rising health care costs. The challenge for developing countries is much larger, as many face already a double health-cost burden: they may still have a high prevalence of communicable diseases among important parts of the population, while rapid population ageing is already putting increased pressure on scarce health-care resources.

Rising health costs should be expected in developed and developing countries alike. The chapter questions, however, whether population ageing is the main driver of increased health costs. In almost all countries, irrespective of their progress in the demographic transition, health costs as a percentage of output have risen over time. Other factors, such as prices of pharmaceuticals, the rising costs of ever-higher qualified health care personnel, new treatment methods and, in general, public pressure for better quality health care may be more important. If such cost-push factors can be contained, it should be well affordable to cope with the increased demand on health services owing to an ageing population, in what are, in any event, countries where levels of income can be expected to increase over time.

The provision of long-term care raises a different set of issues. In some developed countries, such provision tends to be supplied as part of a universal health system which is funded by increased taxation. In other countries, greater reliance is placed on the family and on the individual making provision for such care out of their own income. Yet, rapid changes in social norms, internal migration, greater female labour participation and the breakdown of the traditional extended family system are making the provision of such care especially difficult for many countries. This has given rise to the formulation of policies facilitating long-term care arrangements that offer a "home-like" environment for older persons as an extension of the existing family- or community-based support.

Moving forward

This book discusses the challenges posed by rapid population ageing and by changes in living arrangements with respect to promoting economic growth, ensuring income security for all at older ages, and advancing health and well-being into old age. We conclude that these challenges are large but that they can be overcome through well-focused policies and without excessive strain on available resources. A basic principle for such policies is the full recognition of the potential contributions to society that older persons can make.

The Madrid International Plan of Action on Ageing provides a framework for incorporating the discussion of population ageing into the international debate on development and the implementation of national policies to promote the development of societies for all ages. Yet, it is still necessary for governments and the international community to redouble efforts to mainstream ageing into the international development agenda.

In countries lacking basic pension systems, poverty among older persons tends to be higher than among people of working age and hence policies aiming at improving old-age income security should feature poverty reduction strategies. Employment policies should pay more attention to improving the working conditions and job opportunities of older workers, so as not only to improve prospects for the full participation of older persons in society but also to foster the sustainability of pension systems. Health policies will have to address more explicitly the double burden many developing countries are shouldering: these countries are still facing the challenge of reaching the Millennium Development Goals of reducing maternal and child mortality while at the same time readjusting their health-care systems to meet the needs of a growing older population.

Abuse of older persons and age-based discrimination are problems experienced in many countries. Action is required to redress these negative trends and promote the empowerment of older persons which is essential to ensuring their full participation in society.

Mainstreaming ageing into the global development agenda is crucial to the realization of the objectives identified in the Madrid Plan of Action. Creating, as envisaged, "a society for all ages" requires not only a strong global partnership to advance the commitments endorsed in that agenda, but also a stronger national partnership among all levels of government, civil society, the private sector and organizations for older persons aimed at translating the Plan of Action into practical action.

Chapter II
An ageing world population

Changing population age distributions

The age distribution of the world's population is undergoing a profound and unprecedented transformation. As mortality and fertility have fallen, attaining in many parts of the world levels never before seen in human history, the age distribution has been shifting gradually to older ages in a process known as "population ageing". The shift towards older ages is reflected in rising median ages of populations, increasing proportions of older persons and decreasing proportions of children. All regions of the world are experiencing this change, and those most advanced in the process are already facing the challenge of providing for the needs of a growing population of older persons.

Ageing societies can benefit from declining proportions of children and youth in the population, which imply that the relative weight of young persons in the non-productive ages decreases. Nevertheless, as the age distribution shifts upward, societies must reorient themselves to ensure that persons of all ages, including growing numbers of older persons, have the means or the support needed to maintain a decent standard of living. The present chapter describes the demographic foundations of population ageing and sets the stage for a discussion of its socio-economic implications.[1]

Underlying causes of changing age distributions

The historical increase of life expectancy is one of humanity's major achievements. Early in the history of humankind, the average length of life had ranged probably between 20 and 35 years, reflecting the heavy toll of mortality across the life course and especially among infants and children. By 1900, life expectancy ranged from 45 to 50 years in the industrialized countries of the time and was beginning to increase in other areas as well. One century later, life expectancy stood at about 65 years for the world as a whole and had surpassed 80 years in a few advanced countries. Thus, most of the historical increase in human life expectancy occurred during the twentieth century.

Increasing life expectancy and the major reductions in the risks of death that it reflects constitute one of the key components of the "demographic transition". The other major component of this process of demographic change is the historical reduction in the birth rate or in total fertility, that is to say, the average number of children born per woman. From historical levels of about 6 to 8 children per woman, fertility fell dramatically during the nineteenth and twentieth centuries to reach an estimated 2.6 children per woman worldwide in 2000-2005. By that time, total fertility had fallen below 2 children per woman in several regions of the world, including in many developing countries. Although such changes have been less dramatic in some areas, fertility levels in all regions of the world are lower now than they were a half-century ago.

Table II.1 provides a broad summary of historical trends in two summary measures of mortality and fertility (life expectancy at birth and total fertility), including estimated levels through 2005 and projections until 2050. Life expectancy for the world as a whole rose from 47 years in 1950-1955 to 65 years in 2000-2005 and is expected to continue rising to reach 75 years in 2045-2050. During these same time intervals, total fertility fell from 5.0 to 2.6 children per woman and is expected to continue falling to reach 2.0 children per woman in 2045-2050.

A major consequence of this transition from high fertility and high mortality to low fertility and low mortality has been the enormous growth of world population during the last few centuries, since for most countries the reduction in the death rate preceded the reduction in the birth rate by several decades, creating a sustained period in which the annual number of births greatly exceeded the annual number of deaths. Another major consequence of the demographic transition has been a gradual shift in the age distribution of the world's population from younger to older ages.

Historical stages of changing age distributions

Over the long term, sustained reductions in mortality and fertility lead to older population age distributions, whereas in the short term they produce increases in the proportion of children and youth. As noted already, the demographic transition usually starts with a reduction of mortality, which results in longer survival, especially of children. As a consequence, population growth accelerates and the proportion of children in the population increases, leading to an initial rejuvenation of the population's age structure.

Table II.1.
Life expectancy at birth and total fertility rate for selected countries and groups of countries, 1950-1955, 2000-2005 and 2045-2050

	Life expectancy (years)			Total fertility rate (children per woman)[a]		
	1950-1955	2000-2005	2045-2050	1950-1955	2000-2005	2045-2050
World	47	65	75	5.0	2.6	2.0
Developed countries	67	78	84	2.8	1.6	1.8
Europe	66	78	83	2.5	1.4	1.8
Japan	64	82	88	2.8	1.3	1.9
United States	69	77	82	3.4	2.0	1.9
Canada, Australia, New Zealand	69	80	85	3.5	1.6	1.9
Economies in transition	63	65	74	3.1	1.6	1.8
Commonwealth of Independent States	63	65	74	3.1	1.6	1.8
South-eastern Europe	57	74	80	3.7	1.6	1.8
Developing countries	41	63	74	6.2	2.9	2.1
Latin America and the Caribbean	51	72	79	5.9	2.5	1.9
East Asia and the Pacific	41	70	78	6.1	1.9	1.9
South Asia	39	63	75	6.1	3.2	1.9
Western Asia	43	68	78	7.0	3.5	2.0
Africa	38	49	65	6.7	5.0	2.5

Source: United Nations (2005a).

Note:

(1) Life expectancy at birth is the number of years a child born in the given period would live if the age-specific mortality rates of the period were to remain constant over his or her lifetime; the total fertility rate is the number of children that would be born per woman, assuming no female mortality at childbearing ages and the age-specific fertility rates of the specified region and reference period.

(2) The table shows estimates (until 2005) and medium-variant projections (after 2005).

a Women aged 15-49.

Partly in response to these early changes in mortality, fertility begins to decrease as parents realize that they can have fewer children and still ensure the survival of the number they desire. Other factors contribute as well to a reduction in childbearing, including changes in productive activities as economies become more industrialized, the broadening of opportunities for women outside the home and the increasing availability of effective methods of birth control. Sustained reductions in fertility slow down population growth and eventually produce a smaller proportion of children in the population. Thus, whereas the initial reduction in mortality leads to a younger population (through increased survival of children), the fertility decline that typically follows triggers a long-term process of population ageing.

As time elapses, sustained fertility decline leads to decreasing proportions not only of children but also of young people and eventually of adults of working age. This process is reinforced by continued increases in longevity, which generally have the effect of accelerating the growth of the older population.

Thus, in terms of the effects of the demographic transition on population age structures, one can distinguish three distinct stages. During the first stage, there is a rejuvenation of the age distribution as the proportion of children increases because of increased survival at younger ages. During the second, as a result of fertility reductions, there is the beginning of a decline in the proportion of children accompanied by a rise in the proportion of adults of working age. During the third stage, usually reached after lengthy periods of fertility and mortality decline, the proportions of both children and adults of working age decline and only the proportion of older persons rises.

Although the bulge in the working ages during the second stage of this transition is temporary (lasting, typically, about 50 years), the time period is long enough to have significant implications for economic growth and for many other dimensions of societies. This common feature of the demographic transition has been variously referred to as the "demographic dividend", the "demographic bonus" and the "demographic window of opportunity", with each term alluding to the possibilities offered for raising the rate of economic growth per capita and thus improving the standard of living for the population involved (see chapter IV).

During this phase of the demographic transition, a decline in the proportion (and often the absolute number) of dependent children in the population reduces the costs of providing for educational and other needs associated with this age group, resulting in an increase in the resources available for economically productive investment which, potentially, would contribute to the growth of the national economy. In theory, this demographic bonus provides a window of opportunity for accelerated economic development. However, reaping its potential benefits depends on the availability of productive employment and opportunities for investment and, ultimately, on the existence of social and political conditions that can provide an environment for sustainable growth and development. The experience of many developing countries in cashing in on the demographic bonus has been less fortunate, as evidenced by the large number of growth collapses in the last two decades of the twentieth century (see United Nations, 2006a).

The rapid ageing of the population that occurs during the third stage of this transition poses particular challenges for public policy, as it requires major adjustments in a variety of spheres, particularly health care and old-age support (see chapters V and VI). Such adjustments inevitably raise questions of intergenerational equity in meeting the needs of persons at different stages of life and of the roles of the State, private investment and the family in providing support for dependent populations. Different approaches to solving such problems are likely to affect the distribution of wealth and the distribution and types of opportunities and burdens in relation to age, gender and other social categories.

Regional differences in population ageing

Currently, the age structure of the developed countries is in general considerably older than that of the developing countries. In countries with economies in transition, the age structure is generally younger than that of the developed countries but still significantly older than that of the developing countries. It is expected that all groups of countries will undergo substantial ageing of their populations in the coming decades (table II.2).

According to United Nations estimates, 21 per cent of the population in the developed countries was aged 60 years or over in 2005. This proportion is projected to rise to 28 per cent in 2025 and 32 per cent in 2050. In countries with economies in transition, the average proportion of the population aged 60 years or over is projected to increase from 16 per cent in 2005 to 22 per cent in 2025 and 29 per cent in 2050. In the developing countries, the proportion of the population aged 60 years or over was estimated at only 8 per cent in 2005 but is expected to reach 13 per cent by 2025 and nearly 20 per cent by 2050. Thus, the number of older persons in the developing countries will likely more than double between 2005 and 2025. This increase is much larger than in the developed countries and in the economies in transition, where the number of older persons will grow by about 44 per cent and 32 per cent respectively during the same period.

Table II.2.
**Population by broad age group for the world and groups of countries,
1950, 1975, 2005, 2025 and 2050**

Age group	Population (millions)					Percentage				
	1950	1975	2005	2025	2050	1950	1975	2005	2025	2050
World										
0-14	864	1 498	1 821	1 909	1 833	34.3	36.8	28.2	24.2	20.2
15-24	459	757	1 159	1 211	1 225	18.2	18.6	17.9	15.3	13.5
25-59	991	1 469	2 812	3 593	4 051	39.3	36.1	43.5	45.4	44.6
60+	205	350	672	1 193	1 968	8.2	8.6	10.4	15.1	21.7
Total	2 519	4 074	6 465	7 905	9 076	100.0	100.0	100.0	100.0	100.0
65+	131	232	476	832	1 465	5.2	5.7	7.4	10.5	16.1
80+	14	31	87	160	394	0.5	0.8	1.3	2.0	4.3
Developed countries										
0-14	175	202	170	165	167	27.0	24.3	17.3	15.8	15.6
15-24	105	137	128	118	116	16.2	16.5	13.0	11.2	10.8
25-59	289	360	483	472	440	44.6	43.3	49.1	45.1	41.2
60+	79	131	203	293	345	12.2	15.8	20.6	28.0	32.3
Total	647	830	984	1 047	1 067	100.0	100.0	100.0	100.0	100.0
65+	53	93	153	224	280	8.2	11.2	15.5	21.4	26.2
80+	7	16	39	61	105	1.1	1.9	4.0	5.8	9.8
Economies in transition										
0-14	56	71	57	51	43	29.0	26.6	19.0	17.7	16.5
15-24	39	49	53	36	29	20.4	18.4	17.6	12.3	11.0
25-59	78	113	144	141	113	40.6	42.2	47.8	48.6	43.2
60+	19	34	47	62	76	10.0	12.8	15.7	21.5	29.3
Total	191	268	302	289	261	100.0	100.0	100.0	100.0	100.0
65+	13	23	37	44	56	6.7	8.5	12.4	15.3	21.4
80+	2	3	6	8	14	1.0	1.2	1.9	2.7	5.4
Developing countries										
0-14	634	1 224	1 593	1 693	1 623	37.7	41.1	30.8	25.8	20.9
15-24	316	571	0 978	1 058	1 080	18.8	19.2	18.9	16.1	13.9
25-59	624	996	2 186	2 980	3 498	37.1	33.5	42.2	45.4	45.1
60+	107	184	422	838	1 547	6.4	6.2	8.1	12.8	20.0
Total	1 681	2 975	5 179	6 569	7 748	100.0	100.0	100.0	100.0	100.0
65+	65	116	286	564	1 129	3.9	3.9	5.5	8.6	14.6
80+	5	13	41	91	275	0.3	0.4	0.8	1.4	3.5

Source: United Nations (2005a).

Note: The table shows estimates (until 2005) and medium-variant projections (after 2005).

Figure II.1 illustrates the variation in the ageing process of the different groups of countries by using population pyramids, which depict the distribution of a population of each sex by age. Thus, the figure shows the population distribution estimated for 1950 and 2005 and projected for 2050 for the world, the developed countries, the economies in transition and the developing countries.

Those three broad groups of countries are at different stages of the demographic transition, and their differences in the timing of historical demographic change are reflected in the variability of their current population age distributions. Developed economies are in general well into the third stage of the transition and their populations, which are already considerably older, are expected to age rapidly in the foreseeable future. In 2005, for example, just 16 per cent of Europe's population was under age 15, whereas 22 per cent was aged 60 years or over (annex table A.1). By 2050, the proportion of the population aged 60 years or over in Europe is projected to be 35 per cent.

The ageing process is particularly intense in Japan, where the population is expected to be by far the world's oldest at mid-century. The proportion of persons aged 60 years or over in Japan was 26 per cent in 2005 and is projected to reach 42 per cent in 2050. The United States of America, Canada, Australia and New Zealand are expected to experience a somewhat slower ageing process, as their fertility levels have not fallen as low as those of Europe or Japan. In the United States, the proportion of the population aged 60 years or over is projected to rise from 17 per cent in 2005 to 26 per cent in 2050; in Canada, Australia and New Zealand combined, that proportion is expected to increase from 18 to 31 per cent over the same period.

The countries with economies in transition also find themselves in the third stage of the transition towards lower levels of fertility and mortality and older population age structures. In 2005, 16 per cent of the population of the Commonwealth of Independent States (CIS) and 18 per cent of the population of South-eastern Europe were aged 60 years or over. By 2050, these proportions are expected to rise to 29 per cent and 32 per cent, respectively.

Most of the developing countries find themselves in the second stage of the demographic transition. However, because they have experienced, on average, fairly rapid fertility reductions, particularly in the regions of East Asia and the Pacific and Latin America and the Caribbean, their populations are expected to age more rapidly than those of Europe and other developed countries in the past. In East Asia and the Pacific, the share of the population aged 60 years or over is projected to grow from 10 per cent in 2005 to 28 per cent in 2050, whereas in Latin America and the Caribbean, the corresponding share is expected to rise from 9 to 24 per cent over the same period.

Figure II.1.
Population pyramids for the world and groups of countries, 1950, 2005 and 2050

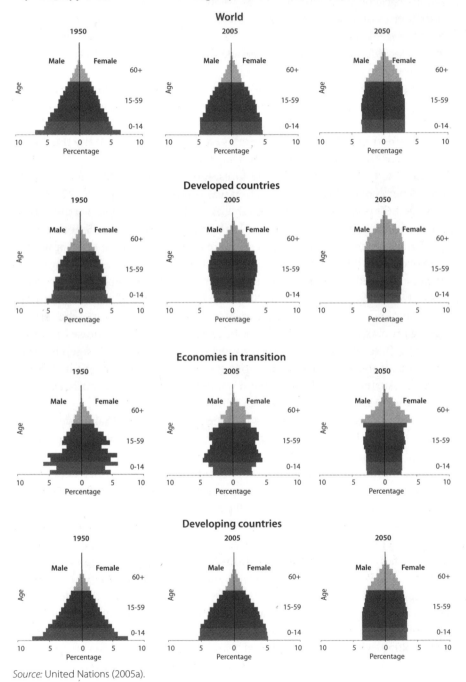

Source: United Nations (2005a).

In Western Asia and South Asia, the ageing process will likely be slower. In the former, the proportion of the population aged 60 years or over is projected to increase from 6 per cent in 2005 to 17 per cent in 2050; in the latter, that proportion is projected to increase from 7 to 19 per cent over the same period. Africa, in contrast, has only recently embarked on the second stage of the demographic transition and still has a very young population. In 2005, 42 per cent of Africa's population was under age 15, whereas only 5 per cent was aged 60 years or over. Because Africa has been heavily affected by the HIV/AIDS epidemic, its transition to low mortality has been interrupted. Furthermore, it is unclear whether or not the incipient fertility reductions experienced by countries in the region will continue over the short term. Even assuming that the fertility decline proceeds at a moderate pace, the African population is expected to remain relatively young well into the twenty-first century.

In general, the speed of population ageing will be faster in the developing countries than it has been in the developed countries. A commonly used indicator of the pace of population ageing is the timespan required for the population aged 65 years or over to increase from 7 to 14 per cent and then from 14 to 21 per cent. Figure II.2 uses this indicator to illustrate the pace of

Figure II.2.
Time period required for the proportion of the population aged 65 years or over to increase from 7 to 14 per cent and from 14 to 21 per cent, selected countries

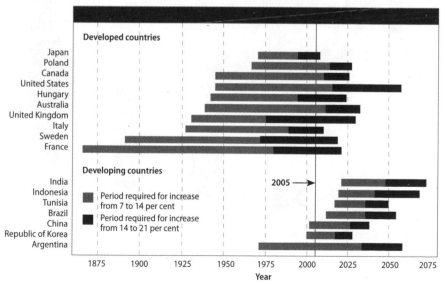

Sources: United Nations (2005a); unpublished tabulations for United Nations (2004a); U.S. Census Bureau (1992).

ageing for selected countries in the developing and developed regions of the world. In many developed countries, ageing has proceeded historically at a moderate pace. In France, for example, it took over a century for the share of the population aged 65 years or over to increase from 7 to 14 per cent, and it is projected that another 40 years will be required for the share to reach 21 per cent. Japan, in contrast, is expected to experience this shift (from a 7 to a 21 per cent share of the population aged 65 years or over) during a span of just 40 years. The pace of ageing is projected to be even faster in some developing countries including China, the Republic of Korea and Tunisia, all of which have experienced very rapid reductions in fertility.

Although populations are generally older in the developed regions, the majority of the world's older persons live in developing countries (figure II.3). In 2005, 63 per cent of the world's population aged 60 years or over lived in developing countries. By 2050, 79 per cent of the world's older population, amounting to nearly 1.6 billion people, will reside in these countries.

Figure II.3.
Size and distribution of world population aged 60 years or over by groups of countries, 1950, 1975, 2005, 2025 and 2050

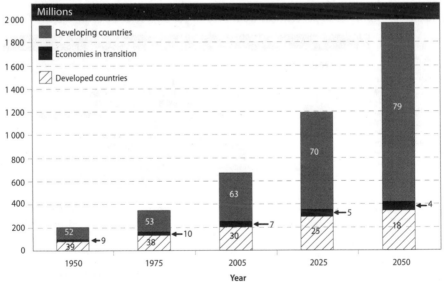

Source: United Nations (2005a).

Note:

(1) The graphs show estimates (until 2005) and medium-variant projections (after 2005).
(2) Percentages are shown inside the bars.

Ageing within the older population itself

A notable aspect of the global ageing process is the progressive demographic ageing of the older population itself. In most countries, the population aged 80 years or over is growing more rapidly than other segments of the older population. The world population aged 60 years or over is expected to nearly triple between 2005 and 2050, whereas the population aged 80 years or over is projected to increase by a factor of 4.5 over the same time period (table II.3). In both of these older-age categories, the proportional increase will be even greater in the developing regions, where the population aged 60 years or over is expected to almost quadruple and the population aged 80 years or over is projected to increase by a factor of 6.7.

The share of the world's population aged 80 years or over is expected to rise from 1.3 per cent in 2005 to 4.3 per cent in 2050. During the same period, the corresponding share is projected to increase from 4.0 to 9.8 per cent in the developed countries, from 1.9 to 5.4 per cent in the economies in transition and from 0.8 to 3.5 per cent in the developing countries. Important variation will remain at mid-century across countries and regions in terms of the share of the total population represented by the oldest age groups. For example, whereas in Japan it is projected that persons aged 80 years or over will make up more than 15 per cent of the total population in 2050, in Africa they are expected to constitute only about 1 per cent of the total population.

Is population ageing inevitable?

Concern over rapid population ageing has generated an intense policy debate, particularly in developed countries, where the historical transition towards older populations is more advanced. An important question is whether this fundamental demographic shift could be altered significantly through policy interventions, or whether population ageing is essentially inevitable (suggesting that policy responses should focus on adaptation rather than on mitigation). To address this issue, it is helpful to examine in more detail the implications of past and future demographic trends for historical changes in the population age distribution, and also to consider the potential impact of policy interventions in matters of childbearing and international migration.

Historical reductions in fertility and mortality

The age distribution of a population results primarily from its past experience of fertility and mortality and to a lesser extent from its migration history.

Table II.3.
Population aged 80 years or over for selected countries and groups of countries, 1950, 2005 and 2050

	Number of persons aged 80 years or over (thousands)			Number of persons aged 80 years or over as a proportion of the total population (percentage)			Number of persons aged 80 years or over as a proportion of the population aged 60 years or over (percentage)		
	1950	2005	2050	1950	2005	2050	1950	2005	2050
World	13 780	86 648	394 224	0.5	1.3	4.3	6.7	12.9	20.0
Developed countries	6 815	39 309	105 082	1.1	4.0	9.8	8.6	19.3	30.5
Europe	4 374	20 568	52 059	1.1	4.1	10.7	8.7	18.7	30.6
Japan	376	6 187	17 159	0.4	4.8	15.3	5.8	18.3	36.7
United States	1 801	10 605	28 725	1.1	3.6	7.3	9.1	21.3	27.5
Canada, Australia, New Zealand	264	1 949	7 138	1.1	3.5	9.4	9.3	19.6	30.5
Economies in transition	1 914	5 852	14 113	1.0	1.9	5.4	10.0	12.4	18.5
Commonwealth of Independent States	1 745	5 365	12 631	1.0	1.9	5.3	10.0	12.5	18.2
South-eastern Europe	169	487	1 481	1.1	2.0	6.9	10.4	11.1	21.5
Developing countries	5 051	41 487	275 030	0.3	0.8	3.5	4.7	9.8	17.8
Latin America and the Caribbean	656	6 700	40 348	0.4	1.2	5.2	6.6	13.6	21.4
East Asia and the Pacific	2 269	19 659	136 814	0.3	1.0	6.1	4.2	9.9	21.5
South Asia	1 403	10 602	68 994	0.3	0.7	2.9	4.9	9.3	14.8
Western Asia	126	994	8 804	0.3	0.5	2.4	4.8	8.3	13.9
Africa	597	3 532	20 069	0.3	0.4	1.0	5.0	7.4	10.4

Source: United Nations (2005a).

Note: The table shows estimates (until 2005) and medium-variant projections (after 2005).

Although increases in life expectancy play a role as well, the historical reduction in fertility levels has been the main force contributing to the gradual upward shift in population age distributions for both developed and developing countries.

Much of the expected future ageing of the world's populations will occur as a result of their current demographic profiles, reflecting earlier changes in fertility and mortality levels plus the cumulative effects of past migration. Although future trends in these three components of population change will help to determine age distributions at mid-century, a powerful momentum for population ageing has already been created by past demographic trends. That is to say, most populations would continue to experience a substantial upward shift in their age distributions even if age-specific rates of fertility, mortality and migration remained constant at today's levels.

Future trends according to alternative projection scenarios

Future effects of different paths of fertility change on the size and age distribution of the world's populations can be assessed by comparing the high-, medium- and low-fertility variants of the United Nations population projections, which are believed to encompass the likely future range of fertility change between now and 2050. For each country or area, the low and high variants assume that from 2005 to 2050 the average level of fertility will be, respectively, half a child below and half a child above the level assumed for the medium variant.

These seemingly small changes in the underlying assumptions are associated with rather large differences in the projected size of the world population in 2050, which would range from 7.7 billion under the low variant to 10.6 billion under the high variant (table II.4). Assumptions regarding future fertility levels also have major implications for the expected pace of world population growth. Under the high variant, world population in 2050 would be increasing by more than 90 million persons annually, a substantially higher annual increment than at present; under the low variant, however, world population would be declining slowly by that time.

In contrast, uncertainty about future fertility levels is relatively less important with regard to expected changes in population age distributions. For the world as a whole, the low variant implies a population in which the proportion of persons aged 60 years or over would be 26 per cent in 2050; according to the high variant, the proportion of older persons in the same year would be 18 per cent. Although these two outcomes differ substantially, both scenarios imply a significant increase compared with the situation in

Table II.4.
**Age distribution estimated for 2005 and according to different
projection variants for 2050, for the world and groups of countries**

Percentage				
			2050	
Age group	2005 estimate	Low	Medium	High
World				
0-14	28	15	20	25
15-59	61	59	58	57
60+	10	26	22	18
Total	100	100	100	100
Number (millions)	6 465	7 680	9 076	10 646
Developed countries				
0-14	17	11	16	20
15-59	62	51	52	52
60+	21	38	32	28
Total	100	100	100	100
Number (millions)	984	918	1 067	1 236
Economies in transition				
0-14	19	11	16	22
15-59	65	53	54	54
60+	16	35	29	24
Total	100	100	100	100
Number (millions)	302	215	261	314
Developing countries				
0-14	31	16	21	26
15-59	61	60	59	57
60+	8	24	20	17
Total	100	100	100	100
Number (millions)	5 179	6 546	7 748	9 096

Source: United Nations (2005a).

2005, when only 10 per cent of persons were aged 60 years or over. Thus, even
if the world experiences relatively high levels of fertility and continued rapid
population growth, substantial population ageing during the first half of the
twenty-first century appears to be inevitable (see annex table A.2).

The same outcome applies to different groups of countries. Even with
relatively high fertility levels in future decades, the proportion of the population
aged 60 years or over in 2050 would be 28 per cent in the developed countries

and 24 per cent in the economies in transition; these values are considerably higher than the corresponding estimates of 21 per cent and 16 per cent for 2005. In the case of the developing countries, the high-fertility variant implies a population in which the projected share of older persons in 2050 (17 per cent) would be more than double the estimate for 2005 (8 per cent); in the low-fertility variant, the projected share (24 per cent) would be triple the estimate for 2005.

Potential impact of fertility policies

Because of the close relationship between fertility trends and changes in the population age distribution, it is worth considering whether policies intended to promote childbearing could be effective as a means of slowing the process of population ageing. Although it appears that such policies can succeed in slowing fertility declines under specific circumstances, it has proved difficult for Governments to change the behaviour of individuals in the direction of increasing their fertility (United Nations, 2004b). Nevertheless, there is a lack of conclusive evidence about the impact of past interventions aimed at increasing fertility levels, as it has been difficult to disentangle the effects of specific policy initiatives from the effects of broader social, political and economic conditions (Demeny, 2000; RAND, 2005).

For similar reasons, designing successful interventions has proved to be extremely challenging, since policies intended to raise fertility can have different effects depending on the political, economic and social contexts within which they are implemented. Another factor that has hampered the implementation of policies intended to reverse fertility declines is linked to the long-term nature of their outcomes. It takes at least one generation before these policies ultimately increase the number of new entrants to the labour force. As a result of this long-term horizon, policymakers generally have few incentives to advocate such policies, which tend to lack popular appeal and therefore do not attract political champions (RAND, 2005).

No single policy intervention seems to have been effective in reversing low fertility. Instead, Governments have used, with modest success, a mix of policies and programmes aimed at directly or indirectly increasing fertility. In France, for instance, generous childcare subsidies have been instituted to reconcile family life with work, and families have been rewarded for having at least three children. In Sweden, several parental policies, including flexible work schedules, quality childcare and extensive parental leave on reasonable economic terms, have allowed many women to raise children while remaining in the workforce (RAND, 2005). It appears that such measures may have had a small positive impact on fertility levels in the countries where they were implemented most aggressively. However, it is important to remember that even a sharp upturn in fertility would not yield a significant impact on the age structure before at least 25 to 30 years, owing to the momentum generated by past demographic trends (United Nations, 2004b).

Potential impact of migration

Although international migration has no direct effect on the size or characteristics of the global population as a whole, it could have an impact on the age distribution of certain national or regional populations, since migrants are disproportionately concentrated in the young adult ages and sometimes have higher fertility levels than native-born populations. In today's world, the developed countries are in general net receivers of international migrants, whereas the developing countries are net senders. The medium variant of the United Nations population projections assumes that the general direction of these flows will remain the same over the next few decades, and it thus reflects the expected rejuvenating effect of international migration on the population of the developed countries.

To assess the size of this effect, another set of projections assuming that there will be no international migration has been calculated. A comparison of the two sets of projections to 2050 for the developed countries shows a difference of 142 million persons in the size of the population at the end of the projection period (table II.5). Furthermore, the projected number of international migrants during 2005-2050 in the medium variant has the effect of reducing the proportion of the population aged 60 years or over by 2.7

Table II.5.
Age structure of the population projected for the developed countries in 2050 according to the medium and zero migration variants

Percentage			
	Projection variants		
Age group (years)	A. Medium	B. Zero migration	Difference (A-B)
0-14	15.6	14.9	0.7
15-59	52.1	50.1	2.0
60+	32.3	35.0	-2.7
Total	100.0	100.0	0.0
Number (millions)	1 067	925	142

Source: United Nations (2005a).

percentage points in 2050, while simultaneously increasing the proportions of children and persons of working age by 0.7 and 2.0 percentage points, respectively. Thus, international migration is expected to slow the ageing process only slightly in the developed countries. This conclusion is consistent with that of other studies, which have found that the impact of international migration on population size and age structure in developed countries is typically rather small (United Nations, 1998; 2001; 2004b).

In particular, a United Nations study on so-called replacement migration (United Nations, 2001) focused on the possible effects of international migration on the population size and age structure of a range of countries with fertility patterns below the replacement level, including France, Germany, Italy, Japan, the Russian Federation, the United Kingdom of Great Britain and Northern Ireland and the United States. An identical exercise was performed for Europe and for the European Union (EU), treating them as if they were each a single country from 1995 onward. The time period covered was 1995-2050, and the calculations were based on the 1998 Revision of United Nations population estimates and projections (United Nations, 1999).

The study considered a number of scenarios with regard to the migration streams that would be needed in order for particular population objectives or outcomes to be achieved. The scenarios focused on three different outcome variables: (a) the size of the total population; (b) the size of the working-age population (aged 15-64); and (c) the ratio of the population aged 65 years or over to the working-age population. In each case, the analysts calculated the level of international migration required to maintain the given outcome variable at the highest level (for the size of the total or working-age population) or the lowest level (for the old-age dependency ratio) that would be attained, hypothetically, in the absence of international migration after 1995.

In performing the required calculations, it was assumed that the fertility rate in all countries and regions would move (upward, in most cases) towards target levels of 1.7 or 1.9 children per woman and, once those levels were reached, that it would remain constant until 2050, the end of the projection period. For simplicity, the age and sex structure of the migrants was assumed to be the same for all countries and was based on historical patterns observed for the United States, Canada and Australia (traditionally, the most important countries of immigration). In addition, the projection methodology assumed that the fertility and mortality levels of immigrants would converge immediately to those of the receiving populations.

Results of the study (table II.6) indicate that, in order for international migration to offset the projected decline in overall population size for countries such as Italy and Japan, and for Europe as a whole (scenario I), the

Table II.6.
Net number of migrants required during 1995-2050 to achieve different population scenarios, selected countries and regions

Country or region	Medium variant	Scenario		
		I. Constant total population	II. Constant age group 15-64	III. Constant ratio 65+/15-64 years
A. Total number (thousands)				
France	525	1 473	5 459	93 794
Germany	11 400	17 838	25 209	188 497
Italy	660	12 944	19 610	119 684
Japan	0	17 141	33 487	553 495
Russian Federation	7 417	27 952	35 756	257 110
United Kingdom	1 200	2 634	6 247	59 775
United States	41 800	6 384	17 967	592 757
Europe	23 530	100 137	161 346	1 386 151
European Union	16 361	47 456	79 605	700 506
B. Average annual number (thousands)				
France	10	27	99	1 705
Germany	207	324	458	3 427
Italy	12	235	357	2 176
Japan	0	312	609	10 064
Russian Federation	135	508	650	4 675
United Kingdom	22	48	114	1 087
United States	760	116	327	10 777
Europe	428	1 821	2 934	25 203
European Union	297	863	1 447	12 736

Source: United Nations (2004).

levels of net migration gains would need to be much higher than in the recent past. For instance, to offset the projected population decline in Europe, the average annual net inflow of international migrants would need to be about twice as high during 2000-2050 (about 1.8 million) as that during 1995-2000 (approximately 950,000, not shown in table). The levels needed to offset the projected decline in the working-age population (scenario II) would be larger still, amounting, in the case of Europe, to an average net inflow of 2.9 million migrants per year during 1995-2050.

However, even these higher levels of immigration would not bring population ageing to a halt. Indeed, much larger flows of immigrants into this same set of countries would be required in order to halt the expected increase in the ratio of persons aged 65 years or over to the population of working age (scenario III). The necessary level would range from an average annual net inflow between 1995 and 2050 of 1.1 million persons for the United Kingdom and 1.7 million for France, to more than 10 million each for Japan and the United States.

Whether these larger numbers of international migrants are within the realm of options open to Governments would depend to a great extent on the social, economic and political circumstances of each country or region. Such scenarios serve chiefly to underscore the point that the ongoing transformation in population age structures has a powerful momentum and that it is impractical to suppose that any policy with regard to international migration will have a major impact on the age structure of most developed countries.

TRENDS IN WORKING AND DEPENDENT AGE GROUPS

Dependency ratios: definition and interpretation

The potential effects of ageing for social and economic development are often assessed using so-called dependency ratios. These ratios compare the size of some group within a population that is considered to be economically dependent to that of another group that is considered economically active. Since precise determinations of the number of persons who are producers (and thus, economically active) and those who are exclusively consumers (inactive) are typically not available, dependency ratios are usually calculated based solely on age ranges.

It is generally assumed that children under age 15 fall into the dependent category and that older persons are more likely to be at a stage of life where they are mainly consumers. Because 65 years has traditionally been regarded as the threshold for old-age dependency, age group 65 or over is used here to calculate dependency ratios. Nevertheless, it is worth noting that the direction of the trends would be largely the same if the dependency ratios were computed using the population aged 15-59 as the denominator and a definition of older persons as those aged 60 years or over. Yet, total and old-age dependency ratios are higher if age 60 is used as a threshold (see annex table A.3).

Three ratios will be considered: (a) the child dependency ratio, which relates the number of persons aged 0-14 to those aged 15-64; (b) the old-age dependency ratio, which relates the number of persons aged 65 years or over to those aged 15-64; and (c) the total dependency ratio, which is the sum of the child and old-age dependency ratios. All dependency ratios are expressed in terms of the number of dependants (children or older persons or both) per 100 persons aged 15-64.

Obviously, this formulation of the notion of "dependency" oversimplifies the reality of people's lives. In most populations, economic activity does not cease at age 65, and persons aged 15-64 are not all economically active. Although persons aged 65 years or over often require economic support from others, older persons in many societies are also providers of support to their adult children (Morgan, Schuster and Butler, 1991; Saad, 2001). Furthermore, not all persons aged 15-64 provide direct or indirect support to children or older persons (Taeuber, 1992). In particular, as the period of training for a productive life increases in the course of economic development, most adolescents and young adults remain longer in school and out of the labour force, effectively extending the period of child dependency well beyond age 15.

These observations suggest that trends in the dependency ratios considered here are merely indicative of the constraints that a society may face as its population ages and unprecedented changes occur in the size of key age groups. Estimation of the likely economic impact of such trends would require more appropriate measures based on information about the number of workers and consumers in a population as a function of age.

Global trends in age-related dependency

Figure II.4 shows the values of the three dependency ratios from 1950 to 2050 for the world, the developed and developing countries and the countries with economies in transition. The total dependency ratio for the world as a whole had increased from 65 dependants per 100 persons aged 15-64 in 1950, to 74 in 1975. This increase in total dependency was due mostly to an increase in the number of children relative to the working-age population, as reflected in the rise of the child dependency ratio. Between 1975 and 2005, the total dependency ratio declined from 74 to 55 dependants per 100 persons of working age, driven by a major reduction in child dependency.

This decline is expected to come to a halt in the coming decade and then to reverse itself, so that the total dependency ratio is projected to be 53 in 2025 and to reach 57 by 2050. This projected increase in the total dependency ratio is due entirely to increased dependency at older ages, since the child dependency ratio is expected to maintain its decreasing trend.[2]

Figure II.4.
**Trends in three types of dependency ratio for the
world and groups of countries, 1950-2050**

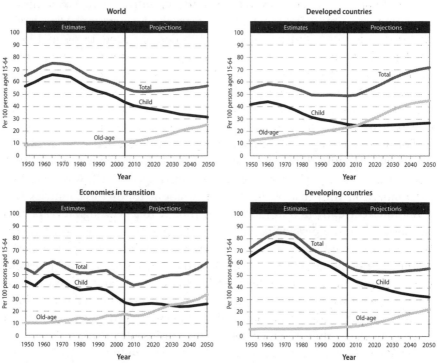

Source: United Nations (2005a).
Note:
(1) The graphs show estimates (until 2005) and medium-variant projections (after 2005).
(2) The total dependency ratio is defined as the ratio of the sum of the population aged 0-14 and
    the population aged 65 years or over to the population aged 15-64. The child dependency ratio
    is the ratio of the population aged 0-14 to that aged 15-64. The old-age dependency ratio is the
    ratio of the population aged 65 years or over to that aged 15-64.

Regional differences in age-related dependency

In developed countries, the total dependency ratio was roughly constant
between 1950 and 1975, at a level of about 54 or 55 dependants per 100 persons
aged 15-64, but had then declined to 49 by 2005. It is expected that the level
observed in 2005 will be a historic low point, since a steadily increasing path
for the total dependency ratio is projected for these regions in the future,
caused by a continually rising old-age dependency ratio. Indeed, by 2050 the
old-age dependency ratio for the developed countries is expected to attain a
value of 45, which is close to the total dependency ratio estimated for 2005.
Adding the dependent children is expected to produce a total dependency

ratio of 72 in 2050, a level that is 37 per cent higher than the average value of this same ratio for the developed countries between 1950 and 2005.

The trends in dependency ratios in the countries with economies in transition are similar to those in the developed countries. After having changed little from 56 dependants per 100 persons aged 15-64 in 1950 to 54 dependants in 1975, and then declining to a historic low point of 42 dependants in 2010, the total dependency ratio is projected to increase to 49 in 2025 and then to 61 in 2050. As in the case of the developed countries, the expected increase in the dependency ratio in the economies in transition is due exclusively to a steady rise in the old-age dependency ratio.

For the developing countries, both the historical experience and the future prospects are quite different. First, their total dependency ratio in 1950, which stood at 71 dependants per 100 persons aged 15-64, was quite high in comparison with that of the developed countries or the countries with economies currently in transition, owing mostly to a very high level of child dependency in the developing countries (65 per 100 persons aged 15-64). Between 1950 and 1975, as the proportion of children in the population of the developing countries increased further owing to reduced mortality, the child and the total dependency ratios soared to 75 and 82, respectively. However, a subsequent reduction in the proportion of children due to reduced fertility, coupled with a rising proportion of persons aged 15-64, led to major reductions in the child and total dependency ratios after 1975.

By 2005, the total dependency ratio in the developing countries stood at 57 and is projected to continue declining until it reaches 52 in 2025. Beyond that point, a slowly increasing trend is expected. Increases after 2025 should be slow, since the rapid rise expected in the old-age dependency ratio is likely to be counterbalanced by continued reductions in child dependency. By 2050, the developing regions as a whole are expected to have a total dependency ratio of 55, a value that is slightly lower than in 2005. However, the composition of this ratio will be quite different in the future, since older persons are expected to account for 42 per cent of the total dependency burden in 2050, up from an estimated 10 per cent in 1950 and 16 per cent in 2005.

In all groups of developing countries considered here, the total dependency ratio (which was already high in 1950) increased to a very high level between 1950 and 1975. This was especially true in Africa and Western Asia, where in 1975 the total dependency ratio reached more than 90 dependants per 100 persons aged 15-64 (annex figure A.1). In that same year, the total dependency ratio was 84 in Latin America and the Caribbean and about 80 in South Asia and in East Asia and the Pacific. In all developing regions except Africa, the total dependency ratio dropped markedly between 1975 and 2005.

This reduction was particularly important in East Asia and the Pacific where, owing to a substantial decline of its child component, a total dependency ratio of 44 dependants per 100 persons aged 15-64 in 2005 became comparable with that observed in the developed countries and the economies in transition. In South Asia and Western Asia, the total dependency ratio dropped to the lower 60s in 2005, and in Latin America and the Caribbean to the mid-50s. In Africa, in contrast, the total dependency ratio in 2005 was still very high, at 81 dependants per 100 persons aged 15-64.

In future decades, Africa is expected to experience a steady decline in the total dependency ratio, with its value projected to reach 55 by 2050. For Latin America and the Caribbean, in contrast, the total dependency ratio is expected to stop declining around 2025 and then start increasing to a level of 57 by 2050. This increase will be caused primarily by the rising weight of the older population. By 2050, the old-age dependency ratio for Latin American and the Caribbean is expected to be roughly equal to the child dependency ratio. In South Asia and Western Asia, the total dependency ratio is expected to decline further to about 50 by 2025 and then to remain stable for the next 25 years.

The future prospects for the total dependency ratio in East Asia and the Pacific are similar to those in the economies in transition, with a slow increase between 2005 and 2025, and a more rapid increase between 2025 and 2050. The old-age dependency ratio in this region is expected to surpass the child dependency ratio by around 2030.

Among the developed countries, Japan stands out as a special case, with a relatively high total dependency ratio in 1950. Between 1950 and 1975, however, that ratio had decreased sharply from 68 to 47 dependants per 100 persons aged 15-64, mainly because of a substantial decline in the child dependency ratio. The old-age dependency ratio in Japan surpassed the child dependency ratio between 1995 and 2000 (annex figure A.2). Thus, in 2005 the older population accounted for almost 60 per cent of the total dependency ratio, which stood at 51 dependants per 100 persons aged 15-64. By 2050, the old-age dependency ratio in Japan is expected to attain a remarkable level (by far the world's highest) of more than 70 persons aged 65 years or over per 100 persons aged 15-64, whereas the total dependency ratio is projected to reach almost one dependant per member of the working-age population.

Europe also experienced a crossover of the child and the old-age dependency ratios (occurring between 2000 and 2005). However, the difference between these two ratios remains significantly lower than in the case of Japan. This recent crossover presages a sharp rise in the future total dependency ratio, which is projected to increase in parallel with the old-age ratio. By 2050, Europe's total dependency ratio is expected to be 77, a very high value similar to that of most developing countries in the 1960s, but in this case determined mainly by a high proportion of older persons rather than of children.

The historical paths followed by the total dependency ratio are similar in South-eastern Europe and CIS. In both groups of countries, the total dependency ratio decreased between 1950 and 2005 but is expected to start increasing within the next decade, reaching by 2050 a level of 66 in South-eastern Europe and 61 in CIS. In both groups, as in most of the developed countries, the expected increase in the total dependency ratio will be driven mainly by the rising weight of the older population. The share of older persons in the total dependency ratio is expected to surpass that of children by around 2020 in South-eastern Europe and by around 2030 in CIS. By 2050, persons aged 65 years or over are projected to constitute 56 per cent of the total dependency ratio in CIS, and 62 per cent in South-eastern Europe.

Ageing within the working-age population

The labour force is itself ageing. For the world as a whole, the proportion of those aged 50 years or over within the population aged 15-64 remained stable in recent decades, at about 17 per cent between 1975 and 2005 (figure II.5). The weight of this age group is projected to grow rapidly in the future, rising to 27.1 per cent in 2050.

In the developed countries, the proportions of the youngest (aged 15-29) and the oldest (aged 50-64) segments of the working-age population were of nearly equal size in 2005. However, starting in 2010 the oldest segment of the labour force is projected to become larger than the youngest component. By 2050, those aged 50 years or over are expected to make up almost one third (31.2 per cent) of the working-age population in the developed countries.

In the countries with economies in transition, the crossover between the youngest and oldest segments of the working-age population is expected to take place between 2020 and 2025. The share of the oldest segment of the workforce in the economies in transition is projected to reach its highest point, 34.8 per cent, in 2045 and then to decline slightly to 32.7 per cent in 2050.

In the developing regions, although the size of the oldest and youngest segments of the workforce started to converge in the 1990s, the youngest segment is projected to remain still dominant by the middle of this century. However, important differences exist within the developing countries. In Africa, for example, the workforce will remain quite young through 2050, whereas in East Asia and the Pacific the size of the oldest segment is expected to surpass that of the youngest segment before 2025 (annex figure A.3).

Figure II.5.
**Distribution of the working-age population by age group
for the world and groups of countries, 1950-2050**

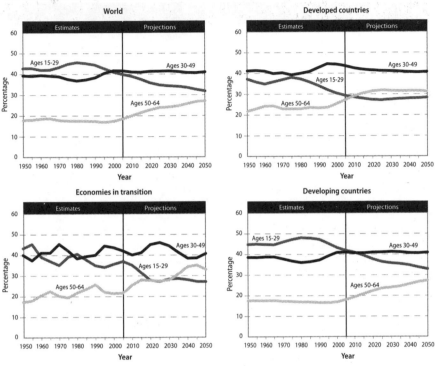

Source: United Nations (2005a).

Note: The graphs show estimates (until 2005) and medium-variant projections (after 2005).

GENDER DIFFERENCES AT OLDER AGES

Numbers of men and women

Because women usually live longer than men, they significantly outnumber men at older ages. While there were 101 males per 100 females in the world population in 2005, among those aged 60 years or over the ratio was 82 men to 100 women (table II.7).

Not only are women more likely than men to survive to age 60, but having once reached that age they can expect to live longer than similarly aged men. Consequently, the proportion of women in the older population tends to rise substantially with advancing age. In 2005, for the world as a whole, women outnumbered men by almost 4 to 3 at ages 65 and over, and by almost 2 to 1 at ages 80 and over.

Table II.7.
**Sex ratio of the population in selected age groups for
the world and groups of countries, 1950, 2005 and 2050**

Age group	Sex ratio (males per 100 females)		
	1950	2005	2050
World			
Total	100	101	99
0-14	104	105	105
15-59	99	102	103
60+	80	82	85
65+	75	77	80
80+	61	55	61
Developed countries			
Total	95	96	96
0-14	104	105	105
15-59	93	100	102
60+	80	76	81
65+	78	71	77
80+	65	49	59
Economies in transition			
Total	79	89	89
0-14	101	105	105
15-59	73	93	97
60+	54	57	65
65+	49	53	59
80+	36	29	38
Developing countries			
Total	104	103	100
0-14	105	105	105
15-59	105	103	103
60+	86	88	86
65+	80	85	82
80+	68	67	64

Source: United Nations (2005a).

Note: The table shows estimates (until 2005) and medium-variant projections (after 2005).

Sex ratios at older ages vary greatly among countries. Female advantage in survivorship has been larger historically in developed countries and countries with economies in transition than in developing countries. As a result, male-to-female sex ratios at older ages tend to be lower on average in the developed countries and the economies in transition than in the developing countries. At present, those low sex ratios in the developed countries and in the economies in transition result from both large sex differences in life expectancy and the long-term effects of the massive loss of young men during the Second World War.

The sex ratio at older ages is particularly low in the economies in transition where, in 2005, there were 57 men per 100 women among persons aged 60 years or over and just 29 men per 100 women among those aged 80 years or over. In contrast, in the developing countries older women outnumber older men by smaller margins because sex differences in life expectancy are generally smaller in these areas of the world. Thus, in the developing countries today there are 88 men per 100 women aged 60 years or over, and 67 men per 100 women aged 80 years or over. Sex ratios at older ages in the developed countries are in-between those found in the economies in transition and those observed in the developing countries.

However, owing in part to an anticipated reduction in the female advantage in life expectancy in the developed countries and the economies in transition, the sex ratio of the population aged 60 years or over in those regions is projected to increase between 2005 and 2050, passing from 76 to 81 males per 100 females in the developed countries and from 57 to 65 in the economies in transition. Likewise, future increases are expected in the sex ratio for those aged 80 years or over in both the developed countries and the economies in transition.

In contrast, sex differences in life expectancy are expected to widen in the developing countries between 2005 and 2050. As a result, sex ratios at older ages are expected to decline, thus exacerbating the imbalance in the numbers of older men and older women in developing countries as a whole. Nevertheless, sex ratios at older ages in the developing countries are not expected to attain the extremely low levels observed in the economies in transition and in the developed countries in 2005.

Gender gap in life expectancy at birth and at older ages

Mortality levels have dropped markedly since 1950. Between 1950-1955 and 2000-2005, the world population gained almost 19 years of life expectancy at birth, but these gains were not shared equally by men and women (table II.8). In most countries, reductions in mortality have been greater for females than for males, thus reinforcing the female advantage in survival to old age. At the world level, the female advantage in life expectancy at birth has increased

Table II.8.
Life expectancy at birth and at ages 60, 65 and 80, by sex for the world and groups of countries, 1950-2050

	1950-1955				2000-2005				2045-2050			
	Both sexes	Female	Male	Diffe-rence	Both sexes	Female	Male	Diffe-rence	Both sexes	Female	Male	Diffe-rence
	Life expectancy at birth (years)											
World	46.6	48.0	45.3	2.8	65.4	67.7	63.2	4.5	75.1	77.5	72.8	4.7
Developed countries	66.6	69.0	64.3	4.7	78.3	81.3	75.2	6.1	83.7	86.6	80.8	5.8
Economies in transition	62.7	65.8	58.8	7.0	65.5	71.2	60.0	11.2	74.1	77.5	70.5	7.0
Developing countries	41.0	41.8	40.2	1.6	63.4	65.1	61.7	3.4	74.0	76.2	71.8	4.3
	Life expectancy at age 60 (years)											
World	14.8	15.5	13.9	1.6	19.2	20.7	17.5	3.2	22.4	24.3	20.5	3.8
Developed countries	17.7	19.3	16.0	3.3	22.2	24.3	19.8	4.5	25.9	28.3	23.4	4.9
Economies in transition	17.9	19.8	15.4	4.4	17.1	19.1	14.4	4.7	20.6	22.9	17.8	5.1
Developing countries	13.0	13.2	12.7	0.5	18.0	19.3	16.8	2.5	21.8	23.5	20.1	3.4
	Life expectancy at age 65 (years)											
World	12.0	12.5	11.3	1.2	15.7	17.0	14.2	2.8	18.5	20.2	16.8	3.4
Developed countries	14.3	15.6	12.9	2.7	18.3	20.1	16.1	4.0	21.7	23.8	19.3	4.5
Economies in transition	14.8	16.3	12.6	3.7	14.0	15.4	11.8	3.6	17.0	18.8	14.6	4.2
Developing countries	10.4	10.5	10.2	0.3	14.6	15.6	13.5	2.1	17.9	19.4	16.3	3.1
	Life expectancy at age 80 (years)											
World	5.7	5.7	5.4	0.3	7.5	8.1	6.7	1.4	9.0	9.9	7.9	2.0
Developed countries	6.4	6.9	6.0	0.9	8.6	9.4	7.4	2.0	10.8	12.0	9.1	2.9
Economies in transition	7.4	7.9	6.4	1.5	6.6	6.9	5.8	1.1	8.2	8.9	6.9	2.0
Developing countries	4.9	4.8	4.9	-0.1	6.8	7.2	6.2	1.0	8.5	9.3	7.5	1.8

Source: United Nations (2005a).

Note: The table shows estimates (until 2005) and medium-variant projections (after 2005).

from 2.8 to 4.5 years since 1950-1955 and is expected to increase slightly to 4.7 years by 2045-2050. However, in recent decades the gap in life expectancy at birth between the sexes has stabilized or even narrowed somewhat in the developed countries.

The female advantage in life expectancy at birth has been particularly large in the countries with economies in transition, where increasing levels of adult male mortality have contributed to increasing the difference between female and male life expectancy at birth, which rose from 7.0 years in 1950-1955 to 11.2 years in 2000-2005. Currently, male life expectancy at birth in the economies in transition is lower than in the developing countries, whereas female life expectancy is six years higher in the economies in transition than in the developing countries.

Women have gained ground relative to men not only in terms of life expectancy at birth but also in terms of survivorship at older ages. Between 1950-1955 and 2000-2005, the female advantage in life expectancy increased from 1.6 to 3.2 years at age 60, and from 0.3 to 1.4 years at age 80. These trends have been similar in different regions of the world and have helped to maintain the low sex ratios among the older population observed worldwide.

CONCLUSIONS

By the beginning of the twenty-first century, most of the world's countries either were experiencing or had already experienced a demographic transition from high to low levels of fertility and mortality. Developed countries have already reached the third stage of the transition, when population ageing is pervasive and rapid. The majority of developing countries and the world population as a whole are in the second stage, when a favourable age distribution gives rise to a potential demographic bonus. There remain, however, some countries that are only at the start of the transition to low fertility and a very few where fertility decline has not yet started.

The changes set in motion by the demographic transition lead to an ongoing transformation of the population age structure, which brings both challenges and opportunities for development. In the early stages of the transition, countries face the challenge of educating large and growing numbers of children and young adults. Later, during the second stage of the transition, an increase in the population of working age creates a favourable age structure and opens up a demographic window of opportunity for economic development. However, in order to benefit from the opportunities created by this demographic bonus, countries need to foster productive investment and job creation.

Equally important is the need to start planning for the time when the demographic bonus ends and population ageing accelerates. In the developed economies, rapid population ageing is already demanding societal and economic adaptations to a new reality. Again, however, there are opportunities as well as challenges, since older people in developed countries remain in good health for longer than ever before and therefore have the potential to continue being productive.

Although the highest proportions of older persons are found in developed countries, this age group is growing considerably more rapidly in developing countries. As a consequence, the older population worldwide will be increasingly concentrated in the developing countries. Already today, when developing countries have a relatively youthful population, they account for 64 per cent of the global population aged 60 years or over. Within 20 years, developing countries will be the home of 71 per cent of the world's older persons.

Ensuring that these growing numbers of older persons have adequate support during old age, access to decent employment should they need or wish to remain economically active, and appropriate health care is likely to prove challenging, as analysed in chapter VI. Policy responses to population ageing should also take into account the fact that women greatly outnumber men at older ages in most countries, especially among the very old.

The worldwide increase in the old-age dependency ratio reflects a situation in which an increasing number of beneficiaries of publicly funded health and pension programmes (mainly those aged 65 years or over) are being supported in many countries by a relatively smaller number of potential contributors (those in the economically active ages between 15 and 64 years). As discussed in chapters IV and V, unless economic growth can be accelerated in a sustained manner, this trend will continue to impose heavier demands on the working-age population (in the form of higher taxes and other contributions) in order to maintain a stable flow of benefits to the older age groups. The increasing burden of old-age support is offset only partially by the decreasing size of the population at younger ages.

Population ageing in future decades is largely inevitable for countries at all levels of development. Although age distributions in the future will be determined in part by ongoing changes in fertility, mortality and international migration, there is also a powerful momentum for population ageing that has been created by past demographic trends. A substantial degree of population ageing is expected over the next few decades in all regions of the world under a variety of plausible scenarios about future fertility levels, and it seems unlikely that policy interventions intended to encourage childbearing in low-fertility countries could substantially alter this expectation. Similarly, although a large rise in the number of international migrants could alter trends in respect of the working-age population, no plausible assumption about international migration levels would have more than a moderate impact on the expected degree of population ageing that will be experienced in future decades by countries all over the world.

In short, the coming changes in population age structure are well understood and thus can be largely anticipated. Ideally, policy responses should be put in place ahead of time to ease adaptation to these long-term demographic changes. Even if population ageing is inevitable, its consequences depend on the measures developed to address the challenges it poses. The subsequent chapters of this report will discuss those challenges.

Notes to Chapter II

1   The analysis presented here is based on the 2004 Revision of the official United Nations assessment of world population trends and prospects (United Nations, 2005a). Although a more recent set of population estimates and projections (the 2006 Revision) has been released, the revised numbers could not be used in the preparation of the present report owing to publication deadlines. Like the earlier assessment, the 2006 Revision confirms that the world's population is on track to surpass 9 billion persons by 2050 and that substantial population ageing is anticipated for all major regions of the world. None of the trends or arguments presented in this report would have changed substantially if the analysis had been based on the revised set of numbers.

2   Even if the world population as a whole were to experience the relatively higher levels of fertility implied by the high-variant projection (see sect. entitled "Is population ageing inevitable?" above for an explanation of different projection scenarios), the child dependency ratio would still decline between 2005 and 2050, implying that the increase in the total dependency ratio will be due entirely to the increase in the old-age dependency ratio (see annex table A.2). Moreover, for all groups of countries, the old-age dependency ratio in 2050 resulting from the high-variant projection would be substantially higher than that estimated in 2005.

Chapter III
Older persons in a changing society

Introduction

The social environment within which people grow older is rapidly changing. The size of families is decreasing, the role of extended families is diminishing, and perceptions of intergenerational support and caring for older persons are rapidly changing.

The implications of these changes in family composition and living arrangements for support and care for older persons depend on the context. In developing countries where older people have limited access to formal mechanisms of social protection, they will need to rely on the family and the local community. However, these informal protection mechanisms have been under increasing stress recently, owing to the process of population ageing itself but also, in some contexts, to a growing participation of women in the labour force and to changing perceptions about caring for parents and older persons in general. Developed countries may need to expand the supply of formal long-term care for older persons, including institutional living, as well as to develop alternative services to allow older persons to age in their homes if they so desire.

The Madrid International Plan of Action on Ageing (United Nations, 2002a) gives major attention to ensuring enabling and supportive environments as a key area of policy and programme action for the well-being of older people. This agenda is concerned not only with the importance of ensuring sustainable systems of formal and informal care, but also with the adequacy of living arrangements and housing; and the possibility for older persons to participate in the political, social, economic and cultural life of society. The growing number of older persons and the changes in living arrangements also increase the risk of abuse and neglect; indeed, abuse of older persons and age-based discrimination are problems signalled in many countries. To redress these negative trends, specific actions are needed. These should be embedded—as argued in the present chapter—into a broader perspective which more fully recognizes and better harnesses the contributions older persons can make to societies. Such measures should ensure greater economic participation and establish adequate mechanisms to guarantee the protection of their human rights and their political empowerment.

This chapter analyses three areas that require better policy responses: the conditions of housing and living arrangements for older persons; their empowerment and political participation; and the legal framework and social awareness that ensure the protection of their human rights. A related concern is how to facilitate greater labour participation of older persons, which is addressed in chapter IV.

CHANGING LIVING ARRANGEMENTS AND HOUSING NEEDS

Trends of declining fertility and mortality rates, as described in chapter II, help to explain profound changes in the size and composition of the nuclear family associated to the decreasing importance of extended families in many parts of the world. Rapid migration from rural to urban areas, mainly as a result of industrialization processes, has been a contributing factor to the decreasing importance of the extended family. More recently, large flows of international migrants have further contributed to this trend. In addition, increasing educational attainment has been found to have an impact on fertility levels and on the composition of the family: families become more nuclear when the level of schooling rises (Oppong, 2006; Bongaarts and Zimmer, 2001; United Nations, 2005b; and chapter III).

Other cultural and social factors, such as delayed marriage and an increase in singleness and divorce rates, also influence the size and structure of families. These reflect important changes in values and lifestyles in countries around the world. Age at first marriage has increased in all regions of the world during the last 30 years (United Nations, 2000) and divorce rates increased significantly in most countries (see figure III.1).

The emancipation of women, including their more active participation in labour markets and increased control over reproductive behaviour through modern contraceptives, has been an important factor in the lowering of fertility rates. In developed countries, childlessness has become a widespread phenomenon. In the western part of Germany, for instance, one third of all men and women born after 1960 are expected to remain childless (Dorbritz and Schwarz, 1996).

All these factors have generated rapid changes in the size and structure of families. Household size has fallen to an average of 3.7 persons in East Asia, 4.9 in South-East Asia, 4.1 in the Caribbean, 5.7 in Northern Africa

Figure III.1.
Changes in divorce rates, selected countries, 1960, 1980 and 2003

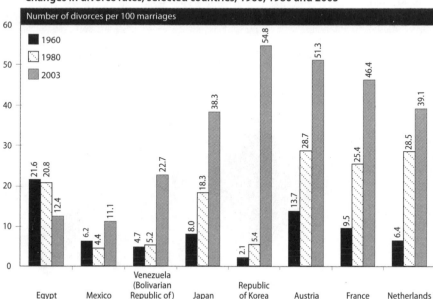

Source: United Nations Statistics Division.

and 2.8 in developed countries (United Nations, 2003). There has also been a shift from extended to nuclear families, including an increase in one-person households. These changes have important consequences for the welfare and living arrangements of older people.

Living arrangements and housing needs[1]

The majority of older persons in all countries continue to live in their own homes and communities, a phenomenon that is sometimes referred to as "ageing in place".[2] In the developing world, the large majority of older persons continue to live in multigenerational households, most of them with their children and grandchildren, and some also with other adults. Only 13 per cent of older people live with a spouse and a very small proportion (7 per cent) live alone (figure III.2). In the developed world, by contrast, the largest proportion of older people live with a spouse in a single-generation household (43 per cent) and another 25 per cent live alone. Older persons in developed countries are more likely to live in non-familial residential settings, but overall only a small proportion of older people in all countries live in centres of institutional care.

Figure III.2.
Living arrangements of older persons[a] in developed and developing regions

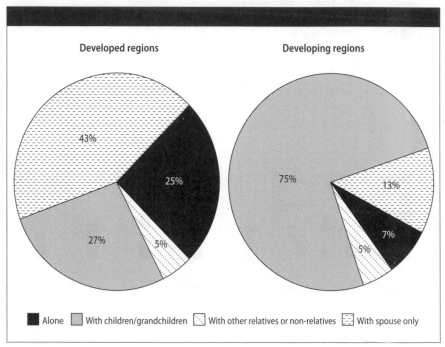

Source: United Nations (2005).
Note: Based on the population in households.
a Aged 60 years or over.

Although living arrangements for older persons vary greatly both among and within countries, in most countries there is a slow but increasing tendency towards solitary living. In developed countries, the proportion of older people living alone in 1994 varied from 14 per cent in Spain to close to 40 per cent in Denmark. In developing countries, that proportion was much smaller (United Nations, 2005b, table II.3). One out of seven or 90 million older people live alone worldwide. This ratio has increased in the majority of regions and countries over the past decades (figure III.3). While the average rate of change is rather modest, the trend is likely to continue and will have important social consequences, especially for women, who are more likely to live alone as, in general, they outlive their spouses. Solitary living may result in increasing isolation and makes caregiving by family members more difficult to arrange. It also increases the need to provide additional support services to enable older people to remain in their own homes (United Nations, 2005b).

Figure III.3.
**Proportion of older persons[a] living alone at
two time points, by sex, averages for major areas**

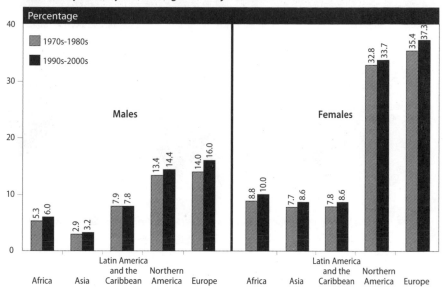

Source: United Nations (2005b).

Note: Based on the population in households. The first time point refers to the latest year in the 1970s or 1980s for which data were available. The second time point refers to the latest year in the 1990s or 2000s for which data were available.

a Aged 60 years or over.

Living arrangements for older persons in the developing world

In the developing countries, the large majority of seniors live with their adult children. In Africa and Asia, on average, about three quarters of those aged 60 years or over are living with their adult children. In Latin America and the Caribbean, the corresponding proportion is about two thirds (figure III.4). The proportion of older persons living alone in developing countries is less than 10 per cent. This share is declining in some countries, but in most of them it is slowly increasing. The exception is Ghana where the proportion of older people living alone has shown a remarkable increase, almost doubling, from 12 to 22 per cent in the period 1980-1998 (United Nations, 2005b, table II.3).

Solitary living in developing countries is particularly problematic because of the generally limited social support programmes for older persons (United Nations, 2005b). In addition, lack of funds and human resources restricts the availability of institutional care in developing countries, as discussed at greater length in chapter VI. In Latin America and the Caribbean region,

Figure III.4.
Living arrangements of older persons[a] in Africa, Asia and Latin America and the Caribbean

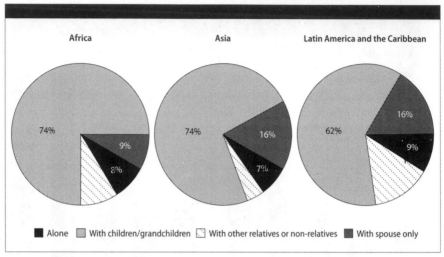

Source: United Nations (2005b).

Note: Based on the population in households.

a   Aged 60 years or over.

for instance, only 1 to 2 per cent of older persons live in institutional care facilities (Pelaez, 2006).

Growing urbanization of the population has been a major dimension of modernization in the developing world. Most developing countries have been experiencing a combination of population ageing and urbanization in a relatively short period of time. It is projected that by 2050, the number of persons aged 60 years or over in the developing countries will be nearly four times greater than it is today, and that the share of older persons residing in urban areas will rise from about 56 million in 1998 to over 908 million by 2050 (United Nations Centre for Human Settlements (Habitat), 1999).[3] The generally wide income disparities between rural and urban areas and the significant migration of younger members of the family to the city increase the probability that older persons in the countryside will become socially and economically vulnerable.

Older persons who relocate from rural to urban areas tend to face different problems. In addition to economic difficulties and a lack of steady income (see chapter V), they often experience a loss of social networks and a lack of supporting infrastructure in cities. Without adequate transportation and opportunities to incorporate themselves in the urban environment, there is greater risk of their being isolated and marginalized, especially when frailty and/or disability restrict their mobility.

Living arrangements for older persons in the developed world

In developed countries, more than two thirds of older persons live either alone or with a spouse (see figure III.2 above). One third live with children/ grandchildren or other persons. Although there is a lack of comprehensive statistics on the number of people living in institutional care centres, such as nursing homes and assisted living facilities, the available information does suggest that only a small share of the older population of developed countries live in facilities for long-term care. Such care is typically reserved for frail older persons who have difficulty managing on their own, are disabled and/ or are in need of specialized medical services.

Institutionalized care was on the increase for several decades in Europe and Northern America, but the escalating cost of providing this type of long-term care combined with the preference of many older people for remaining in their own homes has slowed the growth of nursing homes and assisted living facilities in recent years. Instead, there has been a shift towards more home- and community-based systems of care which have enabled older persons to stay at home. The staggering cost differential is a major consideration. In South Carolina, United States of America, for example, a range of services that enable older persons to remain in their homes, including home-delivered meals, personal care, and adult day services, can be provided for about $822 dollars per year. In contrast, the cost of maintaining someone in a nursing home ranges from $25,000 to $37,000 per year.[4] Estimates of future public-health costs presented in chapter VI may be much higher if population ageing requires the expansion of institutionalized care.

Alternative living and care arrangements for older people in developed countries are growing in importance. The "ageing in place" movement[5] has had some influence on this trend by promoting policies and programmes designed to help older people remain in their own home largely through the support of community-based ambulant care. The variety of services available to older persons in their own homes include personal care, meals, housekeeping, home maintenance, care management, and treatment for health problems. Services in the community include day care, congregate meals, and social centres. Through their availability, these and other programmes enable a growing proportion of seniors to delay or even avoid institutional care.

Sweden is an example of a country committed to providing extensive health and social services to older persons to enable them to live in their own homes. Services provided include personal care and assistance with basic tasks such as cleaning, shopping and meal preparation. These home-help services provided by the municipality are available to all Swedes aged 65 years or over. In 2004, 9 per cent of older people received some form of home-based services (Sweden, Ministry of Health and Social Affairs, 2005).

The Hammond community-care service, in Australia, is another example of an ageing-in-place programme that supports older people with dementia in their own homes. This care package includes support ranging from personal care and home help to medical assistance (Hammond Care Group, 2003). In the United States, different types of planned retirement communities have emerged. These include naturally occurring retirement communities (NORCs) and continuing care retirement communities (CCRC) which feature different types of living arrangements that provide supportive services to community residents. The naturally occurring retirement communities, which have evolved over time as the residents of a community have grown older, provide a range of coordinated health care, social services and educational/recreational activities in neighbourhoods. In New York City, where the NORC movement began, local government and philanthropic organizations provided start-up funding (Vladeck, 2004).

Housing conditions and assistive technology

In developing countries, housing conditions for older people tend to vary significantly depending on their level of income. Tables III.1 and III.2 contain statistics on the conditions of housing in Latin American countries. For the most part, older persons are less likely to be tenants, as well as less likely to live in "poor" areas (that is to say, in shanty towns). Only in Haiti is the proportion of older people who reside in poor areas significantly larger than that of the adult population aged 25-49. In many Latin American countries, older persons are more likely than those in other age groups to live in dwellings constructed using low-quality materials. Such is the case for Bolivia, Chile, El Salvador, Guatemala, Honduras, Mexico, Paraguay, the Dominican Republic and Haiti.

Older persons tend to have less access to the supply of drinking water in the home in countries like Bolivia, Paraguay and Chile, but are in a better position in Nicaragua, Colombia and the Bolivarian Republic of Venezuela. Older people are also more likely to live in dwellings without hygienic restrooms in Bolivia, Brazil, Chile, Ecuador, El Salvador, Honduras and the Dominican Republic. In respect of sewerage deprivation, the elderly are in a worse situation in Chile, Ecuador, El Salvador, Honduras and Mexico.

Interviews of older persons in Egypt, as contained in a report of the United Nations Centre for Human Settlements (Habitat) (1999), revealed poor living conditions for older persons. Systematic evidence comparing the

Table III.1:
Conditions of housing in Latin America by age group

	Percentage that are housing owners				Percentage with dwellings in poor areas				Percentage with dwellings of low-quality materials			
	All (i)	60+ (ii)	50-59 (iii)	25-49 (iv)	All (i)	60+ (ii)	50-59 (iii)	25-49 (iv)	All (i)	60+ (ii)	50-59 (iii)	25-49 (iv)
Bolivia	64	86	80	58	21	11	16	23	55	66	59	51
Brazil	70	82	78	65	1	0	0	1	3	3	2	2
Chile	65	84	76	54	3	2	1	3	10	13	9	9
Colombia	59	82	64	48	1	0	1	1	20	21	20	19
Costa Rica	74	85	85	70	1	1	1	1	5	4	4	5
Dominican Republic	67	86	79	57	45	42	42	45	8	10	8	7
Ecuador	70	85	81	61	..	..	..	..	..	..	..	..
El Salvador	69	80	79	65	6	3	4	6	27	31	25	25
Guatemala	78	87	86	74	..	..	..	..	30	34	29	29
Haiti	67	84	78	58	20	24	20	18	26	32	28	24
Honduras	71	85	83	66	6	2	2	7	10	14	10	9
Mexico	73	86	84	67	..	..	..	..	32	36	30	31
Nicaragua	77	87	88	73	8	6	5	9	22	20	20	23
Paraguay	81	89	89	78	16	16	14	16	2	4	3	2
Peru	76	89	85	68	9	6	7	11	18	11	12	22
Uruguay	64	76	71	50	2	2	2	1	..	..	..	..
Venezuela (Bolivarian Republic of)	76	91	84	69	8	5	5	9	10	8	7	11

Source: Gasparini and others (2007).

Table III.2.
Access to provision of basic housing services in Latin America by age group

Percentage

	Water				Hygienic restrooms				Sewerage			
	All (i)	60+ (ii)	50-59 (iii)	25-49 (iv)	All (i)	60+ (ii)	50-59 (iii)	25-49 (iv)	All (i)	60+ (ii)	50-59 (iii)	25-49 (iv)
Bolivia	77	73	77	78	66	59	67	69	46	52	52	44
Brazil	96	96	97	97	69	69	71	69	56	58	59	56
Chile	95	94	95	96	87	87	90	87	80	78	82	81
Colombia	76	81	76	74	79	80	78	78	57	55	57	58
Costa Rica	96	95	96	96	95	94	95	95	28	34	32	25
Dominican Republic	71	72	73	71	60	57	62	62	23	24	25	22
Ecuador	73	73	73	73	79	75	79	80	45	42	46	46
El Salvador	59	61	66	58	35	31	41	37	32	28	37	34
Guatemala	66	67	71	67	46	46	50	44	38	39	40	37
Haiti	14	15	12	15	4	3	4	4	..	..	..	..
Honduras	35	33	39	35	44	39	47	44	34	29	35	36
Mexico	88	89	90	88	65	64	69	65	71	71	74	71
Nicaragua	61	65	62	61	23	26	25	21	17	20	19	15
Paraguay	70	67	69	72	61	60	62	62	8	10	8	7
Peru	61	64	69	57	58	57	65	56	48	52	58	44
Uruguay	99	99	99	99	94	96	95	93	64	71	68	64
Venezuela (Bolivarian Republic of)	94	95	95	94	89	91	92	89	72	76	77	70

Source: Gasparini and others (2007).

living conditions of older adults with those of other age groups is lacking, but older persons who were interviewed in different neighbourhoods of Cairo were living in overcrowded housing, lacked proper ventilation, and had poor sanitary conditions with inadequate water and waste disposal networks. There were deficiencies in the system of garbage collection and disposal. Most dwellings did have indoor piped water and private baths; however, one third of those interviewed reported having to use group latrines, and a few had only outdoor showers.

The welfare of older people and their ability to continue their pattern of independent living in their own homes can be supported not only by the provision of basic services within the household but also by changes in housing design and assistive technology. Assistive technology, which is a generic term that includes assistive, adaptive, and rehabilitative devices, promotes the greater independence of older persons and people with disabilities by enabling them to perform tasks that they formerly were unable to accomplish or had great difficulty accomplishing.

Important considerations in the provision of housing for older people include accessibility and safety. In Japan, the Construction Ministry has recommended design guidelines for housing to help prepare for a rapidly ageing society (Novelli, 2005). In other countries, more emphasis is being placed on remodelling houses to better meet the needs of older people. A coalition of service providers in Maryland (United States) started a programme known as Howard County Rebuilding Together, which provides home modification support (Horizon Foundation, 2005). Seniors can obtain, as part of a larger ageing-in-place initiative, an assessment of their home, and repairs and remodelling can be provided, if necessary, to make the building safer and more accessible.

There has been a development of assistive technology in both academia and industry in recent years. The relevance of modern information and communication technologies (ICT) and of smart home technologies for living arrangements has increased in the past few years (Meyer and Mollenkopf, 2003). These projects have focused, for the most part, on developing assistive technologies to enhance older persons' functional abilities and adaptive technologies to increase access to information and communication. Such technologies include eldercare robots, elder-centred websites, communication devices and intelligent devices to assist with walking and eating (Hirsch and others, 2000). In Italy, the National Programme for Housing recently funded initiatives that included "neighbourhood agreements" whereby some city councils would promote housing renovation plans supported by new technology (Novelli, 2005).

The introduction of programmes to assist housing design and assistive technology in meeting the special needs of older people is still limited to a few cities, mainly in developed countries. In 1994, the Economic and Social Commission for Asia and the Pacific (ESCAP), with support from the Government of Japan, initiated a programme to promote barrier-free environments in the developing countries of Asia and the Pacific. Specifically, ESCAP issued guidelines for architects, urban planners and engineers on designing barrier-free physical environments and it is supporting pilot projects in Bangkok, Beijing and New Delhi. These three cities have become demonstration sites in the developing world for the promotion of barrier-free environments for persons with disabilities and older persons. China, India and Thailand have produced their own technical guidelines on facilitating better housing design.[6] The introduction of these innovations is very recent and it is still not clear whether this kind of technology can be provided at an affordable cost to a growing population of older people in developing countries.

Implications for care and intergenerational support

The changes in family structures have had a significant effect on patterns of intergenerational provision of care and reciprocity. Co-residence of older and younger family members used to be the central component of lifelong reciprocity arrangements in which adult children provided care for their aged parents in exchange for parental support at earlier stages of their lives. However, changing family structures combined with population ageing have presented formidable challenges to the provision of care across generations. This phenomenon, while evident in all countries, is particularly so in the few developing countries that have experienced demographic ageing in addition to modernization in a comparatively short period of time. Obstacles to family support have increased while formal support systems remain limited (Cowgill, 1972; United Nations, 2005b).

As the proportion of women in the formal labour market increases, adult daughters, who constitute the largest group of personal caregivers for older persons, are more often balancing work and caregiving responsibilities. Stepfamilies resulting from divorce and remarriage create complicated intergenerational relationships. In this context, the developed world is experiencing a growth in the number of older people with fewer adult children available to provide care.

The precise implications of these changes in family composition for living arrangements and support mechanisms depend on the context. In countries where most older people do not have access to formal mechanisms of social security, older persons rely on informal support mechanisms such as the family and the community; but these informal protection mechanisms have been under increasing stress recently, owing largely to the acceleration of demographic transitions, higher economic risks for families, and shifts in paradigms of filial support and reciprocity (Aboderin, 2004; Gomes da Conceição and Montes de Oca Zavala, 2004). Economic insecurity has put pressure on young and able family members to increase their participation in wage-earning activities outside the home including through migration (to domestic and international destinations). Employment opportunities situated away from the current residence of younger workers may have negative implications for the *instrumental* support that older persons traditionally received from children; that is to say, support in the form of preparing meals, and doing laundry, housework, shopping and so on.

At present, not all countries or areas are undergoing major social change. A study by Hermalin (2002) did not find significant shifts in living arrangements of older persons in the Philippines, Singapore, Taiwan Province of China and Thailand. At least two thirds of the cases studied still live with their children. In Thailand, an increase in the proportion of children living nearby seems to have compensated for a modest reduction in co-residence. Major changes, however, are likely to occur in the future. Surveys of women aged 20-39 in Taiwan Province of China indicate that the proportion of those expecting to co-reside with a married son during their old age had declined from 56 per cent in 1973 to 45 per cent in 1986. Likewise, in focus group discussions, adult children in Thailand foresaw that as older persons, the care they received from their children would probably be less than the support they were currently providing to their parents.

Changes in the living arrangements of older people have considerable policy implications in both developing and developed countries. Many developing countries are still facing the challenge of providing basic infrastructure and social services to older people in a context where the lack of adequate formal public and private support programmes increases the vulnerability of older adults. Thus, the expansion of basic services and infrastructure will have to be completed along with the introduction of new forms of informal and more formal care provision. In developed countries, institutional care is more readily available, but larger investment will probably have to be directed towards expanding the number of long-term care facilities required to accommodate the increasing demand for those services expected in the near future (see chapter VI). An additional challenge in the context of a rapidly ageing population in developed countries is the provision of alternative, that is to say, non-institutionalized, support services to allow seniors to remain in their own homes as long as possible.

At this point, it remains unclear what shape the social and institutional arrangements for providing care for older persons will take in the future. Meeting the needs of older persons and ensuring respect for their human rights will require the implementation of a variety of programmes and living arrangements offering a continuum of care, with complementary roles being played by the family, the community and the public sector.

SOCIAL, CULTURAL AND FAMILY CONTRIBUTIONS OF OLDER PERSONS

Older persons have traditionally been active contributors to the social and cultural development of their societies. Certain cultures, most especially the indigenous communities, have long recognized the valuable contributions that their elders make in perpetuating and enriching the social and cultural dimensions of their societies. Ancient cultural norms, beliefs and customs are often kept alive through an informal system of intergenerational transmission, adapted to the local culture and environment. Traditional knowledge is typically passed on orally, and takes the form of stories, songs, artistic impressions, cultural events, rituals, languages and agricultural practices (United Nations, 2005c). When written accounts are scarce, older persons are often the only source of the information needed to maintain the historical record of local communities. For example, the tragic events that took place in Cambodia in the last half-century have been captured in an oral history project that recounts the experiences of older Cambodians during those turbulent times (United Nations, 1997a; HelpAge International, 2001).

Other societies have been less receptive to, and respectful of, the contributions of their oldest members. Older persons in Eastern and Central Europe, for example, are often viewed as contributing to the difficulties the region currently confronts, as they are associated with the old political regimes (HelpAge International, 2002). In a few countries, such as Bosnia and Herzegovina, Moldova and Romania, civil society organizations are helping to counter negative perceptions of older people by creating social clubs offering them opportunities to engage in the volunteer activities of groups for mutual support and assistance to marginalized people.

Grandparenting: contribution to intergenerational cohesion in the family

As the population ages, more attention should be paid to strengthening solidarity between generations, as called for in the Madrid International Plan of Action on Ageing. Often, younger and older generations are at odds, with each group competing for government resources and policy attention. Greater effort should be made to highlight the synergies and interdependence of, rather than the differences between, the generations.

With the changes in family structures, the notion of grandparenting has taken on new dimensions. Older persons play an important role within the family in most countries. When both parents are active in the labour market or when they migrate, older persons (mainly women) act as primary caregivers for children and other family members. The U.S. Census Bureau (2005) reports that 21 per cent of preschoolers are primarily cared for by their grandparents while their parents are working, and 1 in 12 children lives in households headed by grandparents. Hermalin (2002) indicates that the current levels of childcare provided by grandparents to co-resident and non-co-resident grandchildren are significant sources of support (both material and otherwise) in the Philippines, Taiwan Province of China and Thailand. Among poor multigenerational families, older persons often make an important contribution to family income through part-time employment. In Brazil and South Africa, for instance, earnings from the pensions and work of older persons are important sources of income for those households (Lloyd-Sherlock, 2004b; see also chapter V).

In countries with a high prevalence of HIV/AIDS, especially those in sub-Saharan Africa and parts of Asia and the Caribbean, the role of older women as primary caregivers for children is gaining in importance. In sub-Saharan Africa, 30 per cent of households are headed by a person over age 55 and two thirds of these have at least one child under age 15. Many other factors, including violence, incarceration and substance abuse, that are responsible for parental absence from the home, also leave the older generation with major responsibilities for childcare.

Greater involvement of grandparents in childcare and other family responsibilities results in important contributions to the well-being of extended families. Care should be taken, though, that this involvement is not detrimental to the welfare of older adults themselves. Drawing grandparents into assuming greater family responsibilities at the expense of their own health may generate an additional burden for older persons. When older persons must care for children in the absence of younger adults—in what are frequently referred to as skipped-generation households—an additional burden may be imposed on them, in terms of claims on their income, with a consequent deterioration of their living conditions. A close assessment of each particular situation would contribute to the design of sensible policy responses to the challenge of promoting intergenerational cohesion and protecting the welfare of older people.

PARTICIPATION OF OLDER PERSONS IN SOCIETY

As older persons constitute an ever-increasing proportion of the total population, they have the potential to become more influential politically, economically and socially. Fulfilling this potential would be in line with the objectives of the Madrid International Plan of Action on Ageing, which are to ensure that people can age with security and dignity and continue to participate fully in their societies as citizens with full rights. Older persons should be afforded the possibility of becoming more actively engaged in the development process so that their skills, experiences, wisdom and knowledge can be put to use in society for the benefit of all.

In most countries, the position of older persons in society and the opportunities available to them for remaining active participants in the life of the community are often associated with their economic and political power. A growing cohort of older persons, particularly those in high-income developed countries, is carrying substantial weight in the economy and often hold a significant share of wealth. As there is usually a close correlation between economic and political power, older persons who are seen as exercising considerable power in the marketplace will likely translate this power into significant political power and participation. In Germany, for example, those over age 50 own half of the nation's wealth and have the spending capacity of 90 billion euros per year (European Foundation for the Improvement of Living and Working Conditions, 2006a; World Bank, 2006a). Many businesses are responding to the growth of this consumer market by designing products and services especially targeted at older age groups. The emergence of new markets is expanding the job growth potential of the "silver economy" through the creation of new products, services, economic cooperation and networks geared towards older persons.

At the other end of the spectrum, the factors that contribute to a person's vulnerability, namely, poverty, poor health, lack of education, disabilities and absence of influence, become accentuated as a person ages. These factors combine to limit and constrain older persons' ability to participate fully in their communities. For example, low educational levels and illiteracy are major barriers to social and political participation. In 2000, 23 per cent of persons aged 70 years or over in Malta and 25 per cent of those in the same age group in Portugal were illiterate. While these illiteracy rates may be atypical in most developed countries, they do indicate that illiteracy remains a concern for older persons even in high-income countries (United Nations, 2002b).

Although illiteracy rates have been declining over the past 20 years in all regions of the world, they remain generally high in developing countries. Illiteracy rates among those aged 60 years or over in the developing countries dropped from 75 to 56 per cent in the period from 1980 to 2000, and they are expected to continue to fall, reaching 43 per cent by 2010. Yet, major imbalances in literacy achievement across countries remain. Illiteracy rates still exceed 90 per cent in some of the least developed countries in Africa, while they have fallen to below 10 per cent for older persons in countries like Argentina, Tajikistan and Uruguay.

However, as most of the declines in illiteracy have taken place among males, there has been a consequent increase in the literacy gender gap. In 1980, there was a 22 percentage point difference in literacy rates between women and men over age 60. By 2000, this difference had increased to 28 percentage points. In the Economic and Social Commission for Western Asia (ESCWA) region, for example, the illiteracy rate is high among older women because "they were not exposed to educational opportunities at a time when tradition was more in control of their lives, leading to their seclusion, hence denying them the right to education" (El-Safty, 2006, p. 22).

These figures on illiteracy underscore the difficulties that older segments of the population, particularly in developing countries, confront in respect of accessing and processing information that is directly relevant to them. Illiterate older persons are frequently unaware of their rights and the benefits to which they are entitled, including social security benefits. A 2002 survey in Thailand, for example, indicated that only 50 per cent of those aged 60 years or over were aware of the availability of social security for older persons, and that as few as 5 per cent actually received those benefits (Cheng, Chan and Phillips, 2006). Education and literacy are important elements of the process of empowering older persons and expanding their opportunities to continue to contribute to society and to its development. Participation in social, economic, cultural, sporting, recreational and volunteer activities also contributes to increasing and sustaining the well-being of older persons and of the population at large.

In recent years, most developing countries have made substantial progress in expanding the coverage of primary education and reducing the gender gap in educational attainment. It is therefore to be expected that this negative effect of lack of education on empowerment will be substantially reduced over the next 50 years as the current generation of children is transformed into the older generation.

Political participation

The voices of older persons can best be heard through their active political participation at the individual level (through voting in elections), at the group level (through participation in organizations of older persons) and at the government level (through the formation of advisory bodies of older persons). Demographic changes, by themselves, have captured the attention of policymakers with respect to issues that concern older people; at the same time, greater political involvement of older people has been an important factor in drawing attention to their needs.

Voting power

Older individuals have a greater propensity for exercising their democratic right to vote in many countries than those in other age groups. In Kazakhstan, for instance, older persons constitute an active electorate, with 72 per cent of those aged 65 years or over having voted in recent elections, compared with just over 50 per cent of those aged 35-40 (United Nations Development Programme and the United Nations Population Fund, 2005). Similarly, older persons in the United Kingdom of Great Britain and Northern Ireland currently have the highest voting incidence in the population, well above that of younger age groups; during the 2005 parliamentary elections, for example, those aged 65 years or over were twice as likely to vote as those aged 18-24, with the voting rates of these two age groups being 75 and 37 per cent, respectively (International Institute for Democracy and Electoral Assistance, 2006a).

Similarly in the United States, although voting rates of younger age groups have been falling over the past two decades, those for Americans aged 65 years or over have held steady or increased slightly; in fact; older persons now constitute the most active part of the electorate (U.S. Census Bureau, 2005). There is no evidence, however, that older persons constitute a single, unified voting block: they are of different political persuasions and vote for a wide range of candidates. Yet they are becoming an influential force and one to be reckoned with regarding the issues and policies that most affect them, such as the current debates over social security reform and long-term care insurance. The expansion of the Medicare programme in 2003 to include prescription drug coverage represents one result of their growing political impact.

Not all countries share the same tradition of the enjoyment by older people of high political participation and influence. Data from the first round of the 2005 presidential election in Liberia indicate that two groups had the lowest rate of voter turnout: older persons aged 68 years or over and young people aged 18-22 (International Institute for Democracy and Electoral Assistance, 2006b). In other countries, mainly in sub-Saharan Africa, where older persons constitute only 5 per cent of the population, compared with those under age 15 who constitute 41 per cent, relatively low priority is given to policies for older persons. They are also less likely to be sufficiently empowered to be able to draw attention to their concerns.

Organizations of older persons

Organizations of older persons—particularly older women, who often remain voiceless—provide an important means of enabling participation through advocacy and promotion of multigenerational interactions. Furthermore, these groups can help to harness the political influence of older persons and ensure that they effectively participate in the debate and decision-making processes at all levels of government.

There are several examples of successful and influential organizations of older persons, including AARP (formerly known as the American Association of Retired Persons) in the United States, with its 36 million members, and pensioners' organizations in Sweden to which half of all older persons belong. Labour unions also provide older persons with an important means of representation, particularly in Europe where most retired workers remain active union members (Peterson, 2002). These organizations provide information, advocacy, resources, activities and support to older persons, and exert considerable influence in economic and social policymaking.

HelpAge International is a prominent global network of non-governmental organizations whose mission is to improve the lives of disadvantaged older persons. The network consists of affiliate organizations in some 50 countries which are committed to supporting practical programmes, giving a voice to disempowered older persons, and influencing policy at the local, national and international levels (HelpAge International, 2006a). Actions are directed towards encouraging Governments and communities to recognize the needs, values and rights of disadvantaged older persons, and to encompass them in their programmes. In recent years, HelpAge International has been particularly influential in advocating for social pension plans to assist impoverished older persons in sub-Saharan Africa.

There are also a number of prominent international non-governmental organizations that represent the interests of older persons.[7] These include the International Federation on Ageing (IFA), the International Federation of Senior Citizens Associations (FIAPA) and the European Federation of Older Persons (EURAG). Through their various activities, these organizations aim to improve the quality of life of older persons by influencing policies, engaging in grass-roots activities and strengthening public-private partnerships. In addition, they also work to improve the image of older persons by challenging the prevailing stereotypes about ageing, accentuating the contributions that older people make to society so as to counterbalance the emphasis on the economic challenges created by demographic ageing (Global Action in Aging, 2006). Another example is the International Association of Gerontology and Geriatrics (IAGG), an international organization of researchers and professionals in the area of ageing. With its member organizations in 64 countries, IAGG promotes the highest levels of achievement of gerontology research and training worldwide.

Consultation and advisory committees

Several countries also provide for direct consultation and participation of older persons in the design and evaluation of government programmes. The most advanced in this respect have established government offices on ageing at the ministerial or similar level, such as the Department of Health and Ageing (Australia), the Division of Ageing and Seniors of the Public Health Agency (Canada), the National Committee on Ageing (China), the Federal Ministry for Family Affairs, Senior Citizens, Women and Youth (Germany) and the Administration on Ageing (United States).

A number of countries have established independent advisory bodies, composed of academics, representatives from the private sector and non-governmental organizations, to address ageing issues and the concerns of older persons. These advisory bodies, which are typically charged with the task of advising Governments on developing and implementing policies, can serve as watchdogs in the context of government policymaking. Advisory bodies can constitute an important mechanism through which to incorporate opinions and facilitate close and regular monitoring of policy implementation at the local or community level. They can also play a role in evaluating the impact of new programmes and improving their results.

Advisory bodies currently exist in a variety of countries such as Austria, Chile, Guatemala, India and Mexico. Austria, for example, has established an independent council of senior citizens with rights and responsibilities similar to those of a chamber of commerce, which has become a major contributor to discussions on national policy on ageing. Chile has created a National Service for Older Persons which includes an advisory committee composed of representatives of older persons' organizations, academia and institutions working with older persons. Guatemala has a National Council for Protection of the Aged which consults with civil society and organizations of older persons. In India, a National Council of Older Persons, whose membership comprises government representatives (25 per cent), and academics and retired persons from rural and urban communities (75 per cent), is accepted by the Government as a watchdog agency designed to monitor policy on ageing. In Mexico, the National Institute of Older Persons requires that senior citizens be included in advisory bodies concerned with relevant issues. A common feature of many of these advisory bodies is the independence they enjoy which enables them to play a role in monitoring the implementation of the Madrid Plan of Action.

A remaining challenge is to ensure that these advisory bodies become effective mechanisms of broad consultation and representation in respect of the various concerns that affect the welfare of older persons, while taking due account of major differences that may exist in the access to services and benefits by older people in urban and rural areas, based on income group, ethnicity and gender. This would be especially relevant in countries where inequality has traditionally excluded large groups of the population from participation in the political debate. In countries where older persons do not have formal mechanisms for participation in the policy debate, there is the double challenge of improving their opportunities to create organizations and increasing the policy space within the government needed to allow active participation in policy design and monitoring.

EMPOWERING OLDER MEMBERS OF SOCIETY

The International Federation on Ageing refers to the empowerment of older persons as "the ability to make informed choices, exercise influence, make continuing contributions to society, and take advantage of services" (Thursz, Nusberg and Prater, 1995). In this sense, empowerment is closely related to participation.

There are several factors that preclude the more active participation of older persons in society including poverty, poor health, low educational levels, lack of transportation and access to services, negative stereotypes about ageing, and overt or subtle age discrimination (ibid.). The goals in empowering older persons are to overcome these numerous barriers, make optimal use of their potential societal contributions and enhance their life satisfaction.

An important element in the empowerment process is the enforcement of legislative measures to guarantee the rights of older persons that are laid out in national constitutions and international human rights conventions. Recent examples include European Union Council Directive 2000/78/EC of 27 November 2000 establishing a general framework for equal treatment in employment and occupation, which requires member States to enact legislation by the end of 2006 (article 18) that would make age discrimination in employment and vocational training unlawful (see chapter IV). Additionally, some countries have adopted legislation to criminalize elder abuse and increase penalties for certain crimes perpetrated against older persons. Within the Latin American and Caribbean region, for example, some 80 per cent of countries have legislation or policies protecting the rights of older persons, including measures on training and monitoring of abuse and neglect in institutions (Pelaez, 2006). Very often, however, there exist no mechanisms for enforcement.

The first and most essential step in empowering older persons is to guarantee that the legal and justice systems that protect the human rights of citizens are effectively enforced so as to eliminate the risk of marginalization of, and abuse directed against, older persons in a variety of institutional, community and family settings. In some countries, culture and tradition may influence the extent to which older persons risk being discriminated against in mainstream social, economic, political and community life. In the most extreme cases, the denial—or inadequate enforcement—of the human rights of older persons can lead to neglect, abuse and violence.

Fighting neglect, abuse and violence directed against older persons

Abuse and neglect directed against older people are by no means new developments. Scattered evidence suggests that abusive behaviour has been present from ancient times, both within the household and in the society at large. In recent decades, ageing of the population and greater awareness of the need to ensure the welfare of older people have drawn attention to these issues. Although it is generally recognized that abuse, neglect and violence directed against older persons is a serious problem, there has been less attention given to developing the means to assess the extent of the problem in different countries and its evolution over time.

At least three methodological hurdles may explain the absence of systematic data on abuse directed against older persons. The first hurdle concerns the definition of *old age* itself: several countries use different age benchmarks to identify someone as old. In most countries, old age is related to the age of retirement, which varies by country; in some others, the perception of old age is associated with physical decline and inability to meet family and/or work responsibilities (see chapter I). The second difficulty lies in the definition of *abuse*. The International Network for the Prevention of Elder Abuse suggests that "elder abuse is a single or repeated act, or lack of appropriate action, occurring within any relationship where there is an expectation of trust, which causes harm or distress to an older person" and proposes several categories of abusive behaviour: physical abuse; psychological or emotional abuse; financial or material abuse; sexual abuse; and neglect (see World Health Organization, 2002a, pp. 126-127). The third problem is the lack of precise indicators to measure each one of the dimensions of abuse, as defined above, and the absence of reporting mechanisms to facilitate the capture and processing of the information needed to document abusive behaviour properly. Additional complications in respect of the measurement of abuse are related to cultural differences among countries and even within the same country. Overburdening older persons with family responsibilities may be perceived as elder abuse in some cultures, and as part of tradition in others.

The lack of systematic evidence does not mean, however, that problems of abuse cannot be identified. Different instruments used to assess the problem suggest that abusive behaviour directed against older persons is prevalent among their family members, the community and the providers of services. On the other hand, it is difficult to come up with precise estimates of the magnitude of the problem and its evolution over time when there is a lack of information.[8]

Special surveys on domestic abuse were conducted in Canada, Finland, the Netherlands, the United States and the United Kingdom. The evidence, combining all forms of abuse—physical, psychological, and financial abuse plus cases of negligence—suggests that between 4 and 6 per cent of older persons living at home have experienced some form of abuse in these countries (World Health Organization, 2002a).[9]

Across a broader range of studies, such prevalence rates tend to vary quite substantially, however, owing partly to the lack of a common definition of what constitutes abuse, as discussed above. A national survey found that 4 per cent of older Canadians had experienced physical abuse, psychological abuse, neglect or financial abuse after having reached age 65 (Podnieks, 1992). National surveys conducted through telephone interviews in Denmark and Sweden revealed a prevalence rate of 8 per cent using a broad definition of elder abuse, with theft being the most common form (Tornstam, 1989). In the United Kingdom, 5 per cent of older people were found to have experienced verbal abuse, 2 per cent physical abuse and 2 per cent neglect (Ogg, 1993). Research suggests prevalence rates of 0.58 per cent for Australia (Boldy and others, 2005), 2.2 per cent for Costa Rica (Dirección General de Estadística y Censos, 1994), 5.7 per cent for Finland (Kivela and others, 1992) and 8.2 per cent for the Republic of Korea (Cho, Kim and Kim, 2000). However, given the differences in the approaches, periods of reference and definitions used in these studies, it is impossible to make comparisons and draw conclusions on the scope of elder abuse.

Older people living in long-term care facilities are also subject to abuse and negligence. Government reports and personal histories provide some order of magnitude of the degree of exposure to abusive behaviour at the small local level. Unfortunately, there are no data at the national level on the incidence of abuse in residential/institutional long-term care facilities and its evolution over time. However, the figures on abuse in institutional settings that do exist are staggering. WHO (2002a, p. 130) cites data derived from a nursing home in one State in the United States where 36 per cent of the staff had witnessed at least one incident of physical abuse inflicted by a staff member in the preceding year, 10 per cent admitted having committed at least one act of physical abuse and 40 per cent admitted having committed at least one act of psychological abuse. In a survey of a small sample of nursing-home staff in Germany, 79 per cent acknowledged having abused or neglected a resident at least once during the prior two months and 66 per cent having witnessed comparable actions by other staff, with neglect and psychological abuse the most common forms of abuse (Goergen, 2001).

The lack of reliable data is a serious constraint on implementing adequate responses to a problem that appears to be larger than generally recognized. Implementation of the Madrid International Plan of Action on Ageing with a view to protecting the human rights of older people should include specific actions aimed at providing the methodological framework for the generation of consistent data needed to assess the extent of abusive practices against older people, monitor trends over time and facilitate comparisons across countries. Such efforts would have to include actions to overcome the three hurdles that restrict the development of reliable statistics, namely, (a) the lack of a unifying definition of old age, (b) the lack of a common definition and taxonomy of abuse and (c) the need to develop instruments to facilitate measurement and report cases of abusive behaviour directed against older people.

Risk factors for elder abuse and response mechanisms

There are a number of risk factors, including lack of resources, poor training and job-related stress in institutional facilities, negative stereotypes in society, and poverty and disruptive social behaviour that contribute to generating the conditions leading to elder abuse and negligence within the family, institutions and the community. New approaches to the study of abuse include an understanding of the various levels at which the individual interacts—personal, community and societal—and the triggering factors present at each level (World Health Organization, 2002a). In all cases, it has been found that social isolation exacerbates the risk of abuse and mistreatment (Phillips, 1983; Grafstrom, Nordberg and Winblad, 1993; Compton, Flanagan and Gregg, 1997).

Research has determined that domestic abuse directed against older people is more likely to occur in the presence of the following risk factors: alcohol and substance abuse and mental disorders (as they relate either to the older person or to the caregiver), physical impairment, economic dependency, overcrowding in the household, stress and lack of time to care for the elder, among others (World Health Organization, 2002a; Wolf, Godkin and Pillemer, 1984; Anetzberger, 1987; and Paveza and others, 1992).[10] However, these risk factors by themselves are not sufficient to explain cases of abusive behaviour. The dynamics of domestic abuse and the factors that trigger abusive behaviour have not been clearly identified. Better reporting systems are required to improve understanding of the causes and such understanding will lead to better policy responses.

In residential settings, abuse occurs most often when staff is poorly trained and/or overworked and standards of care are low or inadequately monitored. The staggering evidence of abuse in institutional settings presented above requires urgent consideration and a better understanding of risk factors. At the community level, overall social tension, high incidence of poverty, crime and social disruption, and the erosion of intergenerational bonds are factors behind the high incidence of abusive behaviour in general as well as that directed against older people.

Countries have been combating elder abuse and neglect in different ways. Some (for example, Argentina, Canada, Sweden, Turkey, the United Kingdom and the United States) have included coverage of abuse of the elderly under their legal statutes and have created systems for reporting and treating cases of abuse; but many others do not have specific programmes designed to protect older persons from abuse (Podnieks, Anetzberger and Teaster, 2006).

Non-governmental organizations dedicated to improving recognition of, and response to, elder abuse have emerged throughout the world, including the International Network for the Prevention of Elder Abuse, with representation in all six regions of the world. There are several national organizations, including the Japan Academy for the Prevention of Elder Abuse, the Canadian Network for the Prevention of Elder Abuse and the Korean Information Network for the Prevention of Elder Abuse. Local networks at the State and community levels have also been identified in the United States.

While the existence of national legislation and programmes established to respond to cases of abuse and neglect have contributed to protecting the elders concerned, effective mechanisms for preventing such cases and for providing adequate responses to them, require a comprehensive approach at three levels, encompassing (a) the creation of a monitoring system that would give people a window of access to reliable information and effective mechanisms for denouncing cases of abuse and neglect and would also help to make the problem visible to the society; (b) the strengthening of the judiciary system to enable effective enforcement of the national legislation on human rights and appropriate punishment to be meted out to perpetrators; and (c) the development of national training and education initiatives to raise awareness of the problem, to create more positive images of older people and to build adequate skills among the individuals who are taking care of older persons.

These initiatives for the prevention of abuse should obviously be complemented by the provision of adequate services to abused, neglected or exploited older people. In most countries, these services are generally provided through existing health and social service networks and may include medical, psychological and financial services, as well as emergency shelters and support groups for victims of elder abuse and neglect.

Advancing the human rights of older persons

Guaranteeing and protecting their human rights as defined by the Universal Declaration of Human Rights (General Assembly resolution 217 A (III)) constitute an important means of reducing the risk of abuse of older persons and of empowering them. The human rights approach also underlies the principles of the Madrid International Plan of Action on Ageing. In fact, already in 1982, the United Nations had taken a major step forward in advancing the rights of older persons when the World Assembly on Ageing adopted the Vienna International Plan of Action on Ageing (United Nations, 1982), which detailed the measures that should be taken by Member States to safeguard the rights of older persons within the context of the rights proclaimed by the International Covenants on Human Rights (General Assembly resolution 2200A(XXI), annex). This was followed in 1991 by the adoption by the General Assembly of the United Nations Principles for Older Persons (resolution 46/91 of 16 December 1991, annex).[11] These principles continue to constitute the most important international document promoting the rights of older persons in the five areas of independence, participation, care, self-fulfilment and dignity.

The Second World Assembly on Ageing anchored the human rights approach in the Madrid International Plan of Action on Ageing in 2002. The aim of the Madrid Plan of Action is "to ensure that persons everywhere are able to age with security and dignity and to continue to participate in their societies as citizens with full rights" (para. 10). The Madrid Plan of Action also states that "the promotion and protection of all human rights and fundamental freedoms, including the right to development, is essential for the creation of an inclusive society for all ages in which older persons participate fully and without discrimination and on the basis of equality" (para. 13).

Important policy challenges remain in many societies in respect of finding effective mechanisms to ensure that principles of reciprocity, interdependence and equity between the generations apply in practice. Complementary legislation may be needed in some countries to improve the legal framework so as to protect the rights of older persons, prevent their abuse and neglect, and bolster their opportunities for participating in all aspects of social life. A better legal framework will not suffice, however. In addition, societies will need to find adequate mechanisms for preventing age discrimination in labour markets, ensuring intergenerational solidarity through adequate old-age income security systems, and mobilizing the resources needed to provide adequate health and long-term care.

Improving images of older persons

Very often the contribution of older persons to society is obscured by negative stereotypes focusing on the potential problems of population ageing through the projection of images of older people portraying them as a liability to society and a drain on government and family resources. Negative images of older persons may trigger episodes of discrimination and abuse. A more balanced view of ageing—one that gives attention to the authority, wisdom, dignity and restraint that comes with a lifetime of experience—is needed both to increase the self-esteem of older persons and to improve their contribution to development.

The most serious repercussion of stereotyping for older persons is their exclusion from activities and/or social groups. Acceptance of stereotypes by older persons themselves could result in their not seeking help for medical conditions or their not claiming welfare benefits (because ageing stereotypically is equated with poverty) or even in their withdrawing from social relationships, thereby accepting the stigma of isolation and passivity (Victor, 1994).

The sources of stereotypes can be both societal and individual. In societies, stereotypes arise for the most part owing to the lack of adequate information. Individuals may fear growing old because they anticipate stereotypic declines in memory and mobility and the onset of stereotypic age-related diseases (International Longevity Center-USA, 2006). Exaggerated fears of deterioration, dementia and dependency are indeed powerful and can prevent people from planning for the later stages of their life.

Negative images of growing old may also have a negative impact on self-perception, a factor that has been found to be vital to the well-being of older people. People with a positive image of themselves had lower blood pressure and cholesterol levels and maintained a healthy weight. A longitudinal study of self-perception of older men and women found that respondents in the more positive self-perception group lived, on average, 7.6 years longer than those in the more negative self-perception group (Levy and others, 2002).

A creation of a new image of ageing as envisioned in the Madrid International Plan of Action on Ageing will take time. Specific actions have to focus on promoting inter-generational cohesion and interdependence. An increasing number of programmes and campaigns have been launched by both government and non-governmental organizations to counter negative stereotypes of older people and promote more positive images of ageing. For instance, the Office of Older Australians, a division of the Australian Government Department of Health and Ageing, has established a "positive images gallery" which portrays a selection of older Australians at work, in volunteer roles and in leisure-time activities (Office for an Ageing Australia, 2004). In the United States, the Harvard School of Public Health and the MetLife Foundation have launched a national media campaign to "Reinvent aging". This campaign uses news coverage, advertising and prime-time entertainment to promote healthy ageing and to reshape cultural attitudes towards the older years by demonstrating the active and productive role that older people play in society. Argentina launched the Vicente Lopez Parliament on Old Age and the campaign "Old age, first to grow" with the objective of providing a visual depiction of a healthy old age and thus helping to dispel prejudices directed against old persons (Global Action on Aging, 2006a).

An important focus of these various efforts is on showing that older persons constitute an often ignored resource and as such can make an important contribution to strengthening the socio-economic fabric of society. A more balanced perspective requires that the experiences of later life be seen not as one-dimensional, but rather as fluid, complex and heterogeneous (Lloyd-Sherlock, 2004a). Overall, older persons possess higher accumulated stocks of human capabilities and experience, and their contribution to society should be recognized. Removing structural barriers, bringing an end to negative stereotypes and promoting more positive perceptions of older persons would play an important role in furthering improvements in their productive capacity and well-being.

CONCLUSIONS

Most countries of the world are experiencing the rapid ageing of their population with its far-reaching implications for the development of societies. The Madrid International Plan of Action on Ageing expresses the international concern raised by the challenges of adjusting to an ageing world and of improving the quality of life of older persons and recognizing their contribution to social development.

Changes in society simultaneously produced by industrialization, increasing participation of women in the labour force, decreasing family size, diminishing importance of extended families and increasing internal and international migration, among other factors, have important implications for the well-being of older people. These rapid changes are challenging traditional concepts of intergenerational solidarity as ensuring the provision of care and support to older persons; and better-integrated policy responses are therefore required to meet the needs of an ageing population, promote respect for their human rights and facilitate their continuing contribution to social development.

This chapter has identified three areas that require better policy responses: improving the conditions of housing and living arrangements for the elderly; promoting empowerment and political participation of older people; and improving the legal framework and social awareness so as to protect their human rights.

In developed countries, the rapid changes in the composition of the family which are leading to an increase in the number of older adults living alone or with their spouses have implications for the maintaining of intergenerational solidarity and family cohesion. The establishment and expansion of long-term care facilities have been the traditional response to the situation of older people who do not have family support and who need assistance in daily activities. Chapter VI will present cost estimates of future health costs, which would be much higher if long-term care were to expand at the rate required to accommodate the needs of rapidly ageing societies. An alternative to institutionalized long-term care that has been emerging in several countries demonstrates that it is possible, by combining resources from families, communities and the public sector, to provide support and assistance to older persons in their own homes without compromising their quality of life. A larger number of older persons will require assistance in order to be able to live alone in their own home; hence, explicit policy responses will be essential to replicating this kind of initiative in order that those needing support may be reached.

In developing countries, new demands with respect to meeting the specific needs of an ageing population are in competition with the demand for the resources needed to extend the coverage of the most basic services and infrastructure. There are still a large number of older adults who lack access to appropriate water, sanitation and quality housing. Programmes to improve the living conditions of older persons will have to incorporate an explicit objective of equity to ensure that older people, regardless of their level of income or area of residence, have access to a minimum standard of living.

Assistive technology and the redesigning of houses to facilitate the mobility of older persons constitute another area of development where public-private partnerships may prove effective. In developing countries, this objective carries the additional challenge of providing technical solutions at a cost that would make them affordable to those older adults who require assistance.

Empowerment and political participation of older people vary greatly across countries. There are those where older people are better organized and have a tradition of political participation. In many other countries, however, older people are not organized and face great difficulty in voicing their concerns and incorporating their demands into the public debate and the policy agenda. International and national non-governmental organizations have been actively promoting the organization of the elderly as a mechanism for influencing the design and implementation of the policies that affect them. Efforts to organize older persons should be coupled with larger programmes of literacy and continuous education, including information about their human rights, as these are an important element of the process of empowerment.

Building a supportive and enabling environment for older persons requires attention both to their human needs and rights and to their development through social participation. An important element of the contribution of older persons to development encompasses their participation in labour markets, an issue that will be discussed in chapter IV. This chapter has identified the policy challenges that remain to be met with respect to ensuring adequate living conditions for older people and protecting their human rights by enforcing legislation that bolsters those rights, provides safeguards against neglect, abuse and violence, and facilitates their participation in, and contribution to, society.

Further recognition and respect should also be granted to older persons for their authority, wisdom and productivity and for their contributions to their local communities and to the society at large. Active social, economic and political participation and engagement of older persons can ensure a more vital, healthy and meaningful ageing process. Entering the older ages should be equated not with coming to the end of one's productive life, but rather with starting to take advantage of new possibilities and opportunities. The Madrid International Plan of Action on Ageing lays out a framework for achieving these objectives, but in many countries much greater efforts are needed to embed these objectives in national plans of action on ageing and to gain the active support of national stakeholders and international donors for their effective implementation.

Notes to Chapter III

1   The statistical evidence presented in the present section follows the international convention of defining "older persons" as those aged 60 years or over (see also chapter I).

2   See http://www.tsaofoundation.org.

3   The calculations in the Centre's report assume that age structure (the proportion of people aged 60 years or over) is the same in urban and rural areas. This is not necessarily the case: populations in rural areas often have older age structures.

4   This cost differential assumes equal services. Older people living in institutional residences usually require greater assistance in performing daily chores and greater medical attention. The cost comparison in the text above may overestimate actual cost differences, once the type and quality of services provided are accounted for. Cost comparisons may by found at http://www.aarp.org/states/sc/scnews/what_are_home_and_community_based_services.html.

5   "Ageing in place is a gerontological concept emphasizing the importance of, as well as the strategies for, supporting older people in their homes and communities for as long as possible" (http://www.tsaofoundation.org). This concept has stimulated the implementation of a number of policies and programmes designed to help older people remain in their own homes.

6   See http://www.unescap.org/jecf/p04barrier.htm.

7   More information about the international non-governmental organizations working on the ageing issues mentioned here is available from the following websites: http://www.ifa-fiv.org/en/accueil.aspx; http://www.thematuremarket.com/SeniorStrategic/fiapa.php; and http://www.eurag-europe.org/.

8   Similar problems of lack of appropriate definitions and data are confronted when assessing abuse directed against other age groups. These problems prevent any meaningful comparison of the incidences of abuse among different age groups.

9   It should be noted that the results are not comparable across countries because the periods of reference used in registering cases of abuse were different in each country.

10 Additional discussions of the risk factors leading to abuse directed against older people may be found in Homer and Gilleard (1990); Pillemer and Suitor (1992); Coyne, Reichman and Berbig (1993); Anetzberger, Korbin and Austin (1994); Reis and Nahmiash (1998); and Reay and Browne (2001).

11 Available from http://www.un.org/esa/socdev/iyop/iyoppop.htm.

Chapter IV
Economic consequences of population ageing

INTRODUCTION

Ageing will affect the size and composition of the labour force and have important implications for economic growth and the participation of older persons in society. Countries with low and decreasing fertility rates—mostly the developed economies and economies in transition but also an increasing number of developing countries—will face a slower increase or even a decline in the labour supply. A reduction in the number of workers may have negative implications for output growth and for securing the well-being of the population at large. Lower output growth implies that addressing the needs of a larger dependent older population will become a heavier task. Moreover, a gradual "greying" of the workforce is anticipated, as the share of older workers increases in the economically active population worldwide (see chapter II) and older workers undertake to handle a growing portion of the production of goods and services. This shift may impact on the way in which goods and services are produced and on the overall efficiency of the economy.

A particular challenge for economies with declining fertility rates is therefore to sustain levels of material well-being while their labour forces are growing older and eventually shrink in size. This challenge poses a number of economic policy questions, not only about how to increase labour productivity, but also about what can be done to reverse declining trends in labour participation and adjust the retirement age.

Meanwhile, countries where fertility rates are still high or above replacement level (mainly those in sub-Saharan Africa and South and Central Asia, but also developed economies such as the United States of America and New Zealand) will continue to have an expanding labour supply, but over time will also have to deal with the implications of higher old-age dependency ratios. Developing countries confront additional challenges, such as the generation of much larger volumes of remunerative jobs.

Population ageing will affect economic activity and growth performance through other channels besides the labour market. Economic growth bears a close relationship with consumption, investment and savings. Consumption patterns change with age. For instance, older people tend to spend a higher share of their incomes on housing and social services compared with younger population cohorts. Based on current consumption trends exhibited by persons aged 65 years or over in developed countries, it is possible to anticipate, among other things, that the demand for health, long-term care, housing and energy expenditures will likely increase. Consumption patterns owing to population ageing, however, will change only very gradually over time. More importantly, other factors (especially income growth) tend to be more influential in determining the level and composition of consumption expenditures of old and young people alike. Labour earnings are a major component in an individual's income but tend to vary throughout the life cycle, often reaching a peak when that individual is in the prime working years of mid-life. If income declines with age, consumption levels may decline during older ages. Economic growth could then be negatively affected as there is an increasing share of consumers that grow older.

Similarly, the capacity to save may diminish with age, which could impact on the generation of savings in the economy as a greater number of persons grow older. This may have implications for the level of global savings and availability of investment finance, particularly owing to the weight of the countries with ageing populations in the world economy. Again, ageing is but one factor influencing savings behaviour, making projections far into the future subject to considerable uncertainty. On the other hand, implications for financial markets may be more visible. Population ageing is already having an impact on financial markets as an increasing share of household savings flows into pension funds and other financial investment plans for retirement. Institutional investors can play an important role in the deepening of financial markets and in providing additional liquidity for long-term investment projects. At the same time, however, institutional investors largely operate outside of financial market regulation and supervision mechanisms that apply more generally to the banking system. If unchecked, the financial market operations of pension funds could thus be a source of financial instability and influence the effectiveness of monetary policies.

AGEING, LABOUR SUPPLY AND PRODUCTIVITY GROWTH

Asymmetries in labour supply growth

As shown in chapter II, the global labour force will continue to grow over the next 50 years. Yet, relatively high levels of fertility in some parts of the world, accompanied by declining fertility in others, will generate asymmetries in labour-force growth across economies. Relatively strong labour-force growth will take place in low-income countries that are already experiencing significant labour surpluses, while limited gains (or even reductions) in the workforce are projected for most middle- and high-income countries.

Table IV.1 shows the absolute changes in the labour force that have taken place since 1980 and those projected through 2020, by region. Adding to the analysis of chapter II, these projections take into consideration anticipated changes due to gender convergence in labour-force participation rates as well as the demographic composition at the country level.[1]

By 2020, the global labour force will be about 833 million workers larger than it was in 2000, with the bulk of the increase taking place in the developing countries. For the developed countries as a group, the labour force will grow by less than 14 million workers over this same period, owing in large part to increased participation by women. Projections by the International Labour Organization (ILO) indicate that the labour force in Europe, and most particularly in the Russian Federation, will be smaller in 2020 than at present. Additionally, there will be a considerable slowdown in the growth of the labour force in East Asia (China, Japan and Singapore) owing largely to significant declines in fertility rate in the countries of this region, and in Southern Africa as a result of the AIDS pandemic (International Labour Office, 2004a). In other subregions of Asia, the labour force will continue to grow, with the largest increases projected to take place in South-Central and Western Asia.

In Latin America and the Caribbean and Northern America, the labour force will continue to grow during the period 2000-2020, although at a slower pace. Relatively high—albeit declining—fertility rates will support continued labour-force growth in Latin America throughout these two decades. Gradually, however, the rapid decline of fertility levels observed in the region during the past few years will cause labour-force growth to decelerate, especially in the decades beyond 2020. In Northern America (Canada and the United States), labour-force growth is supported mostly by international migration and higher labour-force participation rates. Meanwhile, the labour force will increase rather quickly in most countries of Africa (except for Southern Africa, as noted above) owing to the persistence of high levels of fertility in many countries of this region.

Table IV.1.
Changes in the labour force, 1980-2000 and 2000-2020, by region and sex

Millions

Region	Absolute change from 1980 to 2000			Absolute change from 2000 to 2020		
	Both sexes	Men	Women	Both sexes	Men	Women
World	888.9	510.8	378.1	832.8	480.5	352.3
Developed countries[a]	66.5	22.5	44.0	13.8	-4.6	18.5
Less developed regions[b]	822.4	488.3	334.1	819.0	485.1	333.9
Africa	139.1	83.9	55.2	202.8	122.0	80.8
Eastern Africa	50.3	26.9	23.4	78.4	42.8	35.6
Central Africa	16.6	9.6	7.0	28.3	16.6	11.8
Southern Africa	8.7	5.8	2.9	1.2	1.5	-0.4
Northern Africa	24.9	17.8	7.1	32.4	22.1	10.4
Western Africa	38.6	23.8	14.8	62.5	39.1	23.4
Latin America and the Caribbean	105.0	52.5	52.5	100.7	43.9	56.9
South America	74.4	34.3	40.0	70.6	29.4	41.2
Central America[c]	25.4	15.3	10.1	25.7	12.4	13.3
Caribbean	5.3	2.9	2.4	4.4	2.1	2.4
Northern America[d]	38.8	15.2	23.6	28.0	12.7	15.3

Table IV.1 (cont'd)

Region	Absolute change from 1980 to 2000			Absolute change from 2000 to 2020		
	Both sexes	Men	Women	Both sexes	Men	Women
Asia	588.3	356.9	231.4	505.4	311.5	193.8
South-East Asia	99.3	57.2	42.2	105.8	55.5	50.2
South-Central Asia[e]	205.8	144.4	61.3	285.5	179.8	105.7
East Asia[f]	256.5	133.8	122.7	71.3	47.9	23.4
Western Asia[g]	26.7	21.5	5.2	42.8	28.3	14.5
Europe	13.2	0.4	12.7	-8.9	-11.8	3.0
Eastern Europe[h]	-10.8	-4.6	-6.2	-15.2	-9.0	-6.1
Northern Europe	3.2	0.3	2.9	2.9	0.9	2.1
Southern Europe[i]	8.9	2.0	6.9	3.0	-1.1	4.2
Western Europe	11.9	2.8	9.1	0.3	-2.5	2.9
Oceania[j]	4.5	1.9	2.6	4.7	2.2	2.5
Australia-New Zealand	3.2	1.2	2.0	2.7	1.1	1.6

Source: International Labour Office, "LABORSTA: economic active population estimates and projections", available from http//laborsta.ilo.org (accessed 24 April 2007).

a Comprising all regions of Europe, Northern America, Australia, Japan and New Zealand.
b Comprising all regions of Africa, Asia (excluding Japan), Latin America and the Caribbean and Oceania (excluding Australia and New Zealand).
c Including Mexico.
d Referring to Canada and the United States of America.
e Including Kazakhstan, Kyrgyzstan, Tajikistan, Turkmenistan and Uzbekistan.
f Including Japan.
g Including Armenia, Azerbaijan, Cyprus and Georgia.
h Including Belarus, Moldova, the Russian Federation and Ukraine.
i Including Albania, Bosnia and Herzegovina, Croatia, the former Yugoslav Republic of Macedonia and the former Serbia and Montenegro.
j Including Australia and New Zealand.

Figure IV.1 provides information on labour-force growth at the country level. It shows the projected average annual growth in the period 2000-2020 compared with growth in the period 1980-2000 in 192 countries. Most economies are clustered above the 45-degree line in the figure, thus indicating a deceleration in the rate of growth of the labour force. Economies experiencing acceleration are mainly the high-fertility economies located in Africa, Asia and Latin America.

Figure IV.1.
Labour-force growth, 1980-2000 and 2000-2020

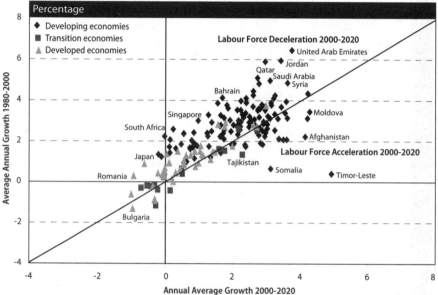

Source: International Labour Office, LABORSTA.

Note: Circles are sized according to projected labour-force size in 2020. Data for the period 2000-2020 are projections.

While an increasing labour force may imply a potential for accelerating growth, and thus improving the standard of living for all (see box IV.1), a declining labour-force growth may have opposite effects and lead to slower output growth. For instance, it has been estimated that employment growth will account for almost half of output growth in the EU-15 until 2010. After 2010, the employment effect on growth becomes neutral, but it should turn negative after 2030 as the labour force shrinks (European Commission, 2005). A similar scenario is likely for such countries as Japan, where the labour force is expected to decline by approximately 8 million by 2020 (International Labour Office, 2005a). This is not to say that there will be no economic growth in this group of countries. Rather, employment will become a drag on growth

Box IV.1.
The demographic transition: first and second dividends for the third age?

Changes in the age structure of the population have the potential to affect the macroeconomy. During the second phase of the demographic transition—after fertility has begun to decline but before the long-term increase in the size of the older population has started—the proportion of people in the working ages rises relative to the dependent young and old population. If this relatively larger workforce is productively employed, a considerable boost to the growth rate of per capita income results. The potential for a surge in the income per capita is known as the "first demographic dividend", and the period during which it occurs is referred to as the "demographic window of opportunity" (see figure). This dividend results from changes in the ratio of the effective number of producers to the effective number of consumers, which is called the support ratio. Further population ageing will lead to additional declines in income per effective consumer as the support ratio declines.

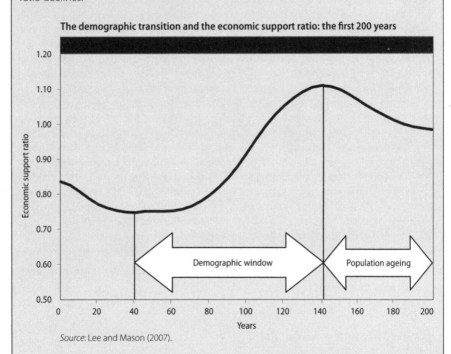

The demographic transition and the economic support ratio: the first 200 years

Source: Lee and Mason (2007).

A higher support ratio can potentially be translated into higher output per capita, which implies that a greater share of national output can be diverted into investment without sacrificing consumption. If some of or the entire first dividend is invested in human and physical capital, a permanently higher economic growth can result. Additionally, depending on the choices made by individuals and the policies pursued by Governments, the first dividend may give rise to a second dividend that will persist well after the demographic window has closed.

Box IV.1 (cont'd)

In theory, the prospects for a second demographic dividend are relatively promising (Lee and Mason, 2007). For several reasons, population ageing leads to an increase in the demand for wealth needed to maintain consumption levels at older ages. First, older people, having accumulated during their working years, hold more wealth on average than younger adults. An increase in the proportion of older people therefore causes an increase in wealth per capita in the population. Second, the anticipation of longer life leads individuals to save more and accumulate more wealth over their lifetimes, reinforcing this effect. Third, with lower fertility, individuals can allocate a larger share of their lifetime earnings to their own consumption, including in old age, again leading them to save more and accumulate more wealth over their working lives. For all these reasons, wealth per capita can potentially rise during the demographic transition.

This potential for increase in wealth per capita, and the rise in income and consumption that it generates, creates the *possibility* of a second demographic dividend. According to Lee and Mason, there is a possibility, in theory, that income per equivalent consumer could be "permanently" higher by 25-30 per cent owing to the second dividend. Yet, the second dividend will be realized only if some or all of the increased wealth generated by the first dividend is invested in assets and not merely transferred from one group to another. Different schemes for old-age income provision will have different implications for the promotion of growth and therefore for the income security of those who will be retiring (see chap. V).

As in any other simulation exercise, the above estimate should be interpreted with caution owing to its sensitivity to implied assumptions about how consumption profiles, returns to assets and economic growth are likely to evolve. In this exercise, productivity is assumed to grow at a constant 1.5 per cent per year as a result of exogenous technological change. Another important assumption is that half of old-age consumption is funded through the accumulation of assets during working ages. This assumption may be unrealistic, especially for low-income countries, owing to the incipient development of financial markets in many of them. Finally, the accrual of the anticipated benefits due to the second dividend presupposes a risk-free rate of return of 3 per cent and an optimistic 6 per cent international real return on accumulated assets, which is expected to decline linearly to 4.42 per cent in 2300.

unless the decline in the labour force can be sufficiently mitigated or labour productivity can be increased.

Offsetting the slower labour-force growth

There is a series of policy options that can be employed to offset the anticipated decline in the labour force and its negative consequences. Migration, outsourcing, increases in fertility and enhanced labour-force participation by both women and older workers are often mentioned. Additionally, improvements in labour productivity can mitigate the negative impacts of slower labour-force growth on economic growth. There is, however, no single labour-market policy or silver bullet that countries should focus on; rather, countries must take into consideration their own outlook for demographic change as well as their labour-market characteristics to determine a policy package that is suitable for their particular situation.

The appendix to this chapter presents a typology for 164 countries and areas according to three main determinants of labour supply growth: fertility, immigration and labour participation rates. These determinants suggest a range of interventions that policymakers could consider to mitigate the projected declines in labour-force growth. For instance, in countries with a low fertility rate and high migratory flows, increasing migration may not be a feasible option. For such countries, for example, Austria, Germany and Spain, increasing participation rates of older workers may provide a way to offset the slowdown in labour-force growth. For others, such as Canada and Switzerland, where both migration and participation rates are already high, efforts perhaps need to be centred on increasing labour productivity.

The scope for increasing fertility rates is limited as discussed in chapter II. Experience has shown that policies may influence the movement of fertility rates downward, but that reversing low-fertility trends through public intervention appears to be difficult. Other policy interventions may therefore be needed in the medium term, such as reducing unemployment, promoting labour productivity improvements and increasing overall labour-force participation.[2] These options are analysed below.

Can migration and offshoring compensate for a smaller labour force?

There seems to be a potential for labour migration, drawing on the large existing pool of both skilled and unskilled workers in developing countries, to meet shortfalls in labour demand in ageing countries. Moreover, the constraints on production capacity caused by a smaller labour force could be offset in part by foreign direct investment (FDI) via the offshoring of production processes (Freeman, 2006).

It is doubtful, however, whether international migration can sufficiently offset the projected increases in dependency ratios. As discussed in chapter II, very large net flows of migrants would be needed to keep the labour forces stable or to significantly affect trends in dependency ratios. For instance, as was shown in table II.6, net migration inflows needed to offset the decline in working-age population in Europe have been estimated at 2.9 million migrants per year during 1995-2050, which is almost triple the annual levels observed during the period 1995-2000 (about 950,000 persons). Large migration inflows such as those just mentioned may not be feasible for various reasons. Recipient countries may encounter political and social difficulties in integrating so many immigrants, while the sending countries may suffer an undesirable brain drain.

The outsourcing of employment to offshore locations, through production facilities' being brought to workers instead of workers' being brought to the production facilities, is another option for dealing with the asymmetries in the global labour supply. As the spread of information and communication technologies (ICT) continues to ease the transferability of both manufacturing and service jobs to offshore locations, global production networks will continue to expand in developing economies with surplus labour. Moreover, with the continued improvement in the education and skills levels of their workforce, these labour-surplus economies will likely attract more offshore jobs, thereby bolstering their competitive wage positions. Estimates for the United States, for instance, have indicated that in the industries that use ICT the most, approximately "3.3 million jobs are expected to move offshore by 2015" (Forrester Research, 2002). Meanwhile, half of the major companies in the United States are currently engaged in some form of outsourcing and an additional number of companies are expected to follow suit in the coming years (Sperling, 2004).

Notwithstanding the above, it is unlikely that offshoring will overcome all the challenges posed by rising dependency ratios and shrinking workforces in countries with ageing population. Although it does alleviate labour shortages by shifting production to workers abroad, offshoring does not offset existing pressures on domestic old-age pension systems brought about by the fact that the retired population is increasing while the contributory base is not expanding (see chapter V). At the same time, offshoring may also result in deteriorating trade balances and increased unemployment owing to cost competition in affected industries. These short- (and medium-) term effects can be mitigated by "wage and investment" compensation mechanisms. For example, wage-cost savings from offshoring would spur increased firm investment and capital deepening in complementary domestic activities, leading to both higher productivity and high economic growth in the domestic economy (Mahoney and others, 2006; Mann, 2003). However, there is no conclusive evidence that such long-term benefits may indeed be reaped.

Boosting female labour participation

The participation of women in the workforce varies considerably across regions. In most countries, increasing female labour participation has been one of the most significant drivers of structural change in the labour force over the past 40 years. Yet, in spite of the impressive gains, female participation rates remain below those of men in every age group (see figure IV.2). First,

Figure IV.2.
World male and female labour-force participation rates by age group, 2005

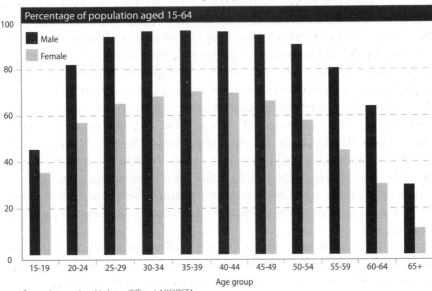

Source: International Labour Office, LABORSTA.

women continue to be disproportionately involved in unpaid housework and caregiving. Second, participation rates of women under age 25 have been falling owing to higher educational opportunities for women, thus postponing their entry in the labour market (International Labour Office, 2006). Nonetheless, improved educational attainment has been credited with raising female labour-force participation (among women aged 25 years or over): the participation rate for women with third-level education is higher than that for women who have completed high school. Similarly, participation rates for women who have completed high school are higher than those for women with very limited educational attainment (Fitzgerald, 2005).[3]

Evidence from developed countries suggests that there is a trade-off for women between work and having children: increased participation of women in the workforce has been accompanied by delayed childbearing and declines in fertility rates (International Labour Office, 2004b). Therefore the challenge for policy intervention is to pay due attention to the need for reconciling the conflicting demands of family and workplace that may arise from increasing female participation. In this regard, employment and social policies need to be directed towards reducing the opportunity costs for women of having children by allowing them to stay in the labour market and maintain their careers.[4]

Participation of older workers in the labour force

Another policy option for offsetting the decline in labour supply is to increase the labour participation rates of older workers. Ideally, older persons should be able to continue working for as long as they wish and for as long as they are able to do so productively. To this end, new work arrangements and innovative workplace practices can be developed to sustain the working capacity and accommodate the needs of workers as they age. At the same time, it is important to combat damaging stereotypes concerning older persons by fostering a positive awareness of their skills and abilities in the workplace (see chapter III). In particular, emphasis needs to be placed on increasing the participation rates of older workers so that the effective retirement age is brought more closely in line with the statutory retirement age (see chapter V). Additionally, those who have reached the statutory retirement age should be given the choice of continuing to participate in the paid labour force wherever practicable.

The definition of "older worker", like that of "older person", is rather fluid (see chapter I). In general, however, those workers aged 55-64 are considered older workers. Labour participation rates of those aged 55-64 are significantly lower than those of persons in their prime working years of 25-54 (see table IV.2) Among men, the decline is most pronounced in the economies in transition, represented by a fall of 38 percentage points, and it is least apparent in Africa, where the drop is about 10 percentage points.

Table IV.2.
Labour-force participation rates, 2005, by region, sex and age group

Percentage of population of working age						
	Age group					
	25-54		55-64		65 +	
Region	Men	Women	Men	Women	Men	Women
Developed countries	91.9	75.3	63.9	44.9	13.4	6.3
Economies in transition	90.7	81.3	52.6	31.2	14.2	7.8
Africa	96.2	61.0	86.5	48.3	57.4	25.8
Asia	96.3	64.2	77.6	35.4	38.0	13.2
Latin America and the Caribbean	94.3	64.3	76.1	37.2	37.2	13.7
Oceania	87.4	73.3	76.0	60.6	51.4	33.4
World	95.1	66.7	73.5	38.7	30.2	11.3

Source: UN/DESA calculations based upon data from the Population Division of the United Nations Secretariat and the International Labour Office (2005b).

The decline in labour-force participation rates is greater among women in all groups of countries. In particular, women in the economies in transition experience a precipitous fall in their labour-force participation upon entering the 55-64 age range, with average rates dropping from 81 to 31 per cent. In developed countries, as well as in developing Asia and Latin America and the Caribbean, women experience a decline of about 30 percentage points in their labour-force participation rates after turning 55. This phenomenon in part reflects the fact that many countries still have lower retirement ages for women despite their relatively higher life expectancy (see chapter II).

Several factors underlie the decline in participation rates for older workers. Poor working conditions, ill health or low job satisfaction may influence the decision to exit the labour force early. Individual preferences also have an impact. For instance, the preferred age of retirement for men in the EU-12 was found to be 58—compared with the early retirement age of 62 adopted in many countries (Howse, 2006).

Institutional arrangements surrounding the organization of pensions systems are also an important factor (see chapter V). In the case of economies in transition, statutory retirement ages may be as low as 60 for men and 55 for women. In developed countries, particularly several Western European ones, workers often choose to withdraw from the labour force prior to the official retirement age (usually 65), as financial incentives make the choice of work over leisure increasingly unattractive. The commonly used "rule of 80" in some developed countries, which combines a person's age and his or her years of experience to determine the point of full pension entitlement, enables a worker to retire in his or her mid-50s upon having completed 30 years of continuous employment. In some instances, developed countries (Denmark and Germany are notable examples) also provide public "pre-retirement" benefits to bridge the gap in years between early withdrawal from the labour force and eligibility for a public pension (Howse, 2006).

Cultural norms and discrimination against older workers are another factor. In fact, a growing body of research in developed countries (McKay and Middleton, 1998; Jensen, 2005) has indicated that age-based discriminatory practices, especially with regard to recruitment, retention and retraining of workers, have contributed to the decline in labour-force participation among workers of pre-retirement age (Leeson, 2006).

Efforts are being made, however—especially in countries where older persons are politically engaged—to combat these negative perceptions and encourage employers to hire older workers. A key initiative, for instance, is the 2000 European Union (EU) Directive establishing a general framework for equal treatment in employment and occupation, including the prohibition of discrimination based on age (Council of the European Union, 2000). To this end, EU member States committed to enacting legislation by 2006 that would make age discrimination in employment and vocational training illegal. In the Asian and Pacific region, Australia, Japan, and New Zealand have established anti-age discrimination legislation to protect the employment rights of older people. The Republic of Korea has enacted affirmative action legislation to promote the participation of older persons in job markets, whereby businesses are required to ensure that at least 3 per cent of their workers are aged 55 years or over. In addition, its Aged Employment Promotion Law identifies 77 types of jobs, ranging from parking lot attendant to bus ticket seller, for which hiring priority should be given to older persons (Cheng, Chan and Phillips, 2006).

Removing disincentives to work and improving working conditions

In addition to the legislation barring discrimination against older workers that has been introduced, there are initiatives to raise the labour participation rates of pre-retirement age workers (primarily those aged 55-64) that focus on creating positive incentives for extending one's working life. These considerations, while applicable to all countries, are particularly relevant for developed countries and economies in transition. In developing countries, participation rates among older workers are relatively high (see table IV.2), largely owing to the limited coverage by formal pension systems (see chapter V).

One important measure that could be taken to encourage people to increase the number of their working years would entail improving working conditions and promoting the overall greater availability of satisfying and adequately paid work. Appropriate adjustments may be needed in the work environment to ensure that older workers have the skills, health and capacity to remain employed into their later years.

Age-related changes in aerobic, cardiovascular and musculoskeletal function may result in decreased breathing capacity, reduced ability to carry out aerobically demanding tasks, and a decline in maximal muscle strength (Harper and Marcus, 2006). Data from the EU, for instance, suggest that the proportion of early departures from the labour force attributable to health problems is higher than that due to dismissal or redundancy (European Commission, 2004).

Reducing the risk of injury among older workers in the later years of their working lives may entail making different job positions available to them that utilize their talents and experience without exposing them to harm. The ILO Human Resources Development Recommendation adopted on 23 June 1975 (International Labour Organization, 1975) suggests that measures be taken to develop work methods, tools and equipment that are adapted to the special requirements of older workers. Sometimes simple adjustments to the workstation or other ergonomic changes are sufficient to accommodate older workers (Benjamin and Wilson, 2005). For those who perform physical work, appropriate modifications may include the use of equipment for lifting, restrictions on the amount of lifting or on the number of physically demanding tasks, and additional rest breaks (Harper and Marcus, 2006). In sum, a shift in focus—towards changing the job to accommodate the worker rather than changing the worker to accommodate the job—needs to be implemented in order to curb the tendency towards early retirement among older workers.

Finally, delaying the transition from work to retirement can be an important ingredient in active ageing as well. It enables older workers to remain engaged in a productive activity through which they retain social status and self-esteem and give structure to their day. If these benefits are not renewed upon exit from the labour force, older persons may find themselves in a situation that "favours passive time use ... underutilizes remaining productive capabilities and fosters disengagement" (Hinrichs and Aleksandrowicz, 2005, p. 3).

Working beyond retirement age

The imposition of a mandatory retirement age means that people must exit their remunerated jobs upon reaching a prescribed age, usually 60 or 65. In many low-income developing countries, mandatory retirement affects only a small share of workers. Therefore, a distinction must be made between allowing people in developed countries to work for as long as they would like and offering older people in developing countries the option of retiring.

Participation rates drop off considerably for workers around age 65, in line with the mandatory retirement age in several countries (see table IV.2). Yet, there are substantial variations across regions and gender. In developed countries and in economies in transition, labour participation rates are about 13-14 per cent for men and 6-8 per cent for women. In Africa and in developing countries in Oceania, on the other hand, labour-force participation remains at relatively higher rates particularly for males over age 65. Among 37 African low-income countries, for example, 36 have labour-force participation rates above 50 per cent for men aged 65 years or over. In 12 of these countries, the labour participation rates exceed 80 per cent. The Congo, where labour participation among older persons reaches 89 per cent, is a case in point. In addition to low pension coverage mentioned above, rampant poverty in the region leads to prolonged labour-force participation. By contrast, among the 33 developed countries included in the analysis, only Iceland, Japan and

Portugal—most likely owing to factors such as cultural norms rather than inadequate pension coverage—have participation rates in the 20 per cent range for men aged 65 years or over. Meanwhile, in 18 of these countries, the labour participation rates are below 10 per cent.

In all, there is a clear inverse relation between levels of GDP per capita and participation rates of older persons (see figure IV.3) which provides an indication of inequalities existing among older persons across countries. Not only are people in high-income countries more likely to live longer, healthier lives, but they also have the opportunity to retire from the labour force and enjoy many years of leisure, thanks to the security of pensions and health-care coverage. Wide disparities in social protection programmes reinforce existing labour-market inequalities, making the notion of working beyond retirement age an option (where allowed) for older workers in developed countries and a necessity for those in low-income countries.

Figure IV.3.
Relationship between labour-force participation rates of older workers aged 65 years or over, 2005, and GDP per capita

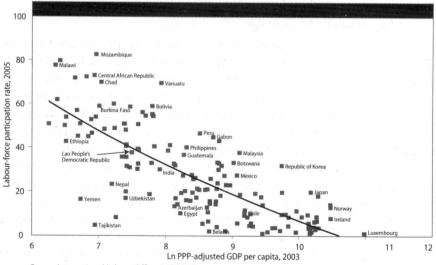

Source: International Labour Office, LABORSTA.

Note: GDP per capita refers to 2003 and was originally expressed in constant international dollars (PPP) of 2000.

Access to knowledge, education and training

Lifelong learning is beneficial to both older persons and society: it facilitates the recruitment and retention of older persons in the labour market and also helps to enhance their participation in society in general. Recent studies, conducted in countries worldwide, have shown a strong correlation between added years of education and increased longevity and improved health in older ages (Lieras-Muney, 2007).

The Madrid International Plan of Action on Ageing (United Nations, 2002a) makes explicit reference to the importance and value of lifelong learning. Specifically, it states that there should be equality of opportunity throughout life with respect to continuing education, training and retraining as well as vocational guidance and placement services. Furthermore, the Madrid Plan of Action stresses the need for fully utilizing the potential and expertise of persons of all ages, thus recognizing the benefits conferred by the increased experience that comes with age. This includes acknowledging and appreciating the value of intergenerational transmission of customs, knowledge and tradition.

The European Employment Strategy also acknowledges that lifelong learning is an important precondition for a longer working life. Within the EU-25, 10.8 per cent of all workers were participating in lifelong learning activities, with the rate slightly higher for women than for men (11.7 compared with 10 per cent). However, participation tends to drop according to age, largely because most countries have not adequately included the needs of older workers in their strategies for lifelong learning (European Foundation for the Improvement of Living and Working Conditions, 2006b). Additionally, policymakers fail to recognize the importance of investing in the education and skill development of people as they age. Throughout the Asian and Pacific region, for example, the concept of lifelong learning has taken hold in only a handful of countries, such as Australia, China, Japan and New Zealand, where the notion of a university of the third age has gained wide acceptance (Leung, Lui and Chi, 2005; Purdi and Boulton-Lewis, 2003).

The importance of providing effective and adequate vocational guidance and training for older workers has also been reflected in the above-mentioned ILO Human Resources Development Recommendation. The Recommendation acknowledges that training for particular groups of the population such as older workers can enhance equality in employment and improve integration into society and the economy. Nonetheless, opportunities for older workers to be engaged in training remain limited. In many contexts, employers seem to be unwilling to invest in the continued training and skills upgrading of workers nearing retirement age, given that the period within which they might reap a return on their investment would be limited (Organisation for Economic Co-operation and Development, 2006a). In Europe, for instance, although access to training for workers increased from 1995 to 2005, training opportunities provided by employers for older workers remained infrequent. According to a recent survey: "(o)nly 1 in 5 of those aged 55 and over report having received training paid for or provided by their employer in the previous 12 months (compared to 27 per cent of all workers). For other categories of training, such as on-the-job training, older workers also fare worse than their younger counterparts" (European Foundation for the Improvement of Living and Working Conditions, 2006a, p. 6).

While there are some exceptions,[5] a majority of older workers beyond retirement age find themselves in unskilled or semi-skilled occupations, owing largely to a perception that their skills are outdated and that they especially lack information technology skills (Chan, Phillips and Fong, 2003). In fact, older workers are less likely than younger workers to use new technologies, such as computers and the internet. Although this difference has been narrowing over the past decade,[6] additional efforts are needed so that older persons and those currently in their middle-age years can upgrade their skills and thus remain competitive in the labour market. Finally, it is important to recognize that older persons themselves can be resistant to training opportunities, especially if they have remained employed performing the same job in the same industry for many years. This may stem from a fear of having to learn something new. Men in particular tend to resist learning new skills. Programmes targeting older workers should take these concerns into consideration and develop measures and incentives that are adequate for addressing them.

The potential impact of increased labour participation on economic growth

How would increasing the labour participation rate of older workers impact on labour-force size and on the growth of output per capita? A decomposition analysis was used to give an idea of the possible growth implication of increased labour participation of workers aged 55-64. The analysis was applied to five economies that are in varying stages of the demographic transition and exhibit different characteristics in terms of older workers' participation rates: fast-ageing Germany, Italy and Japan, and moderately ageing India and the United States.[7]

For the simulations, it was assumed that the participation rates of those aged 55-64 would converge to the rates of those aged 15-54 starting in 2005. These results were then compared with those of a "baseline" scenario where participation rates did not change. (See figure IV.4).

The figure shows that increasing the labour-force participation rate of those aged between 55 and 64 relative to the level of younger cohorts in the labour force would help increase the annual rate of growth of GDP, but only by a small margin. The effect was largest for Germany where the GDP per

Figure IV.4.
Increased participation of older workers in the labour force: impact on the average annual rate of growth of GDP per capita, 2000-2050, selected countries

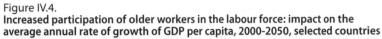

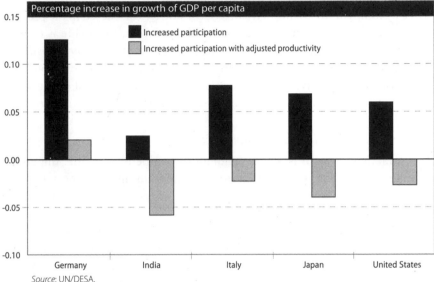

Source: UN/DESA.

capita growth would go up by 0.13 percentage points. For countries where differences in participation rates of younger and older workers were relatively small, boosting participation rates of older workers had negligible impact on the projected rate of growth of GDP per capita. Nonetheless, such an increase in participation rates might contribute positively to the financial sustainability of those countries' pension systems (see chapter V).

The impact of possible lower productivity of older workers on GDP growth (discussed below) was also simulated. Average productivity growth for older workers was assumed—rather arbitrarily—to be 1.5 per cent per year compared with 2 per cent per year for other workers. Under this hypothesis, and with the exception of Germany, increasing the participation rates of older workers would actually result in a lowering of the rate of growth of GDP per capita relative to the baseline scenario where participation rates were not increased. Thus, should a decline in productivity of older workers occur, policies aiming at boosting their rate of participation in the labour force will not be effective in raising the level of output per capita unless those policies are complemented by measures designed to enhance older workers' productivity as well, such as those discussed above.

Ageing labour force, declining productivity?

While it may be possible to partially offset the trend of a declining labour force in some countries through a mix of the policies discussed in the previous section, the changing age structure of the labour force is inevitable as societies continue to age. Accordingly, the following factors need to be considered: (a) the probable impact of the changing age characteristics of the labour force on labour productivity; (b) the potential for increasing overall productivity; and (c) the identification of policy interventions able to raise productivity.

The impact of ageing on labour productivity

If productivity growth is not fast enough to compensate for the impending changes in the labour supply, the burden of maintaining and improving living standards while supporting an increasingly dependent older population becomes heavier.

At the macroeconomic level, productivity is enhanced by, among other things, advances in knowledge, which take the form of innovations, such as new working methods and the development of new technologies, as well as new products. Because innovation implies a certain degree of creativity, and creativity is often higher among the younger members of society (see below), innovation is typically associated with younger workers. It is thus argued that a shrinking proportion of younger workers in the labour force may result in slower advances in sciences and technology which could have an adverse impact on productivity growth.

The impact of ageing on productivity is more readily noticeable at the firm level than at the macro level. A seminal study in this area on "age and learning" (Lehman, 1953), revealed a creative "age curve" showing productivity starting to increase in "creative occupations" such as the sciences, arts and athletics at around age 20, reaching a peak in the period from the late thirties to the mid-forties, and beginning to decline thereafter.[8]

Subsequent studies have supported this thesis and indicated that any decline in productivity associated with age takes place gradually and varies across occupations (see the comprehensive overview of studies by Skirbekk (2003)). For example, occupations where reduced cognitive ability may have an impact on performance, such as in the sciences, would likely witness productivity declines among older workers. Alternatively, in the managerial positions, for example, in professions where experience is a more important factor for job performance, older workers would work just as efficiently as their younger counterparts, if not more efficiently.[9]

The factor of experience can help to offset age-related productivity declines, while changes in organizational structure, more effective use of ICT in specific occupations, and ensuring better access to knowledge, education and training throughout working life have also been identified as means to maintain and improve productivity (European Commission, 2006; Black and Lynch, 2004). Thus, age-productivity profiles may change over time, as technological advancements and structural changes within an economy render some skills related to specific occupations more or less obsolete in the domestic labour market (European Commission, 2006; Nishimura and others, 2002).

Based on the literature, it is possible to argue that as workers continue to age in many middle- and high-income economies, the age profile of the workforce will move away from exhibiting a high share of "peak productivity" workers. Such a scenario suggests that those economies will need to boost their labour productivity growth, which would require a substantial increase in broad capital investments, that is to say, human capital, intangible capital (research and development) and physical capital. Conversely, in low-income economies with a higher proportion of young people, the age structure of the labour force will be moving towards exhibiting a potentially greater productivity. However, non-demographic factors may impede these countries from reaping the benefits of their demographic bonus.

Can labour productivity growth compensate for age-related output changes?

That improvements in labour productivity could offset the impact of population ageing on economic growth raises the question how much productivity would be needed to overcome the impact of ageing and how much productivity would need to increase so as to sustain a certain level of welfare. In the case of Japan, for instance, and assuming all other things being equal, labour productivity would need to grow by 2.6 per cent per year in order to sustain a per capita income growth of 2 per cent annually during the next 50 years. More than 80 per cent of the required labour productivity growth would be needed to overcome the growth impact of population ageing (see figure IV.5). This holds, though to a lesser degree, for other countries with ageing populations like Italy and Germany, and also for the United States. The required productivity growth in all these cases seems, however, within reach by historical standards. Yet, it is equally important to note that at 2 per cent per year, GDP per capita growth is slower than that achieved on average by these economies in the past. Finally, maintaining an annual rate of productivity growth of about 2-2.5 per cent for five decades is not an easy task and may require a sustained policy environment stimulating technological progress and innovation.

Figure IV.5.
Impact of population ageing on required annual average rate of labour-productivity growth, 2000-2050, Germany, Italy, Japan and the United States of America

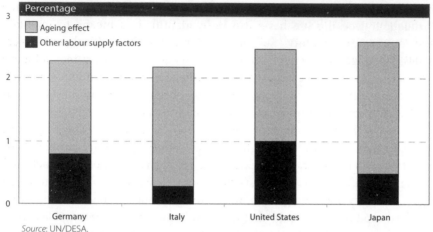

Source: UN/DESA.

Note: The ageing effect is calculated on the basis of a counterfactual exercise: The productivity growth required to generate a certain level of GDP per capita growth in view of anticipated changes in the population age structure is compared with the productivity growth required to maintain the same level of GDP per capita growth in the absence of such changes. It is assumed that the old-age dependency ratio is kept constant at the level observed in 2000.

Investments in the form of broad capital, namely, physical capital, research and development (R&D) and human capital, have long been identified as significant factors in increasing productivity growth.[10] The European Commission has targeted policies designed to increase the quality of investment in R&D, infrastructure and human capital and stimulate the creation of technological synergies within the economy in order to achieve the required higher productivity (Commission of the European Communities, 2006). For example, in addition to initiatives calling for a doubling of the EU research budget, there are initiatives for the creation of regional "innovation poles" and the "European Institute of Technology". These research hubs should attract researchers worldwide and create better linkages between research and industry in order to foster innovation. In the developing economies, technology and innovation policies are often targeted towards specific industries and sectors that have particular strategic importance for growth. Meanwhile, the challenge for many developing countries is also to improve economy-wide productivity by increasing productivity in the traditionally low-skilled informal economy, where a large share of workers is employed. In this regard, increased investment in infrastructure and human capital are equally important for improving productivity (United Nations, 2006a). Additionally, improved access to technology and the creation of forward and backward linkages in the supply chain between the formal and informal sector can enhance worker skills and ultimately lead to higher overall productivity growth (International Labour Office, 2004c). In this regard, while developing countries are in that stage of the demographic transition where a window of opportunity is still open (see box IV.1), the benefits of such demographic opportunity will be realized only with the adoption of the policies necessary to harness the productive potential of the working-age population.

AGEING AND CONSUMPTION PATTERNS

As discussed above, population ageing will affect economic growth owing to its impact on the supply of labour. Yet, this is not the only channel through which the effects of ageing on the economy will be felt. Economic growth also has a close relationship with consumption, investment and savings patterns. Consumption patterns may change as one ages. At the macroeconomic level, such changes can have implications for the demand for goods and services and therefore for investment opportunities, thus influencing patterns of investment and labour allocation in economies with ageing populations. Additionally, the overall level of consumption by older persons may change as well and have a negative impact on economic growth if demand declines.

Life-cycle patterns of income and consumption

Insights generated by economic theory with respect to consumption (and saving patterns) and its relationship with ageing are derived from the life-cycle model and are based on the consumption-smoothing hypothesis (Friedman, 1957; Modigliani and Brumberg, 1954; Ando and Modigliani, 1963). The model indicates a constant trajectory of consumption and a hump-shaped saving pattern. Consumption supported by accumulated savings or intergenerational transfers takes place even in the absence of labour income (see figure IV.6).

The intuition behind the figure is simple: Everyone needs to consume; but the very young and older individuals are less likely to participate in the labour market or earn an income. In order to consume, children rely on parental transfers. Older persons will draw on their accumulated wealth through dissaving and/or receive intergenerational transfers after they leave the labour market. During their working years, individuals tend to earn incomes higher than their consumption levels. The surplus can be used to provide for their dependent children and older persons in the household and saved for old-age income security.

Figure IV.6.
The economic life-cycle profile for the developing world

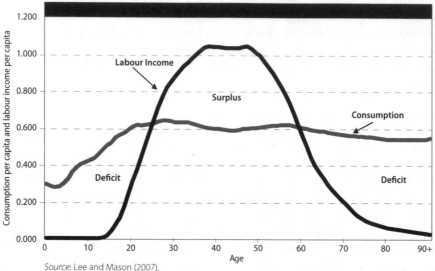

Source: Lee and Mason (2007).
Note: Values based on detailed estimates for a number of developing countries. Values have all been normalized by dividing by the average labour productivity of those in the prime working ages of 30-49.

Available evidence does not, however, always support the model's assumption that consumption levels are relatively stable throughout the life cycle. Empirical studies indicate that there may be a drop in consumption to a lower level following retirement which cannot be explained using the consumption-smoothing model (Banks, Blundell and Tanner, 1998; Bernheim, Skinner and Weinberg, 2001). This finding has given rise to the term "retirement-consumption puzzle". The drop in consumption has been found to be substantial in the United Kingdom of Great Britain and Northern Ireland, but has not been observed in the United States, for example. In countries such as Italy, no abrupt fall in consumption has been noted once leisure was taken into account (Miniaci, Monfardini and Weber, 2003). In the United States, consumption levels for older persons are considerably higher than those for the average person of working age because of increased consumption of publicly supplied goods, more specifically health services (Lee and Mason, 2007). Increased consumption levels during older ages have also been observed in other developed countries such as Japan and Sweden when publicly supplied goods and services were considered. Trends also vary among developing countries and areas: consumption levels during old age remain relatively constant in Taiwan Province of China, but tend to decline in Indonesia and Thailand. In Costa Rica, an initially declining trend at old age is reversed in very old age.[11]

Arguments put forward to explain the retirement-consumption puzzle in the developed countries, where the phenomenon is most conspicuous, include the role played by work-related expenses, which will drop once one retires. Moreover, increased leisure time allows households to purchase goods more efficiently and/or to engage in home production of certain goods. Additionally, in situations where retirement arrives earlier than anticipated, or when there is uncertainty regarding future needs, individuals may cut consumption in order to stretch available resources. Smith (2004) thus concludes that there is no retirement-consumption puzzle once the implications of increased leisure time, or the uncertainties related to the time of retirement, are accounted for.

Even if it may be the case that consumption levels do not decline as one retires, consumption by the retired population may not grow as fast as that of workers, as pension income—the major source of income, on average, for older persons with access to pension systems—grows slower than wages, particularly if pension benefits are not indexed to wages (see chapter V; Schaffnit-Chatterjee, 2007).

Do consumption patterns change with age?

Needs and tastes change over the life cycle. Older people tend to spend a higher share of their incomes on housing and social services than younger population cohorts do (Lührmann, 2005; Lee and Mason, 2007). Figure IV.7, based on household income and expenditure survey data, shows that the shares of housing-related services, energy and health in household expenditure seem to be steadily increasing with age in both the United States and EU. Pursuant to the consideration of current consumption trends exhibited by those aged 65 years or over in developed countries, it is possible to anticipate that the demand for health and long-term care expenditures will likely rise (see chapter VI), while housing and energy expenditures will increase as a result of more time spent at home by the retired population. On the other hand, expenditures on entertainment and transportation may decline, while the share of consumption of basic goods such as food and clothing will remain relatively constant.

Long-run trends in household consumption patterns at the aggregate level appear to reflect those observed above. The shares of health care and energy spending have increased notably in the selected countries since 1970, whereas the shares of spending on food and clothing have declined. Such trends may be expected to continue in the future; however, a closer look at existing trends suggests that the changes in consumption patterns owing to ageing take place

Figure IV.7.
Structure of consumption expenditure by age group, United States of America, 2006, and European Union, 1999

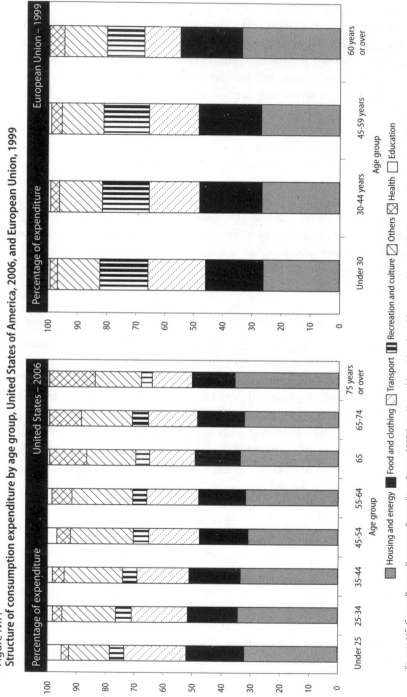

Sources: U.S. Census Bureau, Consumer Expenditure Survey 2005 (http://www.bls.gov/cex/); and European Commission, Eurostat online database 2006 (http://epp.eurostat.ec.europa.eu/).

very gradually and are rather modest in magnitude for the economy as a whole (Lührmann, 2005; Schaffnit-Chatterjee, 2007). Moreover, shifts are gradual.

It is noteworthy that service-related expenditures, especially for health care, and spending on energy have increased their share in total expenditures over time in both relatively older and younger countries (see figure IV.8). It is income that will, no doubt, remain the most important factor underlying the structure and the level of demand in an economy. Thus, when analysing the influence of demographic change on consumption patterns, one needs to consider the relationship between age and income. If income changes with age and old age may imply lower income in some circumstances, as discussed in chapter V, then a growing older population will affect the structure of demand owing not only to aging per se (with its different tastes and needs) but also to the changes in income brought about by ageing. Lower income for a growing number of older persons will lead to lower consumption levels and shift consumption demand towards basic goods. Thus, in projecting the structure of demand in the future, one also needs to take into account (or make assumptions about) possible changes in the purchasing power of older people.

As noted above, the rise in per capita income is the main factor behind the changes in consumption observed in countries included in figure IV.8. As income per capita rises, consumption shifts from necessary goods such as food and clothing towards services. The increase in the share of health expenditures is particularly evident in the United States, most likely owing to the fact that price increases in health care have been relatively more rapid than the growth in prices for other goods and services (see chapter VI). In any case, the structure of demand changes owing not only to changes in tastes and preferences (which may be age-dependent) but also to changes in income level.

AGEING AND SAVINGS DYNAMICS

Changes in the age structure of the population may have important implications for the generation of savings. Based on the description of the behaviour of individuals in the life-cycle model, it may be assumed that economies with high child dependency ratios would have relatively low saving rates. Countries with an age structure dominated by persons in working age may experience faster rates of growth and could potentially have higher saving rates as individuals save in anticipation of their retirement. Meanwhile, economies characterized by high old-age dependency would experience a decline in their savings rates (see above, box IV.1).

Figure IV.8.
Structure of household consumption, selected countries, 1970, 1975, 1980, 1985, 1990 and 1995

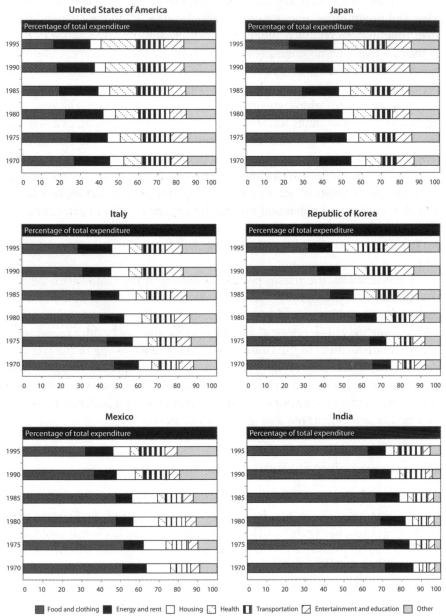

Legend: ■ Food and clothing ■ Energy and rent ☐ Housing ░ Health ▥ Transportation ▨ Entertainment and education ▒ Other

Source: UN/DESA/Statistics Division, National Accounts Yearbook Database online (http://unstats.un.org/unsd/cdb/cdb_source_xrxx.asp?source_code=3).

Table IV.3 presents data on household savings as a percentage of disposable income and old-age dependency ratios for selected developed countries. Net household saving rates have declined in most countries for the last two decades. At the same time, old-age dependency ratios have been on the rise. This would suggest that demographic changes may in fact have important implications for saving rates at least at the aggregate level, but the impact is not uniform across countries.

In France, for instance, household saving rates have remained relatively constant despite higher old-age dependency ratios. In contrast with Germany, in Australia the old-age dependency ratio did not change much, but household saving rates fell precipitously during 1989-2007. Countries with the highest dependency ratios (Japan and Italy) do not have the lowest saving rates. In fact, saving rates are lowest in Australia and the United States, where old-age dependency ratios were also the lowest in 2007. In several countries (Australia, Canada, the Netherlands and the United States), the fall in household saving rates has been more rapid than the increase in old-age dependency ratios.

The differences across these economies may be associated to other factors. For example, highly developed financial markets in combination with financial deregulation in the United States allow economic agents, and the corporate and household sectors, easier access to capital markets both as investors and as borrowers. Owing to reduced constraints on borrowing on the one hand, and the possibility of capital gains on invested funds on the other, the relation between ageing and wage-based saving behaviour, as suggested by the life-cycle model, weakens.

For instance, revaluations of the stock of wealth following fluctuations in asset prices on capital markets also have a powerful impact on household savings. The fact that favourable movements in asset prices lead to an increase in net worth encourages individuals to save less than they would in the absence of such movements, which implies increased consumption and less savings than would otherwise be the case. This outcome has been observed for the United States household sector which has been saving at a declining pace following the wealth effects that originated in gains on the stock market in the mid-1990s and those derived, more recently, from real estate investment. In fact, it has been remarked that the decline in private savings in the United States cannot be attributed to demographic changes, as saving rates for all age groups have declined (Deaton, 2005).

While ageing is not the only factor affecting savings behaviour, and the magnitude of its impact on savings may not be established with certainty, ageing and the resulting increase of retired populations will certainly lead to an expanding number of non-active individuals whose consumption needs

Table IV.3.
Household saving rate and old-age dependency ratio in selected OECD countries, 1989, 1995, 2000, 2003 and 2007

		1989	1995	2000	2003	2007[a]
Australia	Old-age dependency ratio	16.4	17.6	18.3	18.5	19.1
	Household saving rate	7.9	6.7	2.8	-3.1	-1.2
Canada	Old-age dependency ratio	16.2	17.9	18.5	18.6	19.3
	Household saving rate	13.0	9.2	4.7	2.8	1.1
France	Old-age dependency ratio	20.9	23.2	24.7	24.7	25.4
	Household saving rate	8.8	12.9	12.0	12.8	11.5
Germany	Old-age dependency ratio	21.5	22.2	23.3	25.5	29.5
	Household saving rate	12.7	11.0	9.2	10.3	10.2
Italy	Old-age dependency ratio	21.6	23.3	26.9	28.4	31.1
	Household saving rate	24.5	19.4	10.4	11.5	10.0
Japan	Old-age dependency ratio	16.8	21.0	25.2	27.6	31.7
	Household saving rate	13.6	11.9	8.3	4.0	2.4
Netherlands	Old-age dependency ratio	18.4	19.4	20.0	20.6	21.2
	Household saving rate	15.5	14.6	7.0	8.5	5.5
United Kingdom	Old-age dependency ratio	23.9	24.3	24.6	24.4	24.1
	Household saving rate	6.7	10.2	5.1	4.9	5.6
United States	Old-age dependency ratio	18.6	19.2	19.2	18.6	18.5
	Household saving rate	7.1	4.6	2.3	2.1	0.5

Source: World Population Prospects: The 2006 Revision Population Database online (http://esa.un.org/unpp/); World Bank Development Indicators 2005 database; and OECD Economic Outlook No. 80 online database (http://www.oecd.org/dataoecd/5/48/2483858.xls).

Note: Old-age dependency ratio is defined as the number of persons 65 years or over per 100 persons aged 15-64. Household saving rates are expressed as a percentage of disposable household income.
a Estimated.

will have to be satisfied. Thus, one may expect that an increasing share of the income generated by those who are active will have to be transferred to those who are inactive. If income does not grow fast enough, there will be implications for savings (alternatively, the distribution of consumption between workers and retirees will have to be renegotiated or consumption by both will need to decline). For instance, in the case of the United States, calculations of the Department of Economic and Social Affairs of the United Nations Secretariat indicate that on the basis of current consumption levels of active and non-active populations, the share of total consumption in GDP will increase from 71 per cent in 2000 to 75 per cent in 2050. This is a significant but not a dramatic increase. It does indicate, however, that the domestic savings rate may fall by 4 percentage points by 2050. Naturally, the degree as well as the timing of the impact of having an increasingly larger body of non-active consumers is country-specific. The outcome will depend not only on demographic dynamics but also on differences in consumption levels of the various age groups, the desired rate of increase of such consumption levels, and the overall rate of GDP growth.[12]

Implications for global savings

As seen above, the increase in the retired population may exert some pressure on savings, especially in the absence of faster growth. One would expect that the events unfolding in the ageing regions mainly consisting of countries with a dominant presence in the global economy would have an impact on global savings and investment (see figure IV.9).[13] At the global level, the developed countries, with more advanced population ageing, contributed 63 per cent to world total saving and generated 68 per cent of world total investment in 2002. This group of countries, while providing the bulk of world savings, are already entering a stage where the old-age dependency ratio is expected to increase over the next decades. With a share of 16 per cent, China is another important player in the world's supply of savings and is expected to suffer a rapid process of ageing as its old-age dependency ratio jumps from 10 in 2000 to 39 in 2050.

The existence of a significant relationship between global and OECD savings would imply that if ageing is a major driver in respect of the generation of savings, and the rest of the world is unable to grow faster, global savings will decline in the future. Lower global savings may lead to reduced resources available to finance investment and may thus create pressures on interest rates, although the latter will depend on how the demand for investment evolves at the global level.

Figure IV.9.
Global saving and investment per capita by major groups of countries and areas, 1985, 1990, 1995 and 2002

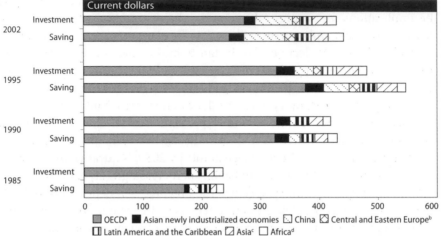

Sources: UN/DESA, based on data from the World Bank Development Indicators 2005 database.
a Excluding the Czech Republic, Hungary, the Republic of Korea, Mexico, Poland, Slovakia and Turkey.
b Including Albania, Bulgaria, the Czech Republic, Hungary, Poland and Slovakia.
c Including all developing economies in East Asia and the Pacific and South Asia and excluding China.
d Including developing countries in sub-Saharan Africa, Northern Africa and the Middle East.

While age may exert an influence on the level of savings, there are many determining factors other than demographic variables as proposed by the life-cycle model. For one, the model applies to household or personal savings only, while the overall level of savings in the economy is also generated by the corporate and the government sectors. Moreover, the relative importance of household or personal savings in the generation of national savings varies across countries and over time in a given country (see figure IV.10). Hence, it is important to be cautious when making claims regarding the dramatic effects of ageing trends on savings patterns. Some of the factors that have an impact on saving and consumption behaviour include: the presence and depth of capital markets, financial innovation and deregulation, the existence of mandatory pension schemes which may affect voluntary saving effort by reducing incentives to save for old age (see chapter V), the presence of bequests that may support saving effort during old age, and fluctuations in levels of income and economic performance in general, as well as simply cultural traits and the institutional framework in place.

Individual behaviour also varies and does not necessarily conform to the assumptions of the life-cycle model. Some individuals may place great value on preserving bequests left to their family and may thus continue to save after retirement. There are those who may choose to utilize their savings earlier on

Figure IV.10.
Gross household savings as a share of gross national savings, Japan and the United States, 1960-2005

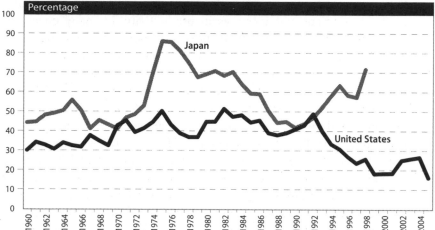

Sources: United States Department of Commerce, National Income and Product Accounts tables (http://www.bea.gov/national/nipaweb/Index.asp), table 5.1 entitled "Saving and investment" (accessed 9 May 2007); and Japan Statistics Bureau and Statistical Research and Training Institute, National Accounts (http://www.stat.go.jp/english/data/chouki/03.htm), tables 03-08 and 03-11-d (accessed 9 May 2007).

in the post-retirement period so as to enjoy life fully while in good health, whereas others might prefer to spread out their accumulated wealth over a longer period of time. Moreover, cohort effects and cultural changes can also impact on individuals, resulting in a saving behaviour that is different than the one foreseen by theory. As a consequence, the hypothesis that people accumulate during working years and decumulate during retirement (thus implying high saving rates for economies where individuals of working age dominate the age structure of the population and low or negative saving rates for ageing countries) needs to be assessed in the larger economic and institutional context of the economy in question.

As it holds for a closed economy, from the accounting point of view savings must equal investment at the global level. As shown in figure IV.9, investment per capita indeed declines at the same pace as savings. Yet, a causal relationship cannot be unambiguously established between these two aggregates. It is not clear that savings drive investment and thus economic growth. Empirical evidence from developing countries, for instance, suggests that higher savings are often the result of faster growth, in other words, that it is economic growth that pushes saving levels up.

In fact, most developing countries "have experienced a discrete increase in domestic savings and investment rate only some time after they underwent a spur in growth" (United Nations, 2005d, overview, p. v). Such growth spurts are in turn related to a variety of external and domestic conditions, including credible and stable policy interventions. Subsequently, growth is sustained by capital investment and increases in productivity. In many developing countries, the bulk of capital formation has been financed by domestic savings and in this regard, constraints on the mobilization of domestic savings in those countries need to be addressed.

Moreover, it is not obvious that a declining labour force necessarily leads to lower investment demand in ageing countries. As seen above, the lower labour supply and the changing structure of aggregate demand may give rise to wage pressure in the ageing economies. Hence, entrepreneurs may well choose to direct their efforts towards higher investment in labour-saving technology and not lower investment in conformity with reduced availability or costlier labour inputs. The speed of technological change and its impact on productivity as well as the resulting obsolescence of existing machinery and equipment are also important factors underlying investment demand. Additionally, in today's increasingly integrated world, investment responds not only to domestic market opportunities but also to opportunities in the global market. Accordingly, the way investment reacts to changes in the size and cost of the labour force, and to the anticipated shifts in the level and composition of demand, together with the necessary technological change and other interventions that allow for increased productivity, will ultimately be crucial for determining and sustaining growth in the future.

Ageing and the Structure and Stability of Financial Markets

While it is not particularly clear whether global and national savings will indeed decline in the future as a consequence of population ageing, the implications for financial markets are already apparent. Increasing amounts of household savings are being directed towards pension funds and other financial investment plans for retirement. Demographic changes together with increasing sophistication of financial instruments and changes in institutional arrangements in many countries have led to an increased presence of pension and mutual funds in the financial markets, with numerous potential implications.

The presence of institutional investors in advanced economies and their rapid rate of growth in many emerging economies are transforming the structure of financial systems around the globe. In the developed economies in the period from 1990 to year-end 2003, assets under management by institutional investors[14] rose from about $14 trillion to $47 trillion and from some 78 to 160 per cent of their aggregate GDP. All three of the major institutional groups (insurance companies, pension funds and investment companies) that are used by households as repositories for retirement savings experienced strong growth during this period (see table IV.4). A number of developing economies have seen a similar surge in the presence of institutional investors. Chile leads with a total asset of pension funds that was equal to no less than 65 per cent of GDP in 2004, followed by Singapore (63 per cent) (Organisation for Economic Co-operation and Development, 2005).

The factors that have induced this shift towards institutional investors vary among countries but a common thread has been the recent emphasis on private pension and retirement funding as government-funded pensions come under pressure (see chapter V). In fact, in those emerging economies that have established fully funded systems, the rise in assets under management by pension funds from 6.3 per cent of their combined GDP in 1992 to 20.3 per cent in 2002 is evidence that shifts of savings into these channels is transforming

Table IV.4.
Assets under management by institutional investors, developed economies, 1990-2004

	1990	1995	2000	2001	2002	2003	2004
	Trillions of United States dollars						
Institutional investors	13.8	23.5	39.0	39.4	36.2	46.8	..
Insurance companies	4.9	9.1	10.1	11.5	10.2	13.5	14.5
Pension funds	3.8	6.7	13.5	12.7	11.4	15.0	15.3
Investment companies	2.6	5.5	11.9	11.7	11.3	14.0	16.2
Hedge funds	0.0	0.1	0.4	0.6	0.6	0.8	0.9
Others	2.4	2.2	3.1	3.0	2.7	3.4	..
	As percentage of GDP						
Institutional investors	77.6	97.8	152.1	155.3	136.4	157.2	..
Insurance companies	27.8	37.8	39.4	45.3	38.4	45.4	44.0
Pension funds	21.2	27.8	52.6	50.1	42.9	50.4	46.4
Investment companies	14.8	22.7	46.3	45.9	42.7	47.2	49.0
Hedge funds	0.1	0.4	1.6	2.2	2.2	2.7	2.8
Others	13.6	9.1	12.4	11.7	10.1	11.5	..

Source: International Monetary Fund (2005), chap. iii, p. 67, table 3.1.

Note: The data may reflect some double-counting of assets owned by defined-contribution pension funds and managed by investment companies. Investment companies include closed-end and managed investment companies, mutual funds and unit investment trusts. Other institutional investors include real estate investment trusts (REITs) and private equity and venture capital funds. GDP is total for OECD countries.

their financial systems as rapidly and effectively as was the case earlier in the more advanced economies. Yet, there are other contributing factors as well: growing wealth, tax incentives, opportunities to diversify holdings, increased liquidity and the contributions to efficiency resulting from technological advances, financial liberalization and product innovation (Davis, 2003).

Pension funds: international capital flows and the home bias

The ageing of populations and the need to set aside resources for retirement together with changes in institutional arrangements have led to a substantial growth of the assets under the management of pension funds in both developed and developing countries. The likely effects of these developments on the volume and direction of international capital flows will depend on the investment strategies adopted by the funds and on the regulations and practices in place in different countries.

Pension funds invest the contributions collected from sponsors and beneficiaries to provide for the future pension entitlements of the beneficiaries. To the extent that international financial markets are not perfectly correlated, international portfolio diversification can reduce the risks as well as provide access to more profitable investments, by providing opportunities for investing in industries and economic activities as well as a wider range of financial instruments that may not exist in home markets. It also provides an outlet for countries where financial and equity markets are small in relation to the volume of pension savings, thereby helping to prevent the emergence of bubbles.

Notwithstanding the above, pension funds in both developing and developed countries display a marked tendency to select domestic over foreign assets. This tendency is commonly known as *home bias*. According to the International Monetary Fund (2005), in 2003 the pension funds of the five biggest economies that are members of the Organisation for Economic Co-operation and Development (OECD) (France, Germany, Japan, the United Kingdom and the United States) invested in aggregate only 14 per cent of their portfolios in foreign assets (5 per cent in foreign equities and 9 per cent in foreign bonds). Pension funds in developing countries also tend to invest mainly in domestic assets (see table IV.5). Additionally, portfolio allocation seems to be country-specific. Institutional investors operating in the developing countries and in European countries—because of either a relatively less developed financial system or the more pronounced presence of welfare State—tend to be more conservative in their investment, as evidenced by their allocation of funds in public and corporate bonds or saving deposits.

Table IV.5.
**Portfolio allocation by pension funds as a share of total
investment, selected countries in Latin America and Europe, 2005**

Percentage	State sector	Corporate sector	Financial sector	Foreign sector	Other assets
Latin America					
Argentina	55.7	13.0	19.8	10.1	1.4
Bolivia	75.8	11.5	8.7	2.5	1.5
Colombia	47.3	19.4	18.8	14.5	0.0
Costa Rica	74.5	2.7	18.9	3.9	0.0
Chile	15.0	23.8	29.8	31.2	0.2
El Salvador	77.7	0.3	15.2	6.8	0.0
Mexico	73.9	12.0	2.0	8.1	4.0
Peru	21.0	52.2	18.8	8.0	0.0
Uruguay[a]	84.5	4.0	9.0	0.0	2.5
Europe					
Bulgaria	43.6	26.4	30.0	0.0	0.0
Poland	62.0	32.0	2.8	1.7	1.5

Source: International Federation of Pension Funds Administrators.
a Pension funds not authorized to invest in foreign assets.

Equity and mutual funds seem to be the class of financial assets preferred by pension funds in Canada, the Netherlands, the United Kingdom and the United States (Organisation for Economic Co-operation and Development, 2005).

The home bias may also be induced by regulatory policy. Many countries have strict investment regulations and impose tight limits on the acquisition of foreign securities and equities to avoid currency mismatches. Some countries often impose limits on foreign allocation or do not allow it altogether. For example, the current ceiling on foreign asset allocation is 5 per cent in Hungary and 10 per cent in Argentina, Colombia and Peru. In the Dominican Republic and Uruguay, pension funds are not allowed to invest abroad, while in Mexico such a restriction was lifted as of October 2005. Limits evolve over time. In the case of Chile, investment abroad had not been allowed initially and was gradually introduced. In 2005, about 30 per cent of funds managed by Chilean pension funds were invested abroad, which has contributed, however, to increased pro-cyclicality of capital flows.

Limits are also common among developed countries. Recently, the Government of Norway announced that the Government Pension Fund will increase its exposure to global equities from the current 40 to 60 per cent (*Financial Times*, April 14/15 2007, p. 4). Tax regulations imposed on Canadian funds, for example, limit foreign investment to 30 per cent of the portfolio. In Italy and Germany, the limit is set at 20 per cent. On the other hand, in such countries as the Netherlands, the United Kingdom and the United States, pension funds are simply subject to a "prudent man rule", which requires the pension fund managers to make sensible investment decisions based on what is perceived as best practice among other institutional investors.

Regulators consider these investment limits necessary to prevent pension funds from taking excessive risks and to thereby protect pensioners' rights and future entitlements. In many circumstances, limits are imposed pursuant to such macroeconomic objectives as promoting the development of local capital markets, retaining scarce resources in the domestic economy, preventing a run on the currency, and facilitating the financing of pension systems reforms (discussed in chap. V). In developing countries, preventing currency mismatches and pro-cyclical flows based on exchange-rate expectations is among the main concerns underlying the imposition of investment limits.

Yet, regulations imposed on investment allocation do not fully explain the small share of foreign assets in pension fund portfolios. Table IV.6 shows that for many countries adopting restrictions on international asset allocation, the share of foreign assets held by the pension funds are on average well below the maximum threshold permitted.

A number of other factors, reflecting pension funds' strategies and the nature of international transactions, contribute to the reduced exposure to foreign assets. Pension fund managers seek not only to maximize returns but also to align the mix of their asset holdings to the structure of their liabilities. In particular, mature pension funds will avoid instruments that entail currency risk and potential capital loss and will prefer domestic bonds instead. Moreover, transaction costs are higher in international asset trading. Gaining access to a foreign market may entail extra costs owing to the registration and the commissions for foreign currency transactions. Also, the relative scarcity of information on foreign markets may represent a significant obstacle to certain investments, particularly where disclosure standards differ substantially from those of home markets (see Ahearne, Griever and Warnock, 2004; and Van Nieuwerburgh and Veldkamp, 2006). Finally, pension fund managers tend to have a liquidity bias in respect of their portfolio allocation, as reflected in high shares of national treasury bills. This liquidity bias may also be partly induced by regulatory provisions.

Looking ahead, it is likely that the absorption of pension fund assets by developing countries will increase in the next 5 to 10 years, provided that these

Table IV.6.
**Limits on and actual foreign assets allocation by pension
funds, selected developed and developing countries**

Percentage	Foreign assets allocation	
	Limit	Actual
Developed countries, 2002		
United Kingdom	PMR[a]	22.9
United States	PMR[a]	11.0
Germany	30.0[b]	7.0
Japan	30.0[c]	22.9
Canada	30.0	15.0
Hungary	30.0	2.5
Poland	5.0	1.6
Developing countries, 2006		
Argentina	10.0	10.0
Peru	8.0	8.0
Mexico	10.0	8.1

Sources: International Monetary Fund, Global Financial and Stability Report, September 2005
(Washington, D.C., IMF, 2005); and International Federation of Pension Funds Administrators.
a Prudent man rule applies.
b Referring to equity issued in other EU countries. On the other hand, the limit on bonds and
equity issued by non-EU countries is 10 per cent.
c No investment limits for public employee funds.

countries are considered attractive enough by pension managers in terms
of their investment strategies. Even assuming that portfolio shares remain
unchanged and home bias persists, as household savings are increasingly
channelled to pension funds, an increase in the overall volume of resources will
naturally translate into an increase in the volume of international investment
of pension funds. While representing an important source of finance and a
growth opportunity for developing countries, these developments may also
generate some worries in the light of the vulnerability of many of the emerging
markets to volatile capital flows.

Institutional investors: transforming financial markets

The increased role of institutional investors as the principal managers of
household savings has brought about positive externalities for financial
development and economic growth. The rise of institutional investors and the
increased supply of financial liquidity have indeed led to the transformation of

financial markets in the direction of enhanced sophistication of the financing mechanisms and a wider range of available instruments in the markets, thus contributing to a further deepening and increased innovation in financial markets in developed economies and supporting financial development in emerging market economies. In the case of the United States, for example, pension and mutual funds contributed to the spectacular rise in the assets of the housing-related government-sponsored enterprises (GSEs) such as Fannie Mae and Freddie Mac and federally related mortgage pools, as well as the group of asset-backed securities issuers that include the finance affiliates of automobile manufacturers, credit card issuers, private mortgage companies and other non-bank lenders (D'Arista, 2006). In emerging markets, the emergence of pension funds has been paralleled by increased equity market capitalization, the development of corporate bond markets and the expansion of debt maturities owing to the long-term nature of pension fund investments and the increased availability of long-term finance. Meanwhile, the greater supply of liquidity brought about by pension funds can also contribute to market stability, as it provides a buffer against potential adverse shocks (Davis, 2005).

On the other hand, the move towards institutional investors and fully funded pension schemes (see chapter V) has allowed new channels for savings to emerge over the past three decades without there being sufficient attention paid to the need to update the bank-centred monetary and regulatory frameworks that have traditionally governed national financial systems. First, it should be noted that the increasing presence of institutional investors has also meant greater competition for the banking sector. As a result, banks have moved towards accepting greater risks by becoming involved in riskier leveraged transactions in order to maintain or expand operations and profits. Additionally, banks (especially those based in the United States) have increasingly relied on non-deposit liabilities for funding as savings move from banks into institutional investors. By tightening the links between the various financial sectors, these developments have led to greater probability that problems in one group of institutions will spill over into others, thus increasing the risk of systemic instability.

Second, monetary authorities (at least in the United States) have lost a great deal of influence over the credit supply as the rise in the market power of institutional investors has led to the transformation of financial markets from a bank-based system into a market-based one,[15] which contributes to increasing pro-cyclicality in financial markets (D'Arista, 2006). For increased pro-cyclicality there are two main explanations. One, the fact that institutional investors are not subject to the central bank's quantitative monetary controls, such as reserve and liquidity requirements, makes it difficult for the monetary authority to conduct counter-cyclical policy. Moreover, the fact that institutional investors act mostly on secondary markets both domestically and internationally compounds the problem. This implies that the monetary authority has lost a great deal of its ability to intervene and sterilize inflows with the existing monetary tools. Two, the reorientation of households' savings towards credit market instruments such as bonds and corporate equities leads to a pro-cyclical wealth effect on household balances: during an upswing, assets prices may rise leading to spending booms while during the downturn, asset prices may fall leading to a decline in consumption, thereby magnifying the swings of the business cycle.

In response to these developments, the Bank for International Settlements (BIS) has proposed a prudential macroeconomic stabilization framework which aims to return to the monetary authorities some of the control that they should have, especially over unchecked credit growth. The framework, however, excludes important functions of monetary policy—those that should be concerned with targeting non-banking financial actors such as the institutional investors among whom most of the financial leveraging has been taking place.

Finally, with increasing liberalization of financial markets across the world, the concentration of capital in the hands of institutional investors may also have implications for the allocation of international capital flows as discussed above. In particular, the role of institutional investors in contributing to the volatility of capital flows and increasing the potential for systemic risk raises questions about the stability of the global financial system and the links forged between institutions and markets worldwide. Reforms should be conducted so as to ensure that international financial markets are also protected from excessive volatility of capital flows. Because most of the capital inflows—especially to developing economies—are destined for secondary markets, they often contribute to increased volatility rather than to sustained economic expansion, while outflows give rise to currency and financial crises. The introduction of capital controls can help to offset the pro-cyclicality and volatility linked to capital flows, in particular portfolio flows, to developing countries, thereby contributing to greater macroeconomic stability in their economies (Ocampo, 2005; Ocampo and Vos, 2006; United Nations, 2006a).

Conclusions

With population ageing, the share of the population in the working ages will shrink and the labour force itself will grow older. This holds especially for the countries, mostly developed, with low fertility rates. In contrast, countries with relatively high fertility levels (primarily low-income economies) will continue to experience strong labour-force growth until 2050, which may open a window of opportunity for accelerated economic growth.

Population ageing could become a drag on economic growth unless the decline in labour-force growth can be controlled or greater efforts are made to increase labour productivity. In most contexts, increases in labour productivity would be required to complement measures that would contribute to stemming the fall in labour supply.

Various measures have been proposed to mitigate the effects of rising dependency ratios, including international migration, outsourcing of employment and increasing labour participation rates.

International migration is often mentioned as a possible tool to ensure an adequate supply of workers in developed countries, but it is not expected that any country will admit the massive numbers of migrants that would be needed to offset population ageing.

The outsourcing of employment to offshore locations is another possibility, but it would fail to address the challenge of mounting old-age dependency ratios. While offshoring alleviates labour shortages by shifting production to workers abroad, it will not reduce pressures on old-age pension systems because employment, and therefore the contributory base of such systems, will not expand.

The analysis of this chapter suggests that the greatest potential for counteracting the projected changes in labour-force growth lies in raising the participation rates of women and older workers. In the latter case, many countries still possess considerable scope for enacting measures aimed at increasing the participation rate of older workers—typically those aged 55-64—by bringing the effective retirement age more closely in line with the statutory retirement age. Yet, these measures will need to be complemented by interventions aimed at raising the productivity of older workers, if in fact productivity tends to decline with age.

There are also a range of options for removing disincentives to prolonged employment, such as altering workplace practices to better accommodate the needs of workers as they age; improving working conditions to sustain working capacity over the life course; countering age-based discrimination; and promoting positive images of older workers. Older workers will also be in a better position to extend their working lives if they are given the opportunity to engage in lifelong learning and on-the-job training initiatives. Such measures are expected to increase economic growth in ageing countries, though the impact may not be very large.

More generally though, worries that ageing populations and ageing workforces will lead to acute declines in economic growth appear unfounded. The analysis provided in this chapter indicates that the productivity growth required to sustain a given level of per capita GDP growth compares favourably with that of past experience. Yet, sustaining relatively high productivity growth for prolonged periods may be a challenge, which underlines the importance of continued efforts to upgrade skills and promote technological development.

Countries with growing and still relatively young labour forces may be able to accelerate growth. However, in order to reap this demographic dividend, they will need to deal with a different set of issues. Rather than be concerned about impending labour shortages, they should remain focused on creating decent employment opportunities, especially for the growing numbers of young people expected to enter the workforce. Boosting employment rates in the formal economy will help to raise tax revenues and set the stage for expanding social protection schemes where they are currently underdeveloped, thereby enabling older workers to retire with financial security. Productivity growth is also important for developing economies with respect not only to supporting an expanding older population, but also to raising overall living standards and reducing poverty.

By many accounts, population ageing is expected to have implications for patterns of consumption, investment and savings. Understanding whether and how population ageing will affect these aggregates is crucial to anticipating how economic growth and development may unfold in the future. Although economic theory offers some clear conceptions of this relationship, in reality it remains rather difficult to predict how ageing will influence future consumption and growth patterns.

Consumption needs and tastes change over the life cycle. It has indeed been established that older people, in contrast with younger population cohorts, tend to spend a higher share of their incomes on housing and social services. Population ageing thus could lead to substantial changes in the composition of the demand for goods and services.

A closer look at existing trends suggests, however, that these changes occur slowly over time. Furthermore, levels of consumption are more closely related to income than to the demographic structure. This complex reality makes it difficult to predict future trends in consumption, as the growth of incomes for older persons in the coming decades is a subject of relative uncertainty.

Similarly, the implications of ageing for savings patterns are difficult to gauge. It is often assumed that economies with high levels of child and old-age dependency have relatively low national saving rates, while economies with large shares of working-age population have high savings rates. Ageing may indeed exert an influence, but there are many other factors determining savings behaviour and the level of savings in the economy.

It is clear, however, that an increasing share of available (household) savings flows into pension funds and other financial investment plans for retirement. Institutional investors, which typically manage such savings, have already become the main players in financial markets. These investors manage not only large amounts of household savings from developed countries, but also, increasingly, household savings from developing countries where the importance of privately managed capitalized pension systems has grown. Institutional investors contribute to the development and deepening of financial markets in developed countries and emerging market economies, but in doing so, they largely operate outside of financial market regulation and supervision mechanisms that apply more generally to the banking system. If unchecked, the financial market operations of pension funds could thus be a source of instability and enhanced market speculation. Also, as increasing financial investments are intermediated outside of the banking system, monetary authorities are losing some control over credit growth, thereby limiting the effectiveness of monetary policies. Improved (international) regulatory measures are needed to avert possible financial market destabilizing effects of the operations of large pension funds and to prevent the income security of older persons from being jeopardized.

Notes to Chapter IV

1   For further discussion of the methodology for estimates and projections, see: http://laborsta.ilo.org/.

2   For example, in the case of Italy, calculations of UN/DESA indicate that a gradual reduction in the unemployment rate from 11 per cent in 1999 to 4 per cent by 2025 would imply an average annual rate of growth of gross domestic product (GDP) per capita of 2 per cent during the period 2000-2050 compared with a rate of 1.8 per cent in the absence of such a decline (see note 7 below).

3   At the same time, however, in the United States there is evidence of a reverse trend, as an increasing number of highly educated professional married women are dropping out of the labour force to care for their young children, either for short periods or at least until their children reach school age (Mosisa and Hipple, 2006).

4   In the United Kingdom of Great Britain and Northern Ireland, for example, companies demanding high-skilled labour are offering a new service to women workers returning from maternity leave called "maternity coaching". The service represents an attempt to retain women of middle and senior rank who companies feel may leave owing to the stress of working in a high-pressure environment while raising a newly born child (Maitland, 2007).

5   In some Western Asian countries, for instance, older workers have been offered opportunities for education and training through special programmes in such areas as improving/acquiring computer skills, with the aim of preparing them for productive work (Economic and Social Commission for Western Asia, 2002). A number of companies in Europe have established age management policies to deal with their ageing workforces. A good-practice example can be found in Austria, where the global steel company Voestalpine adopted a programme designed to respond to the challenge presented by its ageing workforce. The programme, known as LIFE (Light-hearted, Innovative, Fit, Efficient), aims to retain older workers; integrate new workers; promote the transfer of know-how from one generation of workers to the next; and improve safety through better ergonomics. Training is also an important part of the programme, and every employee is granted at least 33 hours per year to spend on projects and training (European Foundation for the Improvement of Living and Working Conditions, 2006a).

6   In the case of computers, the gap is expected to decline further over time. Of course, new technologies may emerge that give rise to the same phenomenon.

7   This decomposition exercise is based on the accounting identity which states that the overall output of GDP is equal to the product of the number of workers (L) and their individual level of productivity (ε). In mathematical terms, this may be expressed as $GDP = L.\varepsilon$. Accordingly, the rate of growth of GDP per capita is approximately equal to the sum of the growth rate of employment and the growth rate of labour productivity less the rate of population growth, that is to say, $(\widehat{GDP}/N) = \hat{L} + \hat{\varepsilon} - \hat{N}$. With employment growth given based on the number of persons anticipated to be engaged in the labour force and labour productivity growth assumed to be at 2 per cent annually, it is possible to derive the annual rate of increase in output per capita. Conversely, one can estimate the necessary labour productivity growth by assuming a constant growth in GDP per capita. The labour force was projected based on forecasts of population of working age (15-64) derived from the World Population Prospects: The 2004 Revision, Population Database. Participation rates for the period 2000-2020 were derived from the ILO database on labour statistics (LABORSTA), available from http://laborsta.ilo.org/ and assumed to remain at the 2020 level for the remainder of the period of analysis.

8   Specifically, Lehman found that chemists reached their peak productivity between the ages of 26 and 30. In mathematics, physics, botany, electronics and practical inventions, peak productivity was achieved between the ages of 30 and 34.

9   There may have been some bias present in these surveys associated with how the pertinent variables were being measured. Measurement of cognitive abilities, for example, ignored experience and managerial abilities, which often increase with age, while surveys relying on supervisors' evaluations were subjective and might have been biased against older workers (Börsch-Supan, 2004).

10   See, for example, earlier studies such as Romer (1986); Mankiw, Romer and Weil (1992); Coe and Helpman (1995); and Lichtenberg (1992).

11   National Transfer Accounts Database (lead institutions: Population and Health Studies Program, East-West Centre and Center for the Economics and Demography of Aging, University of California at Berkeley), available from http://www.schemearts.com/proj/nta/web.

12   Per capita GDP was assumed to grow by 2 per cent per year, on average, during the period 2000-2050. Consumption includes both private and public consumption and was estimated to increase also at 2 per cent per year, on a per capita basis, for both active and non-active populations. Data on consumption levels for the various age groups (under 15, 15-64 and 65 years or over) for the year 2000 were derived from Lee and Mason (2007), while population data were obtained from the Population Division of UN/DESA, World Population Prospects: The 2004 Revision Population Database.

13   From the accounting point of view, investment equals savings at the global level. The difference in some years was due to errors and omissions and also to the fact that not all countries were included in this exercise.

14   Institutional investors include insurance companies, pension funds, investment companies, hedge funds, real estate investment trusts (REITs), and private equity and venture capital funds. Investment companies include closed-end and managed investment companies, mutual funds and unit investment trusts.

15   In a bank-based system, banks dominate credit allocation and financial intermediation, whereas in a market-based system these roles are shared with the financial markets which supply credit through trading of equities and securities.

APPENDIX

Grouping of countries and areas by fertility, immigration and labour-force participation rates

Fertility	Immigration	Labour-force participation rates	Country or area			
High	High	High	Jordan	Saudi Arabia	Qatar	West Bank
	High	Low to moderate	Belize Côte d'Ivoire	Gabon Gambia	Oman Libyan Arab Jamahiriya	
	Moderate	High	Comoros	Congo	Ghana	Namibia
	Moderate	Low to moderate	Burkina Faso	Syrian Arab Republic		
	Low	High	Bangladesh Benin Bolivia Burundi Cambodia Cape Verde Central African Republic Chad Democratic Republic of the Congo	Djibouti Ethiopia Guinea Guinea-Bissau Kenya Liberia Malawi Mauritania	Mozambique Nepal Niger Pakistan Paraguay Philippines Rwanda Senegal Sierra Leone	Somalia Sudan Swaziland Tajikistan Togo Uganda Yemen Zambia Zimbabwe
	Low	Low to moderate	Afghanistan Angola Bhutan Botswana	Eritrea Guatemala Haiti	Honduras Lao People's Democratic Republic Lesotho	Madagascar Mali Nigeria

Appendix table (cont'd)

Fertility	Immigration	Labour-force participation rates	Country or area			
Moderate	High	High	Kazakhstan Kuwait			United States
		Low to moderate	Bahrain Brunei Darussalam Costa Rica	France Guadeloupe Ireland	Israel Lebanon Martinique	Reunion
	Moderate	High	Bahamas	Iceland		
		Low to moderate	Kyrgyzstan	Malaysia		
	Low	High	Azerbaijan Brazil Colombia Ecuador	Indonesia Mongolia Myanmar Panama	Peru Thailand Turkmenistan Uruguay	Venezuela (Bolivarian Republic of) Viet Nam
		Low to moderate	Albania Algeria Argentina Chile Democratic People's Republic of Korea	Dominican Republic Egypt El Salvador Guyana India	Iran (Islamic Republic of) Jamaica Mexico Morocco Nicaragua	South Africa Suriname Tunisia Turkey Uzbekistan

Appendix table (cont'd)

Fertility	Immigration	Labour-force participation rates	Country or area			
Low	High	High	Canada	China, Macao	Switzerland	Spain
		Low to moderate	Australia	Croatia	Latvia	Sweden
			Austria	Cyprus	Luxembourg	Ukraine
			Belarus	Estonia	Netherlands	
			Hong Kong, SAR	Germany	Singapore	
	Moderate	High	Denmark	Norway		
		Low to moderate	Armenia	Greece	Russian Fed	UK
			Belgium	Portugal	Slovenia	
	Low	High	China			
		Low to moderate	Bosnia-Herzegovina	Georgia	Malta	Serbia-Montenegro
			Bulgaria	Hungary	Mauritius	Slovakia
			Cuba	Italy	Poland	Sri Lanka
			Czech Republic	Japan	Korea, Rep	Trinidad and Tobago
			Finland	Lithuania	Romania	

Sources: Population Division of the Department of Economic and Social Affairs of the United Nations Secretariat, Trends in Total Migrant Stock: The 2005 Revision: CD-ROM documentation available from http://www.un.org/esa/population/publications/migration/UN_Migrant_Stock_Documentation_2005.pdf (accessed 21 February 2007); Population, Resources, Environment and Development (PRED) Databank: The 2005 Revision; and International Labour Office, LABORSTA: Economically active population estimates and projections: 1980–2020.

Note: Countries classifed as follows:

(1) Total fertility rate (TFR):
High fertility = TFR ≥3.0; moderate fertility = 1.80 ≤ TFR < 3.0; low fertility = TFR < 1.80

(2) International migration as a share of population (MIG):
High migration = MIG ≥ 10 per cent of population; moderate migration = 5 per cent ≤ MIG < 10 per cent; low migration = MIG < 5 per cent.

(3) Labour-force participation rates of population aged 15 years or over (LFPR):
High LFPR = LFPR ≥ 65 per cent; low-to-moderate LFPR = LFPR < 65 per cent.

Chapter V
Old-age income security

INTRODUCTION

Living standards often decline for people at older ages. Reduced economic opportunities and deteriorating health status frequently increase vulnerability to poverty as people age. Such conditions vary greatly, however, across contexts and groups of older persons and livelihood strategies tend to differ accordingly. In developed economies, the main source of livelihood and protection shifts from employment to pension income as one reaches a given retirement age. In developing countries, few have access to pensions and most have to rely on other sources of income. In fact, 80 per cent of the world's population do not have sufficient protection in old age to enable them to face health, disability and income risks (International Labour Organization, 2002). This would mean that in developing countries alone, about 342 million older persons currently lack adequate income security. That number would rise to 1.2 billion by 2050, if the coverage of current mechanisms designed to provide old-age income security is not expanded. The demographic transition poses an enormous challenge with respect to ensuring the availability and sustainability of pensions and other systems providing economic security for an ever-larger number of older persons in both developed and developing countries.

For the unprotected, the notion of retirement does not exist; they must continue to rely on their work, which is a greater challenge for those in advanced age (80 years or over). To survive, older persons also count on the support of the family and the community, which, if also resource-constrained, may not be able to offer solid social insurance. In this regard, older persons who are single, widowed or childless (particularly women) face an even higher risk of destitution. Meanwhile, countries with formal pension systems have been successful in reducing, if not eliminating, poverty during old age.

Yet, the sustainability of existing pension systems has been increasingly put in question. Increased longevity, faulty programme design, mismanagement, and insufficient economic growth and employment-generation have undermined the financial viability of many of these systems. Additionally, the increase in the old-age dependency ratio, as described in chapter II, will place significant pressure on both formal and informal support systems if economic growth (and the generation of decent jobs) cannot be accelerated and sustained. At the same time, smaller family sizes and the reduced importance of the extended family will alter the availability and patterns of informal support as well (see chapter III).

Pension systems should ensure income security during old age for all and, as a minimum, need to provide benefits that place recipients above the poverty line or any other socially acceptable minimum standard. Issues of solidarity, accessibility, affordability and sustainability are at the core of old-age pension system design and reform. In practice, these principles appear to be best approached through national pension systems designed on the basis of several pillars addressing specific needs, complementing one another, and tailored to particular circumstances. For instance, in a country with a large informal sector, universal coverage could be attained through a pillar offering minimum benefits. This minimum benefit should be made available preferably on a universal basis. The analysis in the present chapter shows that a universal social pension scheme which offers benefits equivalent to the international (extreme) poverty line can be affordable for the majority of developing countries, including most low-income countries. Another pillar could be introduced providing basic pensions for those segments of society holding formal jobs. In this pillar, pensions could target a minimally accepted wage-replacement level. Moreover, this pillar should build in the necessary incentives for consistent participation while including solidarity mechanisms directed towards those contributors who are less well off in order to enhance their benefits. Last, those more affluent segments of society should be encouraged to complement the public pensions with their own accumulation of savings, either through private pension or employer-sponsored schemes or through other forms of asset accumulation, upon which they can draw when they retire.

Pension systems may be privately or publicly administered, but ultimately the responsibility to guarantee, regulate and supervise the delivery of a basic pension lies solely with the government. Several countries introduced structural reforms in their pension schemes, moving from a pay-as-you-go (PAYG) scheme with defined benefits to a fully funded defined-contribution system (see box V.1 for definitions). Ultimately, these systems, the latter in particular, cannot guarantee income security during old age. Moreover, pension systems would still have to adjust in order to cope with the anticipated increases in demographic pressures: as the dependent population increases,

Box V.1.
Pension systems: a multitude of arrangements

There is great diversity in respect of the design of old-age pension systems. In systems that are contributory, beneficiaries (and their employers in some cases) are asked to contribute to the financing of the benefits. Such contributions often take the form of a tax on labour income. Entitlement to future pension benefits is contingent on one's having a minimal history of employment or self-employment. The government may also participate in the financing of contributory schemes with funds from general revenues (or specifically earmarked taxes) for the purpose of subsidizing low-income workers, of covering administrative expenses and/or of making up deficits. Non-contributory systems, an alternative, are often financed with general taxation revenues and generally provide a flat benefit. These systems can be universal (covering the entire population) or targeted (covering only a target group, say, the poor). The targeting mechanism may be based on a means test, that is to say, access to benefits may depend upon recipients' meeting certain criteria (for instance, that their income must fall below a certain level).

Pension benefits can be financed on a pay-as-you-go basis (PAYG), where the contributions paid by the current generation of workers into the system are disbursed to pay benefits to retirees and no accumulation of financial assets occurs. Conversely, benefits can be pre-funded, that is to say, paid using resources accumulated previously in a fully funded (FF) system, by which each generation finances its own pension. Under a fully funded system, pension reserves should total 100 per cent of the present value of all pension liabilities owed to current contributors.

Defined-benefit (DB) schemes refer to pension plans that guarantee the application of a predefined or prescribed formula determining, for instance, a certain wage-replacement level.

Defined-contribution (DC) schemes prescribe a periodic contribution, and future benefits depend on the level of contributions made and the returns on the investment of those contributions. Pay-as-you-go systems often operate on a defined-benefit basis. Recently, however, some countries have been reforming their pay-as-you-go systems and introducing a defined-contribution approach, whereby current contributions are used to finance current benefits; such schemes thereby retain the characteristic of a pay-as-you-go system. Under these schemes, however, in contrast with traditional pay-as-you-go schemes, contributions are credited to a "notional" individual account which earns a "notional return" based on a predetermined formula; in other words, resources are not actually put resources into a depository, thereby making the approach a pure accounting exercise. As the overall accumulated notional principal and return later determine one's pension benefit, such approaches can be considered defined-contribution schemes.

more resources will be needed if a certain level of welfare is to be maintained for all and the burden is not to become too heavy for the working population. This is not to say, however, that current pay-as-you-go systems need not be reformed. This chapter indicates some of the adjustments that should be introduced, which could go a long way towards ensuring the financial sustainability of current systems while providing a minimum degree of income security for all based on solidarity among and between generations.

OLD AGE AND INCOME POVERTY

Information on the incidence of poverty among older persons is scattered, not readily available and often not comparable across countries or regions as data are derived using different methodologies, concepts and period coverage. Yet, it is possible to say that, in general, for countries where formal pension systems or old-age public transfers have extensive coverage, older persons are likely to be less affected by absolute poverty than the rest of the population.[1] This is the case both in developing countries, such as Argentina, Brazil, Chile and Uruguay, and in developed economies. In the United States of America, for instance, the poverty rate for the total population in 2004 was higher (at 12.7 per cent) than that among those aged 65 years or over (at 9.8 per cent) (Social Security Administration, 2006; U.S. Census Bureau, 2006). In fact, the expansion of old-age pension coverage and increases in benefits have been important factors behind the decline in the incidence of poverty among older persons in the United States, from 35 per cent in 1960 (Engelhardt and Gruber, 2004) to less than 10 per cent at present.

Estimates of poverty among older persons in other developed countries with extensive pension coverage are often based on a concept of relative poverty. Related studies tend to use a definition of the poverty line based on a share of the median income. Being poor according to the relative poverty concept does not necessarily imply that a person or a household is unable to afford a minimum of basic goods and services. Rather, because it measures people's positions relative to the mean or median of the distribution, relative poverty should be seen in this context more accurately as an indicator of inequality. In this regard, available data show that in some developed countries older persons are overrepresented in the bottom of the income distribution. In Denmark, for instance, 47 per cent of persons aged 65 years or over belonged to the bottom two deciles of the income distribution in 1996, while the corresponding figure was about 30 per cent for Greece, Portugal and the United Kingdom of Great Britain and Northern Ireland (Heinrich, 2000). Relative poverty seems to be higher among older persons than in the rest of the population in the majority of developed countries shown in figure V.1a. In the case of the United States, for instance, relative poverty remained stable in the 1980s and 1990s, thus indicating that older persons have not shared the increases in standard of living realized by the rest of the population (Engelhardt and Gruber, 2004). Similar trends were observed in Ireland in the late 1990s as the income of older persons had not grown at the same pace as the median income (Förster and d'Ercole, 2005).

Figure V.1a.
**National and old-age poverty headcount ratios,
selected developed economies, circa 2000**

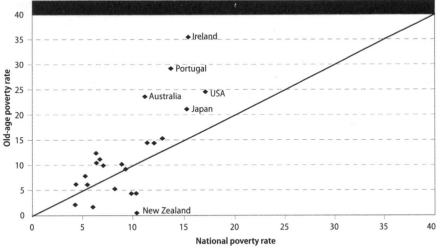

Source: Förster and d'Ercole (2005).

Note: Old age refers to those aged 65 years or over. Poverty rates are estimated on the basis of 50 per cent of the median per capita income.

For countries without or with limited pension systems, poverty among older persons tends to be comparable with the national average (see figure V.1b) but is often higher than among the working-age populations. In the absence of access to old-age pensions, the greater risk of falling into poverty at older ages is typically caused by the limited job opportunities and/or reduced working capacity of older persons. Available evidence for Latin America indicates that older people (aged 60 years or over) are not necessarily more likely to be unemployed than other age groups of the labour force (Gasparini and others, 2007). Rather, when employed, older persons tend to work fewer hours and to receive lower wages than younger cohorts.

More education generally provides access to better-paid jobs. The incidence of illiteracy is still relatively high among older persons in developing countries. As older persons also have fewer years of completed schooling, when they do continue to work they are more likely to have a low-skilled job. In Brazil, for instance, the incidence of poverty among those aged 60 years or over with no schooling was at 33 per cent in 1997, whereas poverty affected only 6.5 per cent of older persons with eight years of schooling (Paes de Barros, Mendonça and Santos, 1999). The risk of falling into poverty at old age may also relate to family size. Older persons in Latin America tend to live in smaller households and are therefore less able to benefit from the sharing

Figure V.1b.
National and old-age poverty headcount ratios,
selected developing economies, 1997-2005

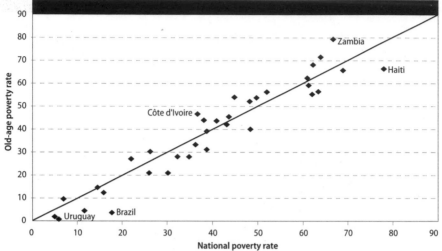

Sources: Gasparini and others (2007); and Kakwani and Subbarao (2005).
Note: Old-age poverty refers to those individuals aged 60 years or over.

of goods in the household, that is to say, they do not gain as much as those in larger households from economies of scale in consumption (Gasparini and others, 2007).

Large differences in poverty incidence also exist between beneficiaries and non-beneficiaries of pension schemes. For instance, in the case of the United States, while the poverty rate among pension beneficiaries was 7.7 per cent in 2004, the corresponding figure for non-beneficiaries was significantly higher at 25.4 per cent (Social Security Administration, 2006). Also, in other contexts, the impact of old-age pensions on poverty reduction can be considerable. In the absence of pension benefits, and all other things being equal, poverty among older persons would be much higher.[2] Table V.1 presents evidence for a group of Latin American countries. The case of Brazil stands out, as 85 per cent of those aged 60 years or over living in rural areas receive pensions. The incidence of poverty among this group lies at 3.5 per cent (poverty line at $2 purchasing power parity (PPP) per day); it would lie at 51 per cent in the absence of such benefits (Gasparini and others, 2007).

Even when the level of benefits is less than the monetary value of the poverty line, old-age pensions may help reduce the intensity of poverty and they can reduce household economic vulnerability by strengthening livelihood strategies and crowding in other support mechanisms that provide for income security. For instance, a significant proportion of beneficiaries of

Table V.1.
Proportion receiving pensions and poverty headcount ratio for persons aged 60 years or over, nationally and by urban/rural, selected Latin American countries, 2001-2005ᵃ

Percentage	National			Urban areas			Rural areas		
	Proportion receiving pensions	Old age poverty incidence		Proportion receiving pensions	Old age poverty incidence		Proportion receiving pensions	Old age poverty incidence	
		Including pension income	Excluding pension income		Including pension income	Excluding pension income		Including pension income	Excluding pension income
Argentina	56.4	4.5	39.5	56.4	4.5	39.5	..	..	..
Bolivia	11.1	42.1	50.4	19.4	19.4	30.9	2.7	67.7	72.3
Brazil	77.3	3.7	47.9	75.7	3.7	47.2	85.2	3.5	51.3
Chile	54.5	1.8	22.7	57.9	1.6	21.4	37.9	2.9	29.1
Dominican Republic	11.2	14.7	17.1	13.9	12.4	15.3	7.0	18.1	19.8
Ecuador	10.7	33.3	39.2	17.6	24.6	32.9	4.2	41.6	45.2
El Salvador	14.1	31.2	35.6	20.0	21.4	27.4	4.2	47.6	49.2
Guatemala	10.6	28.0	30.6	15.1	20.6	25.0	5.9	35.8	36.5
Haiti	0.9	66.4	68.8	2.5	60.0	63.4	0.1	69.5	71.4
Honduras	5.4	39.2	41.3	9.7	22.2	25.3	1.7	60.8	61.6
Jamaica	14.0	54.0	60.6	17.3	56.4	65.2	11.9	52.0	56.8
Mexico	20.1	27.1	40.4	25.4	20.4	35.4	7.3	44.0	53.0
Nicaragua	10.4	40.1	43.5	14.5	33.8	37.9	3.8	50.3	52.5
Panama	38.7	12.4	38.8	52.0	4.8	32.2	18.5	23.9	48.8
Paraguay	12.2	21.0	27.2	17.7	14.5	23.2	5.0	29.6	32.4
Uruguay	77.9	0.8	20.2	77.9	0.8	20.2	..	..	..
Venezuela (Bolivarian Republic of)	17.1	28.1	41.1	17.1	28.1	41.1	..	..	..

Source: Gasparini and others (2007).

Note: Poverty line at $2 purchasing power parity (PPP) per day.

a   Results of a simulation exercise.

the rural pension in Brazil reported using part of their pension to purchase seeds and tools to support agricultural production (Delgado and Cardoso, 2000). Furthermore, pension incomes are often shared with other household members. In Namibia, for instance, over 70 per cent of the pension income was shared among household members, and was spent on food as well as on education for grandchildren (Palacios and Sluchynsky, 2006). In this regard, pension-sharing can be a factor in reducing the overall degree of poverty. Naturally, the impact on poverty will depend on the size of the pension benefits and on the absence of offsetting reductions from other sources of income. If pension benefits are too small, sharing will imply minimal income gains on a per capita basis for household members. Yet, even in this case, pensions may contribute to poverty reduction if benefits are used for improving the educational or nutritional status of household members.

Old-age pensions do not necessarily eliminate poverty and large differences in welfare among pensioners do exist. The incidence of poverty tends to be higher among older pensioners, as pension benefits and a longer history of contribution favour younger cohorts. Female pensioners tend, in general, to be poorer than their male counterparts, partly owing to the fact that older women often have not participated in the labour market and have not acquired a pension on their own. Living longer than men, and having survived their husbands, they receive survivor's benefits which are lower than regular old-age pensions. In the case of the United Kingdom, for instance, the survivor's pension is typically 50 per cent of the couple's pension, while income from other State benefits also declines after widowhood (Whitehouse, 2000). Additionally, as mentioned above, household arrangements may have a compounding effect on poverty; for instance, older persons living alone will not be able to benefit as much from economies of scale in consumption as those living in extended households. Consequently, one typically finds a higher incidence of poverty among both male and female pensioners who live alone; and older women are more likely to be poor than older men, as women are more likely to live alone in old age (see table V.2 and chapter III).

The increase in female labour-force participation may mitigate the risk for women of falling into poverty during old age in the coming decades. However, as long as women continue to have shorter working lives than men and to earn lower salaries, the level of pension benefits will likely be lower and provide insufficient income security at old age. Additionally, if pension benefits have originated in fully funded schemes and are determined on a defined-contribution basis (see box V.1 for definitions), the annual pension income will be lower than men's owing to women's greater longevity. In all, the incidence of poverty tends to be higher among older women, and more so among those living alone.

Table V.2.
Incidence of poverty among persons aged 65 years or over and among persons aged 65 years or over living alone, by sex, selected developed countries, 1996

Percentage				
	Male	Female	Female living alone	Male living alone
Austria	9.2	12.6	17.9	12.0
Belgium	11.5	15.1	20.2	6.2
Germany	6.9	11.5	12.8	7.8
Denmark	9.8	10.8	12.4	11.9
Spain	4.1	5.4	3.6	3.7
France	8.3	10.8	12.9	11.4
Greece	23.9	26.6	30.4	24.1
Italy	7.4	9.6	11.5	7.5
Netherlands	4.0	4.3	5.6	4.6
United Kingdom	11.7	18.1	25.6	16.9

Source: Heinrich (2000).

Note: Poverty rate has been established at 50 per cent of the median per capita income.

This does not mean that older persons living with a partner or in a multigenerational household will necessarily be less vulnerable to poverty. Other factors may come into play. If anything, co-residence tells very little about how income is generated and consumption allocated within the household. In some instances, large households may be a symptom of poverty in themselves, rather than a source of support and intergenerational solidarity (Lloyd-Sherlock, 2006).

The risk of, and vulnerability to, poverty vary at the individual and country levels, reflecting differences not only in the availability and adequacy of old-age pensions but also in the patterns and the dynamics of traditional social insurance mechanisms and household coping strategies. Nonetheless, poverty was found to be higher than the national average in sub-Saharan households headed by older persons, whether they lived alone, with their adult children or in the company of their grandchildren.[3] A study of 15 sub-Saharan African countries showed that the incidence of poverty was significantly higher in 8 countries among households where older persons were living with children, usually their grandchildren (Kakwani and Subbarao, 2005). In fact, it has been established that "(a)mong the older persons who do not live alone, those living with grandchildren but not with children are in general the ones with lower indices of material well-being" (United Nations, 2005b, chapter V, p. 109).

In such living arrangements, often called "skipped generation households", adult children are absent largely owing to mortality from HIV/AIDS and older persons are the sole breadwinners and caregivers for young children. Over 60 per cent of orphaned children in South Africa and Zimbabwe, and 50 per cent in Botswana, Malawi and the United Republic of Tanzania, live with their grandparents. In Namibia, the proportion of orphans living with their grandparents increased from 44 per cent in 1992 to 61 per cent in 2000. This phenomenon is not restricted to Africa: in Thailand, half of the orphans live with their grandparents (Zimmer and Dayton, 2003). Owing to limited coverage of formal social security mechanisms and the disastrous impact on entire communities, these older persons continue to work as they shoulder the responsibility for caring for their orphaned grandchildren.

SOURCES OF ECONOMIC SUPPORT AND LIVELIHOOD FOR OLDER PERSONS

The livelihood strategies of older people vary greatly across countries and regions, but they are likely to be more complex and diverse in developing countries than in developed economies. In developed economies, with strong and extensive pension provisions and deep capital markets, the main source of livelihood and protection shifts from employment to pension income as one reaches a given retirement age.

In developing countries, few have access to pension benefits and most have to rely on other, often insecure sources of income. Those who were poor during their prime working years have a high probability of remaining poor during old age. Those who were above the poverty line but who have been unable to accumulate enough funds to finance consumption also face the risk of poverty in old age. Informal support mechanisms, such as the family and the community, usually do not provide a stable and reliable source of income and can provide only limited insurance. Operating on a small scale, they cannot pool risks in order to provide greater protection against income shocks and guarantee a certain level of benefits, as do insurance systems provided by the State.

During old age, people tend to rely on four main income sources: (a) private transfers from the family and social networks; (b) public transfers from pensions and other cash transfer programmes; (c) labour earnings; and (d) financial and other assets, including private pensions.

Available data suggest that the composition of the various income sources is context-specific. The importance of private transfers tends to fall as the average income level rises, which appears to be the case, for instance, in Japan, the Republic of Korea and Taiwan Province of China (see table V.3).

Table V.3.
Main sources of income during old age as a proportion of total income, selected countries, and Taiwan Province of China, selected years

Percentage					
	Year	Labour earnings	Private transfers	Public transfers	Assets and other
Japan	1981	31.3	15.6	39.9	10.5
	1988	24.5	9.0	56.4	9.7
	1999	19.0	2.6	65.0	13.4
Republic of Korea	1981	16.2	72.4	2.0	8.7
	1994	37.6	44.3	3.5	10.6
Taiwan Province of China	1986	29.8	67.8	1.2	1.2
	1993	42.8	53.2	1.6	2.4
Thailand	2002	39.3	35.4	7.3	18.0
United States	2000	15.2	7.2	36.8	40.9

Sources: Barrientos (2007); Lee and Mason (2007); United Nations Population Fund (2006).

This trend could indicate that the higher the level of the mean income of the population, the smaller the importance of private transfers as a source of income during old age.

The relative importance of the various sources of income also tends to vary with the age and gender of the head of household. In the case of the United States in 2004, for instance, those aged 65-69 derived a greater share of their income from earnings through work (about 32 per cent) than those aged 75-79 (14 per cent). Meanwhile, publicly provided pensions are a relatively more important source of income for older women (51 per cent of annual income) than for older men (35 per cent) (Employment Benefit Research Institute (EBRI), 2006).

Labour earnings during old age are more important in developing countries than in developed ones. Issues of access to labour markets and employability of older persons were discussed in chapter IV and the discussion will not be repeated here. In contexts of widespread poverty, however, continued labour-market participation will most likely intensify poverty conditions during old age as labour productivity may decline as age advances. This is not to say that older persons should not seek to remain engaged in labour markets if they so desire. It is highly unlikely, however, that those whose labour earnings were not sufficient to place them above the poverty line during their working age years will command higher labour income when they age. Under these circumstances, continued engagement in labour markets per se will not be sufficient to guarantee an old age free of poverty.

In developed countries, contributory pension schemes constitute the main policy instrument for ensuring income security during old age and provide regular and reliable income transfers in old age (Diamond, 1996). Financial and other assets accumulated during people's working life are relatively more important income sources in developed countries than in developing ones. Developed countries have deeper capital markets, providing a wide range of financial instruments for savings, while higher average incomes provide more room for savings during working life.

Such conditions are more restricted in developing countries. Asset accumulation is a part of the livelihood strategies utilized by people in developing countries, including the poor. More often, however, assets are used to smooth consumption, as a buffer, during times of adverse shocks, such as a bad harvest, rather than to provide for income security during old age. Even when assets are accumulated to provide resources during old age, they may prove to be an insecure source of such resources in many developing-country contexts. The returns from and the value of assets may be highly volatile. For instance, in rural societies, while cattle can be an important asset, they, like other animals, may die during an episode of drought, or sale proceeds may be lower than anticipated as other individuals (hit by the same shock) also try to sell their cattle (Dercon, 1998).

Private transfers are a main source of income during old age in much of the developing world. Such resource flows may take the form of monetary support, transfer of assets or in-kind support in the form of food, clothing, shelter and time for care. Generally, children are the largest providers of private transfers to older persons. Other relatives or friends, but typically those who are members of the extended family, may sometimes also contribute (Hermalin, 2002). The probability of receiving family support is higher when older persons reside with their children or other relatives than when they live alone. Co-residence is a more important determinant of the likelihood of older persons' receiving private transfers than the fact that they have children who are still living (United Nations, 2005b).

It is quite possible, however, that private transfers turn out to be unreliable sources of income. First, reliance on family networks might not fully protect older persons against poverty, particularly in situations where these networks are themselves vulnerable to adverse shocks. Second, in most contexts, such transfers are voluntary and based on informal arrangements which may be subject to change. Only in a few countries has the obligation of the family to provide support to older parents been formally set out in the constitution or other legislation (Bongaarts and Zimmer, 2001). Such legislation does exist in China and Singapore, for instance. In the case of Singapore, policies have been adopted according to which the family has primacy as the primary source of income support and care for older persons, and the economic support of aged parents by their children is governed by law (Chan and others, 2003).

The importance of private transfers in providing income security at old age is likely on the decline in many contexts owing to the reduction of family size, the rise in the number of older persons living alone and the changes in attitudes about care for older persons (as discussed in chapter III), although there exists no systematic empirical evidence in this regard. Hence, whether poverty at old age can be avoided in developing countries will greatly depend on the possibilities of extending the coverage, and ensuring the adequacy of the level of benefits, of formal pension schemes.

FORMAL PENSION SYSTEMS: ENSURING INCOME SECURITY DURING OLD AGE

The inability of informal mechanisms to provide for adequate and reliable income security in old age underlines the urgency to improve and expand formal mechanisms so as to ensure economic support for all older persons. Formal mechanisms are already present in most countries in one form or another. Occupational or employer-related pension schemes have a long history: the first publicly managed and broad-based scheme was introduced just over a century ago in Germany under Otto von Bismarck, its first Chancellor.

Germany is credited with having been the first Western industrialized country to adopt (in 1889) a formal mechanism for instituting an old-age and invalid public pension programme, in this case, a contributory pension plan wherein workers, upon reaching the retirement age of 70, would be entitled to a regular pension payment. Pension payments were financed by contributions from those currently working. Hence, this scheme was labelled pay-as-you-go. The German pension scheme has served as a model for many pension systems around the world; and in the course of the twentieth century, the majority of developed economies also introduced formal public pension programmes through one means or another

Social security was established as a right in the Declaration concerning the aims and purpose of the International Labour Organization adopted in Philadelphia, Pennsylvania, on 10 May 1944, and is integral to the implementation of the Universal Declaration of Human Rights (10 December 1948)[4], which states that "(e)veryone ... has the right to social security and is entitled to realization ...of the economic, social and cultural rights indispensable for his dignity" (article 22) and that "(e)veryone has the right to a standard of living adequate for the health and well-being of himself and of his family, including ... necessary social services, and the right to security in the event of unemployment, sickness, disability, widowhood, old age or other lack of livelihood in circumstances beyond his control" (article 25).

Public pension schemes are often also an important tool for effecting income redistribution within cohorts, in particular to lower-income groups, with the aim of reducing poverty among those who were previously in low-paying occupations and thus unable to accumulate wealth. Yet, the extent to which formal schemes provide income *security* for older persons varies significantly. There are large disparities in terms of coverage, adequacy of benefits and contribution costs of old-age pension systems not only among but also within countries.

The available cross-country evidence suggests that the share of the labour force contributing to a formal pension scheme increases with per capita income. On the other hand, as indicated in figure V.2, a few countries, including Armenia, Belarus, Georgia, Kyrgyzstan and Ukraine, have a pension coverage that is higher than might be expected given their level of gross domestic product (GDP) per capita. The importance of social pensions in these countries suggests that a commitment to universality does indeed matter.

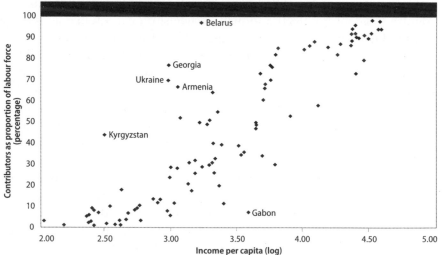

Figure V.2.
Contributors to public pension schemes as a proportion of labour force, by income per capita[a]

Sources: Palacios and Pallarès-Miralles (2000); and World Bank (2005).

a Latest observation between 1988 and 1998.

Lower coverage in many developing countries is partly the result of the way in which contributions are generated and collected. Only a few countries finance the provisioning of public pensions through general taxation (in other words, only a few have non-contributory pension schemes). More often, public pension schemes are financed through contributions levied on wage-related income (contributory schemes). In such cases, the eligibility for pension benefits is contingent upon prior participation. Thus, the contributory approach typically excludes self-employed and other workers in informal sectors for whom participation is at best possible only on a voluntary basis. There are a number of countries, however, that have successfully introduced old-age pension schemes for some segments of informal workers and are considering extending such coverage more broadly. This is the case for India (see box V.2).

Given the relationships observed in figure V.2, one might expect that with economic growth and industrialization, pension coverage would also increase in developing countries. This has not been the case, however—not even in the more advanced developing countries. In many contexts, the liberalization of labour markets, which occurred during the 1980s and 1990s, have limited the expansion of wage employment in the formal sector and left the informal sector as the major employer (Gill, Packard and Yermo, 2004; Rofman, 2005). Pension coverage in Latin America, for instance, has not improved in the last 15 years, as most employment growth has come from the informal sector and pension system reforms have failed to increase coverage (Economic Commission for Latin America and the Caribbean, 2006; and see the analysis on pension reforms below).

Even in countries where coverage is extensive, income security in old age may be in jeopardy as the sustainability of existing pension systems is increasingly questioned. Countries with weak growth and weak employment performance over longer periods of time will, of course, feel a larger strain as they attempt to keep their pension schemes financially viable. High prevalence of early retirement practices as well as rising costs of welfare-indexed benefits may further undermine the sustainability of pension systems. In some cases, problems have been compounded by mismanagement, poor investment decisions and bad governance of the pension systems themselves, leading to their bankruptcy or to drastic reductions in benefits for pensioners.[5]

It is believed that, with population ageing, many existing pensions systems—not only many private (that is to say, employer-provided) schemes, but also public schemes in many developing and developed countries—will become too costly. In developed economies, there is an overall perception that pension systems have become unaffordable, with public spending on old-age pension

Box V.2.
Expanding social security in India

The share of India's population that is over 65 years of age is expected to triple to 15 per cent in 2050, up from about 5 per cent in 2005. The provision of income security through traditional earnings-based arrangements is mainly constrained by the fragmentation of the labour force. Approximately 92 per cent of the labour force (more than 362 million persons) does not have any income security protection, as they are informally employed. Of these workers, 337 million work in the unorganized sector and 26 million in the organized, but small-scale business sector (comprising all unincorporated enterprises employing less than 10 persons). A total of 235 million are employed in the agricultural sector.

India has undertaken a number of pension reforms in the recent years. These have been largely confined, however, to the formal and public sector pension systems. Examples are the New Pension Scheme entailing the introduction of a defined-contribution scheme for new entrants to government service in 2004. In the formal private sector, an "employee provident fund" and an "employee pension scheme" are operational as part of the Employee Provident Fund Organization. These are mandatory schemes for workers in 177 defined industries earning below 6,500 rupees (Rs) ($156) per month in establishments with more than 20 workers. They covered only about 15 million workers in 2004 (Shah, 2005).

The provision of old-age income insurance to the vast majority of workers in the *informal* sector is limited and fragmented. Numerous central and State government programmes have been introduced. The National Social Assistance Programme, launched in 1995, is a case in point. It provides the poor and destitute over age 65 who have neither a source of income nor the support of family members with an old-age pension of Rs 200 ($5) (about half of the poverty line) through the National Old Age Pension Scheme.

Despite the introduction of similar initiatives, only 6 per cent of the informal sector (21 million) had access in 2000 to social security entitlements—largely welfare assistance—provided by the central and State government schemes: about 5 million were covered by central government schemes, 10 million by State government schemes and 6 million by the National Old Age Pension Scheme. In addition to the central and State governments, there are non-governmental organizations involved in the provision of social security. Non-governmental organization-sponsored programmes reach an estimated 5 million informal workers and provide health and life insurance with old-age pension provision being relatively sidelined (National Commission for Enterprises in the Unorganized Sector, 2006).

Several proposals have been made aimed at providing social security to informal workers. In 2001, the National Commission on Rural Labour recommended that, inter alia, a means-tested old-age pension be paid to all over age 60. In 2003, the National Commission on Labour made several recommendations, including a basic benefits package of death and disability insurance, health insurance, maternity coverage and old-age benefits.

Recently, the National Commission for Enterprises in the Unorganized Sector put forward a comprehensive proposal for extending coverage to workers in the unorganized sector. The draft unorganized workers social security bill calls for a comprehensive package providing to workers in informal employment a *national minimum social security,* which includes universal health and life insurance benefits as well as old-age security (in the form of old-age social or non-contributory pensions to poor workers and a provident fund to all others). Although the scheme excludes workers and farmers having an income of more

Box V.2 (cont'd)

than Rs 6,500 per month, it would cover some 300 million workers (83 per cent) in the unorganized sector and also provide coverage (through the health and maternity insurance component) for up to four dependent family members per contributor (Sengupta, 2007).

Significantly, while the proposal foresees the existence of a provident fund, earning a guaranteed rate of return of 10 per cent, for contributing workers, it also calls for a *universal* old-age pension for workers aged 60 years or over who are below the poverty line, with a benefit equal to that of the National Old Age Pension Scheme. The scheme envisages financing from daily contributions by workers, employers and the government of Rs 1 ($0.25) each for each participant. When the employer is absent, which is the case for the majority engaged in the informal sector, the government would provide the employer's contribution. The total contributions of Rs 1,095 ($26) per annum are to be split in order to provide for sickness and maternity insurance (Rs 380), life insurance (Rs 150) and old-age security (Rs 565) (National Commission for Enterprises in the Unorganized Sector, 2006, p. 96). The benefits provided will include, for example, coverage of hospital costs up to Rs 15,000 per year to workers and their families, sickness allowance for hospitalization beyond three days, a life insurance of Rs 15,000 ($360) per beneficiary, and maternity benefits of up to Rs 1,000 ($24).

The Commission has detailed at some length how the scheme is expected to operate (including registration procedures and mechanisms for collection of premiums and disbursement of benefits) and has also clearly indicated that such a national scheme is indeed affordable. After five years of operation of the scheme, all 300 million informal workers would be covered and total costs would reach 0.48 per cent of GDP per year. The central Government would bear responsibility for the cost of all pension benefits for those below the poverty line. All other costs would be shared with individual States which would bear one quarter of the costs.

The challenges for implementing such a comprehensive scheme include ensuring that individuals continue contributing and that employers do not shirk their obligation to contribute. Tracking the eligibility for benefits may prove to be another challenge in practice. However, with sufficient political will, such hurdles can be overcome and the emergence of such a scheme will no doubt contribute significantly to providing greater income security in old age to informal sector workers.

benefits having already surpassed in 2003 10 per cent of GDP in countries such as Austria, France, Germany, Greece, Italy, Poland and Sweden (Organisation for Economic Co-operation and Development, 2007). The costs of public pension schemes are forecast to increase to 20 per cent of GDP in countries such as Cyprus, Portugal and Slovenia during the first half of the present century owing to population ageing (European Commission, 2006).

The expected impact of population ageing on the financial sustainability of current pension schemes adds urgency to the need for reform. Pay-as-you-go pension schemes are considered particularly vulnerable, as a dwindling number of workers would have to support an increasing number of pensioners. Moreover, in some countries, the impact of the HIV/AIDS epidemic exacerbates the pressure exerted by natural population ageing on pay-as-you-go systems by disproportionately affecting those of working age and thereby eroding the contributory basis of pension systems.

Consideration of pension systems design and reform, including coverage expansion, is therefore relevant to both developed and developing regions and countries, as schemes must be made readily available and accessible, economically sustainable, and financially affordable, while providing meaningful benefits for all to allow for economic security and old age free of poverty.

Sustaining and expanding pension systems

How pensions should be provided is the subject of considerable debate. The economics of pension systems are too complex and too context-specific to be encompassable by a "one-size-fits-all" framework. Pension systems also reflect societal preferences in terms of the redistribution of resources within and among generations. More importantly, pension schemes also indicate who should participate. As discussed above, any pension system should be built on the notion of providing income security for all.

Those with the capacity to participate in the financing of their future pension benefits should do so not only to ensure equity but also to realize their rights and duties as citizens of a given country (Economic Commission for Latin America and the Caribbean, 2000). Thus, it may be useful to approach pensions systems as constructions comprising several layers or "pillars", as suggested in various studies by the World Bank (1994) and Holzmann and Hinz (2005), and as evidenced in the practice adopted by many countries. The different layers of the system should be tailored to specific country conditions and social preferences. For instance, in countries where formal labour markets are dominant, a single basic public pillar may be sufficient to provide income security in old age, one whose financing could be based on earnings-related contributions, as is the case for most pension systems in many developed countries. In such cases, the benefit level could be determined as a function of earned labour income, with the aim being to attain a certain wage-replacement level. At the same time, the system should offer the appropriate incentives so as to ensure consistent participation during a specified period of time. Moreover, solidarity mechanisms should be built in so that workers with lower incomes and/or workers with unstable and insufficient work history can also be provided with a minimum benefit.

Countries where employment is largely informal or where there are dual labour markets could perhaps consider two basic public pillars: one non-contributory, offering minimal flat benefits, and the other contributory, along the lines described above. Moreover, it is important that the design of public pension schemes not intensify existing inequalities. For example, the disincentives to participate that contributory schemes may create for lower-income and informal sector workers should be avoided. In particular, contributory and non-contributory pensions should be available simultaneously for low-income groups, with the non-contributory element gradually declining in relation to the pre-retirement income (Economic Commission for Latin America and the Caribbean, 2006). Finally, individuals who have the capacity to do so should be encouraged to make provisions for their own old-age income security (through private or employer-sponsored old-age saving schemes or the accumulation of other assets) in order to complement income to be received from publicly provided pensions.

The way in which pension systems are designed will influence exposure to, and distribution of, risks and consequently the degree of income security in old age. Under unfunded pay-as-you-go systems, pension rights constitute a claim against future GDP and are enforced through future contributions and/or taxes. This claim is subject to political risk directly and to macroeconomic and demographic risks indirectly. In regard to the latter, a deterioration of macroeconomic conditions or adverse demographic developments imposes a heavier burden on the future cohorts of workers, thus making the claim more difficult to enforce. In a fully funded system, pension benefits will depend on the value of accumulated assets and, in this case, they are directly subject to an investment risk and the volatility of returns on such assets (Turner, 2003).[6] In a defined-contribution (DC) scheme, pension beneficiaries bear most of the risks, including that of not being able to systematically contribute to the system. In its purest form (without minimum pension guarantees), a defined-contribution system offers no insurance. The possibilities for intragenerational distribution and poverty relief are also more limited. In defined-benefit (DB) systems, risks are largely borne by the sponsor or provider of benefits, inasmuch as there is a promise that the pension will correspond to a certain fraction of the retiree's wage (Barr, 2006).

In any case, and perhaps more importantly, the ability of any pension scheme to generate adequate benefits and to remain affordable is rooted in the capacity of the country concerned to sustain economic growth.

The centrality of output growth for pension sustainability

While focusing on reform of formal pension systems, it is also essential to recognize that economic growth is necessary in order for an economy to provide income security for those who are retired. As discussed in chapters II and IV, the ongoing demographic transition implies that fewer workers will be providing for a larger number of non-working consumers. In the long run, the support of larger dependent populations—without a lowering of the standard of living—hinges essentially on faster economic growth. This is especially true for developing economies with low pension coverage and where the informal sector dominates economic activity. An increase in formal sector employment widens access to pensions by strengthening participation in contributory schemes, hence improving income security in old age. Additionally, the relative expansion of formal sector employment will further contribute to increased sustainability of pensions in pay-as-you-go schemes by broadening the contributory base, thus reducing the pressures of ageing on such schemes.

Much of the debate on pension reforms and pension system design concentrates, however, on the financial aspects of the two predominant pension schemes, without paying due attention to the question of output growth. Yet, any pension-related "asset" acquired by today's working population—either as a financial asset, in the case of a pre-funded system with individualized accounts, or as a promise by the public sector through a pay-as-you-go scheme—is a claim on future output. Thus, economic growth is at least as fundamental for the sustainability of a pension regime as the design of the regime itself.

The macroeconomic implications of pension system performance may in turn influence the growth prospects of the economy. For instance, increasing deficits of public pension systems could raise public debt, which in turn could put upward pressure on interest rates and crowd out private investment, thus affecting economic growth negatively. Rising pension deficits could also lead to higher taxation, which in turn could increase labour costs and lower disposable household incomes and depress employment and output growth accordingly. Such possible macroeconomic implications underline the need to strive for financially balanced pension systems. On the other hand, the impact of pension funding mechanisms—fully funded or pay as you go—on savings is less clear. Although higher contribution rates may increase compulsory saving, overall higher mandatory savings may be offset by a reduction in voluntary private savings or savings elsewhere in the economy (see below). Further, the standard argument assumes that higher savings rates will always lead to higher productive investment, generating a permanent increase in real output per capita.[7] In reality, however, the link between an increase in savings and increased investment is more complex, and not all savings necessarily will end up in investments that lead to faster growth (Barr and Diamond, 2006). Finally, it may also be the case that efforts to build up financial assets to support consumption in old age lead to a reduction in effective demand during the period of saving for such assets which could in turn could be detrimental to economic growth.

Reforming pension systems I: fine-tuning system design

Two types of contributory pension system reforms have been undertaken: (a) strengthening existing systems by changing underlying parameters (*parametric* reforms) and (b) radically changing system design (*structural* reforms). Parametric reforms have been implemented in virtually every pay-as-you-go scheme and are much more widespread than structural reforms.[8] This type of reform is attractive largely for political reasons, as these reforms are easier to implement and likely more acceptable to the public than those entailing a more fundamental change.

Countries have introduced measures on both the revenue and expenditure sides to ensure the affordability of such schemes. One common adjustment has consisted in increasing the contribution premium paid into social security systems. There are limits, however, to the exercise of this option owing to the distortive effects high contribution rates have on labour markets, on both the demand for, and the supply of, labour. Other possibilities include the reduction of pension benefits (as undertaken in Greece, Hungary, Italy, the Republic of Korea, Portugal and Switzerland), the tightening of pension eligibility requirements (Germany, Italy and the United States) and changing the indexation of benefits (Germany, Japan and Sweden). In fact, every member of the European Union (EU-25) has undertaken some form of adjustment of the parameters defining its social security schemes (Zaidi, 2006). Changes to parameters related to retirement age, the pension formula and the contribution rate were part of the reform package in the majority of cases.

In a growing number of countries, increasing the retirement age, despite being unpopular, is being considered or has been already effected. For instance, in the United States, the retirement age is to increase to 67 in 2027, while in France the latest reform proposes to increase the number of years of contribution required to receive a full pension by one year, between 2009 and 2012, as well as to base future increases on changes in life expectancy as of

2012. Such measures attempt to reduce the gap between the increases in life expectancy and the retirement age, which can be considerable.[9] Currently, life expectancy at retirement in developed countries is already 18 years higher than the statutory retirement age of 65 that is common in many of them (see table II.8).

An increase in the retirement age is also expected to boost revenues as the length of the average working life is extended. At the same time, old-age pension expenditures will decline as retirees benefit from the system for a shorter period. In fact, this measure is potentially so effective that in the case of the United States it has been estimated that "if the normal retirement age were increased to 70 by 2030, about half of the current long-term deficit in social security would be eliminated" and that "(i)f the age of early retirement were increased at the same time from 62 to 67, the currently projected deficit would essentially disappear" (Bosworth and Burtless 1998, p. 293).

An increase in the statutory retirement age will help to improve the viability of pension schemes only if accompanied by policies that also increase the *effective* age of retirement. This may require changes in labour-market conditions for older workers as discussed in chapter IV. Among industrialized countries, the age at which early retirement benefits can be retrieved ranges from 53 in Italy for some occupations to 62 in the United States, while in most of those countries the regular retirement age is 65. In most countries, however, people retire before they turn 65. Early retirement is promoted by many pension schemes: According to Gruber and Wise (2005, p.5): "Once benefits are available, a person who continues to work for an additional year will receive less in social security benefits over his lifetime than if he quit work and started receiving benefits at the first opportunity."

This implies that the number of pensioners will be much larger and benefits will have to be paid over a longer period than would be the case without early retirement, thus putting an unnecessary burden on pension systems. Problems affecting many pay-as-you-go systems therefore seem to stem largely from the fact that there are a larger number of years of retirement, not only because of increased longevity but also, and perhaps more importantly, because of a shorter working life involved. The European Commission (2006, p.12) has in fact argued that "member States are facing a problem of retirement rather than a problem of ageing". An increase in the *effective* retirement age from approximately 60 years to the statutory age of 65 years is probably the single most potent parametric reform option in the European Union. According to some estimates, it would reduce the increase in social security contributions required to finance future benefits by 40 per cent, as compared with the scenario where no changes in the retirement age would be made.[10] Delaying the retirement of workers and having them stay longer in the workforce (discussed in chapter IV) can go a long way towards sustaining pay-as-you-go systems, provided labour markets, reacting accordingly, are able to retain those workers.

Reforming pension systems II: introducing notional accounts

A number of countries have carried out a structural reform of their pay-as-you-go system without moving into a fully funded scheme. These countries introduced individual capitalization with defined contribution benefits while maintaining the pay-as-you-go form of their public pension scheme, having recognized that *parametric* reforms of pay-as-you-go schemes, as outlined above, offer an only partial solution to deficiencies in the design of pension systems. Additionally, in many pay-as-you-go defined-benefit schemes, the link between contributions and benefits typically is not completely transparent to participants (especially when benefits are based upon an incomplete earnings profile). Thus, the incentive for continued labour-force participation once the minimum age eligibility for benefits has been met is weak, particularly if early retirement does not entail an actuarial reduction in benefits.[11]

In pay-as-you-go defined-contribution schemes, or so-called notional defined contribution (NDC) systems, individuals' contributions are registered in "notional" individualized accounts, the balance of which is credited with a notional annual return (see box V.1). Benefits depend on each individual's accumulated (notional) fund balance, that is to say, they are based on a complete contribution history and not just on a given number of years of contribution as is the case in most defined-benefit systems (Economic Commission for Latin America and the Caribbean, 2006). Thus, there is a priori no need to introduce a retirement age, as individuals themselves can decide when to retire, based on the annualized benefit they would receive. Such schemes are therefore designed to address the issue of early retirement.

Pay-as-you-go defined-contribution schemes can, in principle, resolve the sustainability problem faced by many pay-as-you-go defined-benefit schemes, as no future defined-benefit obligations are incurred by the system. Rather, future benefit obligations depend on the rate of return. In particular, the rate of return that is credited to individual accounts can be linked, for example, to productivity changes, current and prospective demographic changes, wage growth, and so on. Thus, benefits are automatically adjusted with changes in the relevant parameters. For instance, in Latvia, the formula defining the notional return is based upon the growth of total contributions. In Sweden, it is based upon the growth rate of nominal wages, whereas in Italy it will follow the growth rate of nominal GDP.[12]

It is therefore possible to ensure that the pay-as-you-go defined-contribution scheme remains financially sustainable by adjusting the rate of return on contributions which will lead to a commensurate adjustment of benefits. Thus, reforms such as these facilitate maintaining financial sustainability of pension systems while retaining an important intergenerational solidarity component. Like any other individual capitalization system, however, such a scheme does not guarantee that everyone will have a pension and at least a minimum level of benefits, because benefits are based on each individual's contributions. This being the case, notional defined contribution reforms need to be complemented by measures that will ensure universal coverage and a minimum level of pension benefits (see below).

Reforming pension systems III: switching to fully funded systems

It is frequently argued that fully funded schemes remain financially sustainable because benefits depend on the amount invested and the returns on such investment. The United Kingdom was among the first nations to move towards a funded provision of pensions in 1980, but only partially. Chile adopted a more radical approach in 1981 by replacing the publicly administered pay-as-you-go defined-benefit pension scheme with a mandatory privately managed fully funded defined-benefit scheme (see box V.1 for definitions). Several other Latin American countries have introduced similar reforms.[13] Structural reforms have also been implemented in Central and Eastern Europe and, to a lesser extent, in South and East Asia. Kazakhstan, for instance, switched completely to a fully funded scheme in 1998. Other countries have maintained their pay-as-you-go scheme while introducing a fully funded pillar. These include Bulgaria (2002), Hungary (1998), the former Yugoslav Republic of Macedonia (2003) and Estonia (2002).

Transition costs and public finances

While fully funded systems with individual capitalization can be financially sustainable in principle, the transformation of a pay-as-you-go system into a fully funded system has negative implications for public finances, as the pension obligations contracted under the old system have still to be honoured while pension contributions are being channelled to the new system. Pension funds typically provide much of the financing for these fiscal costs, as they tend to invest large shares of their portfolio in Treasury bonds. There are, however, macroeconomic implications. The related increase in public sector debt may put upward pressures on interest rates, thus further increasing the fiscal costs of the transition, and may affect private investments. The rising public sector debt may affect interest rates, thus increasing the cost of the transition and having implications on private investment.

An important issue in structural pension reform is how to deal with, and finance, the transition from the existing scheme. In the case of a multi-pillar system, where fully funded and pay-as-you-go systems coexist, the burden of transition is often placed directly on contributors, who are required to contribute a given amount to the fully funded scheme in addition to what they contribute to the pay-as-you-go scheme. In Sweden, for example, workers contribute 2.5 per cent of wages to a fully funded, defined-contribution system, which operates alongside the public pay-as-you-go system.

When the fully funded system replaces the pay-as-you-go scheme, however, workers who have contributed to the system, but are not yet retired, need to be compensated for their past contributions if they opt to switch into the new system. Current retirees need to continue receiving their pensions as contracted under the old system but this will occur in the absence of payment of contributions from current workers who have moved to the new system. On the fiscal side (and assuming there are no changes in pension benefits), the government may run a larger deficit, which will have to be financed by higher taxation, cuts in public spending or an increase in the public debt, thus making the implicit pension debt explicit.

The experience of Argentina has shown that reform leading to fully funded schemes can have a significant economic impact on public finances. Argentina's reform of the pay-as-you-go system in 1994 led to a significant increase in public debt as the financial position of the social security system showed increasing deficits after 1994. The balance of social security contributions and expenditures was positive at 0.6 per cent of GDP in 1993, but turned into a deficit of 2.6 per cent of GDP by 2001. It contributed to an unsustainable public debt situation which came to a head during the economy-wide crisis of 2001.

In the case of Chile, the cost of financing the operational deficit of the old pension system plus the cost of "recognition bonds" – issued to compensate workers who had switched to the new system but had accrued pension rights— averaged approximately 3.9 per cent of GDP per year during 1981-2004, having peaked at 7.1 per cent of GDP in 1984 (de Mesa and Mesa-Lago, 2006). The costs have decreased over time, but are expected to persist up to 2038 (in the case of recognition bonds) and up to 2050 (in the case of the operational deficit), signalling the fact that transition is long-term, particularly when the pay-as-you-go system is abolished with a "bang" instead of being phased out gradually.

The above cases illustrate how costly reforms can be (naturally, there is also a cost incurred by *not* reforming the system, where unsustainable) and also point to the need for a strong fiscal framework to support such reform.

Other impacts of the structural reforms

The claim that reforms leading to fully funded systems contribute to increasing savings, discussed previously, cannot be validated in many countries. Evidence from Latin America does indicate, however, that savings may have increased in response to the pension reform, but the precise impact is difficult to establish, as pension reform is often a part of wider reform efforts (Holzmann and Hinz, 2005).[14] Moreover, if the objective is to increase savings, reforming the pay-as-you-go schemes need not be discarded. In particular, it has been estimated that raising the retirement age in a pay-as-you-go scheme could, through higher savings, increase GDP in Europe up to 13 per cent (European Commission, 2006).

Fully funded individual capitalization has been credited with offering superior rates of return. It is often ignored, however, that the higher return is a reflection of higher risk. While explicit capital returns may exceed the implicit returns on a pay-as-you-go scheme, the volatility of capital returns is also significantly higher. As a result, by shouldering the investment risk—which may be very difficult, particularly for those in low-paying jobs—participants are exposed to the possibility of significantly lower returns should their portfolio sustain large losses towards the end of their working lives.

Moreover, with benefits tied to contributions (and their return), involuntary interruptions to the payment of these contributions will imply lower pensions and increased risk of economic insecurity during old age. Additionally, when comparing returns, it is important to adjust administrative costs and charges, which can absorb a considerable amount of the returns. Such charges can amount to up 25 per cent of contributions (compared with charges of approximately 0.5 per cent of contribution income to the publicly managed pay-as-you-go defined-benefit scheme in the United States) (Thompson, 2001). Administrative charges lower the net returns for beneficiaries. For instance, 1 per cent of administrative fees charged over the working life of a contributor will imply a 20 per cent reduction in the value of the pension to be received (Diamond, 2004, as cited in Barr, 2006).

For Chile, after 25 years of experience with pension reform beginning with the replacement of a pay-as-you-go scheme by a fully funded scheme with individual accounts, the outcome in terms of coverage has not been overly satisfactory. Despite the popularity of the fully funded system in the early years of reform, overall coverage declined relative to the pre-reform era from 71 per cent of the employed population in 1975 to about 64 per cent in 2000 (de Mesa and others, 2006), partly owing to low participation rates of the self-employed, as participation is not mandatory. Increased informalization of the labour market has also been a factor.

Additionally, the closer correlation between contributions and benefits notwithstanding, the private capitalization systems have failed to increase the number of contribution payments by participants. It has been estimated that in Latin America, contribution densities (the ratio of the number of contribution payments made to the number of months the individual was of working age) of a large share of participants in fully funded, defined-benefits systems are insufficient to ensure their receiving a retirement pension or to generate adequate pensions (Economic Commission for Latin America and the Caribbean, 2006).

Through the introduction of individual accounts, the social insurance component of social security is reduced, as these accounts limit the extent to which the scheme can function as a tool for redistribution within a generation and for the alleviation of poverty. In systems without individual capitalization, redistribution can take place depending on how benefits are calculated. For instance, lower-income individuals may receive greater benefits (in relation to their contributions) or have the value of their benefits adjusted under more favourable terms compared with the adjustment received by higher-income retirees.

With individual capitalization, benefits are dependent on the value of contributions made and on their return. In such circumstances, workers in low-paid jobs may be unable to amass a minimum amount of income as pension benefits even if they duly contribute to the pension schemes. Moreover, contribution densities are much lower among lower-income groups, compared with those better off, and even more so among women. Women often have an interrupted and shorter employment history than men owing to childbearing and child rearing. Lower-income workers are frequently more reluctant to contribute to pensions, particularly if they are self-employed (and hence also more prone to periods without employment) and contributions are not mandatory, as is the case for Chile. As noted above in the section dealing with the sources of income of older persons, pensions are particularly relevant to the low-income workers, as these are most likely to have been unable to accumulate any (substantial) assets to complement their public pensions and therefore most likely to be threatened with destitution.

Some redistribution may therefore be necessary either within or outside the pension systems in order to not exacerbate income differences and to prevent poverty in old age.

Indeed, in the case of Chile, additional reforms are being considered owing to dissatisfaction with the current system. Minimum pension benefits financed by the Government out of its general revenues may not be available to any participant whose accumulated funds do not allow for a certain level of pension. Many participants will in fact be unable to meet the minimum requirement of 20 years of contribution needed to qualify for the minimum pension; and it has been projected that approximately 45 per cent of women who are currently between the ages of 45 and 50 will not qualify.[15] Those not qualified to receive the minimum pension can apply for a social assistance pension; however, since the number of social assistance pensions is limited by the level of funding made available annually, not every eligible person who applies will receive one. Proposals for new pension reform in Chile therefore include, inter alia, a broader-based solidarity pension, financed by general taxation and provided on a means-tested basis. This reform would ensure a monthly pension to workers who were unable to save towards their retirement.[16]

Solidarity, accessibility and affordability: moving towards universal coverage

Issues of pension affordability are country-specific. With greater formal employment-generation, faster economic growth and improvements in the asset base of low-income households, the capacity to contribute to old-age pensions increases and the need for non-contributory pensions declines. In the meantime, however, for those living in poverty, the capacity to contribute is limited—if not impossible—and benefits need to be supported by other segments of society.

The simplest minimum pension scheme designed to ensure old-age income security would be a universal transfer equal to the poverty line granted to all those above a certain age. Such a scheme could be entirely non-contributory, that is to say, beneficiaries would not directly participate in the financing of benefits. Benefits might be financed through general taxation (as, for example, in Mauritius), by some "solidarity tax" imposed on those participating in contributory earning-related schemes (as in Colombia) or by some specific earmarked tax (as in Brazil, for instance). Alternatively, benefits could be delivered on a contributory basis, but in that case access by those unable to contribute would need to be facilitated by subsidization.

A simple exercise was conducted to assess the cost of universal non-contributory pensions for those aged 60 years or over in developing countries and in economies in transition. The exercise assumed a basic pension equivalent to $365 per year or $1 per day (expressed in international dollars, that is to say, in purchasing power parity (PPP)), which corresponded to the international threshold used to define extreme poverty. The pension would be made available to all those aged 60 years or over. The exercise also assumed that the universal pension could remain constant in real terms at $365 per year during the entire period 2005-2050. Further, it was assumed that GDP growth would be sustained at the average rate achieved during 1990-2005. However, for countries with a rate of growth of more than 5 per cent, the growth assumption was capped at the 5 per cent level. Countries with negative growth performance during the period 1990-2005 were not considered in the exercise.

The results are presented in figure V.3, which shows that the costs of providing a universal old-age pension scheme with benefits equal to the international poverty line does not appear to be very high for the majority of the 100 countries considered in the exercise. For 66 countries, the cost would be less than 1 per cent of GDP in 2005 and for 34 the cost would be less than

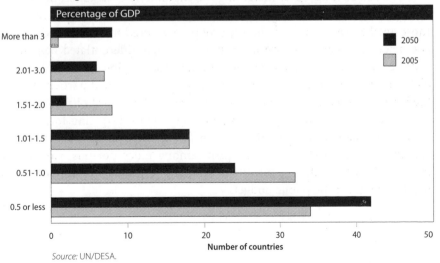

Figure V.3.
Simulated costs for developing countries of a universal social pension scheme designed to keep older persons out of extreme poverty, 2005 and 2050

Source: UN/DESA.

Note: Universal pensions are estimated at $1 per day for those aged 60 years of over. The annual rate of GDP growth for the period 2005-2050 is assumed to be equal to that observed in the period 1990-2005.

0.5 per cent of GDP. Additionally, costs could be kept relatively low, during the entire period, as for the majority of countries the rate of GDP growth would be comparable to, or faster than, the rate of growth of the population aged 60 years or over. For many of the poorest countries however, the burden would be more substantial (see annex table A.4 for detailed results by country).

In all, universal old-age pensions schemes offering benefits equal to the extreme poverty line seem to demand only a relatively small share of the GDP currently. Even if the cost of these programmes as a share of GDP is relatively small, it is still not clear whether they are affordable for low-income countries. Besides constraints such as the limited fiscal resources mentioned above, there is the fact that spending on social pensions might have to compete with public spending on what, like education and health, are typically qualified as priorities, or spending in areas, such as defence and debt service, in which countries often allocate a significant amount of resources. A cost of a universal old-age pension scheme of 1 per cent of GDP would absorb about 10 per cent of tax revenues in countries such as Cameroon, Guatemala, India, Nepal and Pakistan, among others, and would be equivalent of the size of the health budget in Bangladesh, Burundi, the Comoros, Côte d'Ivoire, Equatorial Guinea and Myanmar, to name just a few. Interestingly enough, some of these countries (Bangladesh, India and Nepal) are already providing non-contributory pension benefits, though not in all cases on a universal basis (see annex table A.5).

Costs can be lowered by increasing age eligibility. For instance, in the case of Nepal, benefits are paid only to those aged 75 years or over, instead of to those aged 60 years or over, the age group considered in this chapter. Other countries, like Mauritius, are moving towards age-differentiated benefits in order to lower costs by, say, providing a modest pension for the "youngest old", who may be able to complement income by continued participation in the labour market, and a relatively larger one for the "oldest old" (Willmore, 2006). Costs could also be lowered by reducing benefits. Targeting, for instance, through a means test, is another option for lowering costs, particularly in contexts where poverty is not frequent among older persons. Conversely, in countries where old-age poverty is rampant, targeting would not provide much savings for the public budget.

Conclusions

Empirical evidence suggests that older persons living in countries with comprehensive formal pension systems and public transfer schemes are less likely to fall into poverty than younger cohorts in the same population. In countries with limited coverage of pension systems, old-age poverty tends to parallel the national average. The majority of persons in developing countries face, in the absence of formal pension coverage, considerable income insecurity during old age.

With, on average, only 20 per cent of their populations covered by social security benefits, developing countries face considerable challenges with respect to expanding formal protection so that old age can be free of poverty. In this regard, low-income countries often face a double challenge. On the one hand, the State's capacity to raise revenues is limited and tax revenues tend to amount to a relatively small share of GDP (about 10 per cent on average).[17] On the other hand, the demands on scarce resources are multiple so that provisioning of old-age income security may be imperilled by the costs of achieving other social goals.

In developed countries, well-regulated labour markets have made it possible for employment-based contributory pension schemes to cover almost the entire population. Thus, older persons living in countries with comprehensive pension systems are considerably less vulnerable as regards falling into poverty, but their economic security is in jeopardy as pension systems become financially unsustainable.

Although demographic change can create problems for old-age pension schemes, from an economic perspective these problems are not insoluble (see also Barr, 2000, p. 34). In particular, the financial resources available to a pay-as-you-go system depend on the level of wages and employment rather than on the ratio of young to old (non-retired to retirees). By the same token, resources available for consumption for older persons (both in a fully funded and in a pay-as-you-go system) will depend on the goods and services produced by those of working age and on how much consumption workers are willing to forgo in favour of dependent populations.

Output growth is essential for the sustainability of pension systems, particularly if the income distribution between active and non-active populations is not to be altered significantly and a given level of overall well-being is to be sustained. This is not to say that current systems are not in need of reforms and that systems in financial imbalance do not have negative consequences for the growth prospects of the economy. As discussed in this chapter and in chapter IV, steps to eliminate the perverse incentives of early retirement and other design flaws in current pension schemes and, to tap the large pool of inactive workers, including those in involuntary retirement, as well as to increase labour productivity, can potentially go a long way towards saving social security as we know it. This implies maintaining a system that provides a sufficient degree of risk-sharing and guarantees a socially acceptable level of benefits, so that old age will be free from poverty for all.

The design of pension systems and their reform thus need to be based on a broad approach. Pension systems have to be tailored to country-specific conditions. In this regard, pension systems can be approached as constructions consisting of multiple layers or pillars adjusted to the prevailing characteristics and needs of different segments of society.

Financial sustainability should be an important guiding principle in the design of any pension system, but not the only one. There is no point in having a financially viable system that provides inadequate benefits or does not reach all older persons. It is worth recalling that old-age pensions were introduced to address the risk of income insecurity, or poverty, in old age. As discussed above, the incidence of poverty among older persons is higher in countries where pension coverage is incipient. Social insurance has been the preferred mechanism for pooling the risks among a large enough number of individuals in order to protect them as much from suffering economic vulnerability during old age as from suffering financial shocks because of unemployment, disability and ill health during their working life.

It is precisely the safeguarding of social insurance that has been the one important component missing in reforms that have focused on building pension systems centred on individual capitalization schemes. More generally, the move from a defined-benefit to a defined-contribution system (pre-funded, notional or otherwise) shifts the economic risks entirely to the pensioners. In a defined-benefit scheme, risks are largely borne by the sponsor or provider of benefits. For this reason, most countries that moved towards a fully funded defined-contribution system did introduce guarantees of minimum levels of pension benefits. This, however, has not solved the problem of ensuring adequate income security for all. For one, coverage has not improved. Moreover, not all participants may qualify for receipt of the minimum pension or may be able to accumulate enough funds to ensure a certain wage-replacement level. Therefore, solidarity mechanisms targeting lower-income contributors need to be strengthened in these systems.

In fact, the move to a dominant fully funded scheme with individual accounts and paying benefits on a defined-contribution basis is no longer seen as the main ingredient in pension reform, but rather as only a component with respect to increasing protection in old age. Recognition of the need to undertake reform yet still maintain existing pay-as-you-go schemes whereby social insurance and an adequate level of wage replacement can be ensured has resurfaced. Furthermore, the failure of reforms of the contributory pillar as regards addressing the lack of access to old-age pensions for informal sector workers and persisting poverty in old age, especially in developing countries, is now increasingly being recognized.

Accessibility should be an equally important guiding principle in the design and reform of pension systems. Emphasis on earnings-based social security schemes will necessarily lead to exclusion of large proportions of the population, particularly in developing countries, thus increasing the vulnerability of older persons to poverty. In this context, non-contributory pensions are distributional mechanisms designed to improve the economic security of older persons. It is clear from the experience of developing countries such as Brazil, Mauritius, Namibia, Nepal and South Africa that non-contributory pension schemes substantially reduce the risk that older persons and their families will fall into (extreme) poverty.

Finally, affordability of old-age income security systems should be considered a guiding principle. Public resources are finite and, for many developing countries, insufficient to meet all social needs, hence trade-offs between development goals may have to be considered. International development assistance may help overcome a lack of resources, but ultimately it is the societies themselves that will have to decide on how to address the issue of conflicting interests with respect to the distribution of resources. In many instances, though, small distributional shifts can make a large difference. Along the same lines, it was shown that the cost of a social pension scheme providing a one dollar-a-day benefit to the entire old-age population would be less than 1 per cent of GDP for most developing countries. Thus, even for many low-income countries with large informal sectors, it would seem that introducing and maintaining a basic layer of non-contributory social pensions represent an affordable option. More generally, in most developing countries, there is a need to ensure that sustainable non-contributory programmes are an integral component of pension systems aiming to provide a minimum degree of income security for all during old age.

NOTES TO CHAPTER V

1   Absolute poverty indicates that a person or household is unable to afford a minimum basket of goods and services.

2   Results were obtained through a counterfactual exercise that computed poverty rates after excluding pensions from total household income. The implicit (and strong) assumption inherent in this exercise was that in the absence of a pension system, older persons' income would be reduced by the amount of the pensions they received, which might not be the case. Without pensions, older persons may receive transfers from relatives or the community or remain in the labour market in order to offset the loss in income.

3   Exceptions do exist, however: in Madagascar, Mozambique and Nigeria, children were found to be much worse off than the elderly (Kakwani and Subbarao, 2005, p.2).

4   General Assembly resolution 217 A (III).

5   For instance, in the United States, more than 23 corporate pension plans in excess of $100 million each have defaulted owing to bad governance. The largest default occurred in 2005 when United Airlines left an underfunded pension plan of about $9.8 billion to be rescued by the Pension Benefit Guaranty Corporation (PBGC).

6   Portfolio allocation and investment strategies by pension funds are discussed in chapter IV.

7   An alternative view suggests, along Keynesian lines, that it is aggregate demand—and not savings—that drives investment. Entrepreneurs decide on the volume of investment in part based on expectations of increases in aggregate demand. Past changes in aggregate demand act as estimates of changes expected in the future. Hence, for the economy to grow faster, consumption rather than savings should be encouraged. Capital deepening due to higher investment will then give rise to productivity growth and lower unit costs which will make room for both higher real wages for workers and higher profits for firms. In turn, this will lead to the higher savings needed to finance the increase in investment.

8   Schwarz and Demirgüç-Kunt (1999) found that of 82 countries reforming social security, only 21 had adopted "major" reforms involving a substantive change of system.

9   For instance, when pensions were initially introduced in Germany in 1889, the average life expectation at birth (44 years) was 26 years lower than the retirement age of 70. Accordingly, only a small proportion of workers (approximately 17 per cent of males and 21 per cent of females) lived long enough to qualify.

10   If the effective retirement age is raised to 65, the social security contribution rate would still need to be increased by 20.5 per cent by 2050 (from about 16.1 per cent in 2000). However, if the effective retirement age stays unchanged, then the contribution rate will have to be increased to 27 per cent (European Commission, 2001, p. 191, table 5, and p. 199, table 8).

11   This explains the relatively high labour participation rate in the United States, where benefits *are* actuarially reduced in response to early retirement, so that retirement at, say, age 62 entails an actuarial reduction of 20 per cent of the full pension; this reduction will be increased to 30 per cent by 2027 when retirement age reaches 67 (Munnell, 2006).

12 Germany did not explicitly introduce a notional defined contribution system, but its scheme does have features that mimic those of such a system. The German scheme includes a "sustainability factor" which adjusts pension benefits so as to take account of changes in the dependency ratio (Zaidi, 2006).

13 Public pay-as-you-go defined-benefit schemes were entirely abolished in Bolivia (1997), El Salvador (1998), Mexico (1997) and the Dominican Republic (2003) and workers are now required to join the mandatory fully funded defined-contribution scheme. In contrast, workers in Colombia (1994) and Peru (1993) have the choice of opting for either a pay-as-you-go defined-benefit scheme or a fully funded defined-contribution scheme. On the other hand, hybrid systems exist in Argentina (1994), Uruguay (1996) and Costa Rica (2000), where a public component based on the pay-as-you-go principle (partly funded in Costa Rica) pays a defined-benefit basic pension and a fully funded defined-contribution scheme with multiple types of administration pays a supplementary pension.

14 De Mesa and Mesa-Lago (2006, p. 154), for example, emphasize this point in the case of Chile, indicating that tax reform contributed to the large increase in corporate savings. Acuña and Iglesias (2001) provide a brief overview of empirical studies on the impact of reform on savings, concluding that "it is therefore clear that in Chile's case, empirical studies have been insufficient to resolve the question of the impact of the reform on saving" (p. 40).

15 Furthermore, at about 25 per cent of the average wage, minimum pension benefits are insufficient to ensure income security in old age.

16 See http://ipsnews.net/news.asp?idnews=36003.

17 World Development Indicators online Database (WDI Online), available from http://devdata.worldbank.org/dataonline/ (accessed 20 March 2007).

Chapter VI
Health and long-term care systems for ageing societies

INTRODUCTION

The health profile of populations has changed in parallel with the demographic transition. The importance of communicable or infectious diseases has declined and that of non-communicable or chronic diseases has increased. This phenomenon is referred to as the epidemiological transition. Its implications, particularly for the delivery of health and long-term care services to older persons, will be examined in the present chapter.

In most developed countries, the epidemiological transition took place in the nineteenth and the early twentieth century. Developing countries are now at various stages of the transition, but taken as a group they are forecast to face a dramatic shift in the early part of the twenty-first century. There will be a major shift in the occurrence of deaths from predominantly among younger ages to mainly among older ages and from deaths due to communicable disease or maternal or prenatal causes to deaths due to non-communicable disease. Global HIV/AIDS deaths are projected to rise dramatically; on the other hand, the proportion of deaths due to non-communicable diseases is projected to rise from 59 per cent in 2002 to 69 per cent in 2030 (Mathers and Loncar, 2006). Ischaemic heart disease and stroke followed by cancer, chronic lung diseases and diabetes mellitus will become the main causes of death in the world. Notably, these causes of death share many of the same key risk factors: tobacco use, unhealthy diets, lack of physical activity and alcohol abuse.

The demographic and epidemiological transition in developed countries took place over a long time span. Increased life expectancy reflects improvements in nutrition and the success of public-health interventions on various fronts, including improvements in public systems for providing clean drinking water and for disposing of human and animal wastes and for ensuring the quality of food products, such as through the pasteurization of milk. Educational campaigns promoting healthy practices in matters of infant care, personal hygiene, sound nutrition, use of tobacco, alcohol and other drugs, sexual habits and so on have also contributed.

Many of these interventions were made possible thanks to substantial advances in medical knowledge dating from the middle of the nineteenth century. Improvements in the medical treatment of sick individuals advanced dramatically in the latter half of the twentieth century, especially following the development of antibiotic drugs as well as therapies for the effective management of cardiovascular disease. Most developed countries are already preparing for population ageing and have undertaken scenario analyses of the social and economic implications, in part out of concern for possible future strain on national and budgetary resources, especially in relation to the financing of pension and health and long-term care systems.

The demographic transition in developing countries is taking place at a much faster pace. The health-care challenge for these countries is therefore generally much larger, as their health-care systems still have many deficiencies in respect of addressing diseases for which the younger population is most at risk, while the rapid ageing process has already led to much greater demands for health care by older persons. Out of an estimated 58 million deaths in the world from all causes in 2005, chronic diseases accounted for 35 million (60 per cent); and 80 per cent of chronic deaths are considered to have occurred in low- and middle-income developing countries, primarily because these countries contain most of the world's population, but also, partly, because the developing world is experiencing rapid ageing and the need to address the greater health needs of older persons (World Health Organization, 2005, pp. 2 and 4). Concurrently, communicable diseases still constitute the major causes of death in many developing countries. Many developing countries thus face a double burden of disease: the large death toll and ill health associated with both communicable and non-communicable diseases.

Developing countries need to expand and reform their heath-care systems so as to manage the double burden of disease. The establishment of prevention programmes to delay the onset of diseases and of formal systems for catering to the special needs of older persons, including long-term care if needed, is required. Moreover, such expansion must be accompanied and supported by a strong political commitment to expand health-care coverage and strengthen the administrative capacity of various levels of the Government. An additional reason for increased involvement of different levels of government is that family- or community-based informal support for older persons is under growing pressure due to falling fertility rates, smaller family sizes, increased longevity of older persons and changing cultural norms regarding caring for older persons, as discussed in chapter III.

This chapter argues that, while the challenges are large, they are not insurmountable. The analysis shows that population ageing is a factor, but not always the main factor, in rising health costs. Estimates of future health costs for an ageing population vary and are subject to much uncertainty, but, as analysed below, most studies concur that the impact of ageing per se would be to increase public-health expenditures by a range of from about 1 to 3 percentage points of gross domestic product (GDP) over several decades. Similar figures apply for the future increase in public spending for long-term care in the developed countries, although very much depends on the design of systems of health-care delivery and financing.

Other factors besides ageing are pushing up health costs and much will depend on whether the prices of health-care provisioning and medicine can be contained. The challenges will differ from context to context and will reflect the stages of the demographic and epidemiological transitions that countries have reached. Action will be required on many levels to provide in an affordable manner for the health needs of the whole population, including older persons. Taking into account the expected speed of the demographic and epidemiological transitions, all levels of government will have to re-examine the way in which health-care services are provided to the population in general and to older persons in particular; the way in which the system that eventually emerges is financed by both public and private sectors; and the ways in which the ability of society to offer special programmes for older persons can be enhanced. However, there is little question but that the size of the health sector in the economy and public expenditures on that sector will tend to increase over time, even if efforts are made to contain the increase in costs; but as this expansion has been foreseen and is taking place over time, it should normally be manageable in a country that sees a steady rise in per capita incomes. As much of this expansion can be foreseen as part of a long-term trend, economies can be made to adjust to it gradually over time.

EPIDEMIOLOGICAL TRANSITION AND POPULATION AGEING

Mortality decline and the epidemiological transition

In pre-transitional, high-mortality populations, infectious and parasitic diseases were the dominant causes of sickness and mortality, and a large proportion of deaths occurred at younger ages. Mortality rates were high across the age range, but infants and young children were particularly vulnerable. Chances of survival improved, especially among children, as the risk of *infectious* disease was reduced through improvements in sanitation, hygiene, nutrition and medical therapy. As more and more individuals survived to adulthood and even to old age, they were increasingly exposed to the risk factors associated with *chronic* diseases. Over time, non-communicable, chronic and degenerative diseases became the foremost causes of morbidity and mortality, so that the vast majority of deaths now occur at older ages in the countries that have completed this transition.

In developing countries, this transition started later than in developed countries and was particularly rapid in the second half of the twentieth century. Large differences remain in the epidemiological profiles of various regions. Figure VI.1 illustrates regional differences in the breakdown of causes of death into three major groups: (a) communicable, maternal and perinatal, and nutritional causes; (b) non-communicable chronic diseases; and (c) injuries. In the figure and the following discussion, countries and other areas are grouped into regions according to the classification framework used by the World Health Organization (WHO).

In Africa,[1] 70 per cent of deaths in 2005 were attributable to the first group of causes, whereas 23 per cent were due to chronic diseases, reflecting the fact that this region is still at an early stage of the epidemiological transition. Sub-Saharan Africa, in particular, has been severely affected by HIV/AIDS, with an estimated 24.7 million HIV-positive individuals in 2006, although in several

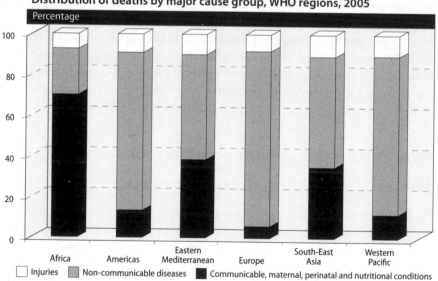

Figure VI.1.
Distribution of deaths by major cause group, WHO regions, 2005

Source: UN/DESA, based on WHO Global Bureau of Disease projections for 2005, available from http://www.who.int/entity/healthinfo/statistics/bod_deathbyregion.xls (accessed 5 January 2007).

affected countries, the pandemic has slowed or reversed a downward trend in mortality. Moreover, associated infectious diseases, such as tuberculosis, have continued to rise. Available data indicate that by 2006 more than 25 million people worldwide had died of AIDS and an additional 39.5 million were living with HIV (UNAIDS 2006; UNAIDS and World Health Organization, 2006).

Two other WHO regions, South-East Asia[2] and the eastern Mediterranean,[3] also have a substantial burden of disease from the first group of causes, but more than half of the deaths in these regions are now due to non-communicable diseases. In Europe, on the other hand, the vast majority of deaths are attributable to non-communicable causes.[4]

The differing epidemiological profiles of the various regions reflect their age patterns of mortality. For the developing world as a whole, deaths in 2000-2005 were distributed relatively evenly across the age span, with 29 per cent taking place under age 15, 30 per cent among adults aged 15-59, and 42 per cent among adults aged 60 years or over. In sub-Saharan Africa, however, children under age 15 had the highest number of deaths (estimated at 47 per cent of total deaths), reflecting the large burden of communicable, prenatal and nutritional causes. Another 38 per cent of deaths, many of which were caused by the HIV/AIDS epidemic, took place among adults aged 15-59; maternal mortality, injuries and chronic diseases leading to early death were also important causes. The patterns observed in sub-Saharan Africa mark a strong contrast with those in developed countries, where deaths were concentrated among persons aged 60 years or over (80 per cent) and only 1 per cent among children under age 15. Yet, non-communicable diseases are becoming increasingly important as causes of death in low- and middle-income countries; moreover, they tend to occur at younger ages than in high-income countries (World Health Organization, 2006b).

With continued medical advances, most developed countries experienced sustained declines in mortality in the second half of the twentieth century as deaths from non-communicable diseases, particularly cardiovascular disease, took place later in life. France, where between 1971 and 2002 the estimated level of life expectancy at age 65 rose from 16 to 21 years for men and from 21 to 26 years for women (United Nations, 2006b), is a representative case among developed countries. With increased longevity, death has become increasingly concentrated at advanced ages: for example, in 2000-2005, more than 80 per cent of deaths in France took place at ages 65 and above and 50 per cent occurred at ages 80 and above.

In some countries, mortality has increased even if the epidemiological transition has taken place, owing to assorted social, economic and behavioural causes, including accidents, violence and substance abuse, which are often a reflection of stress caused by the profound changes in socio-economic conditions (Kinsella and Phillips, 2005). In the countries of Eastern Europe, infectious diseases had been largely controlled by the 1960s, but mortality from cardiovascular disease continued to rise; and during the period of central planning, the region did not see the health advances witnessed by its Western neighbours, some of which had started off with lower life expectancy (United Nations, 1997b, p. 25). In the early 1990s, several countries of the former Soviet Union experienced a marked worsening of mortality from cardiovascular disease and external causes, particularly for men. In the Russian Federation, the death toll in recent years has been particularly high for working-age males.

HEALTH AND DISABILITY IN THE OLDER POPULATION

While episodes of communicable disease can have disabling consequences, non-communicable diseases, such as cardiovascular disease and cancer, often bring about a long period of poor health and diminished functioning. In addition, some non-fatal (but often chronic) conditions can have an important impact on the quality of life and health-care costs for older individuals. Examples of such conditions include hearing and vision loss, musculoskeletal conditions such as osteoarthritis, and cognitive impairments including Alzheimer's disease and other dementias.

With populations ageing rapidly in developed countries, as well as in many developing countries, the evolution of the health status of older persons has broad implications. Increased life expectancy is usually considered to be a favourable outcome of social and economic development, but how healthy are the added years of life? If medical treatments postpone deaths from chronic conditions but do not delay the onset of the conditions themselves or their disabling consequences, the result could be an expansion of morbidity and disability over the life course of individuals. Alternatively, if the same forces that delay death also delay the onset of chronic conditions, then morbidity and disability could be contracted into a shorter period (representing the so-called compression of morbidity).

Little information is available about long-term trends in the incidence or prevalence of chronic disease and morbidity. One set of data provide information about white veterans of the Union Army of the United States of America, who fought in the American Civil War of 1861-1865. These veterans had been subject to regular medical check-ups and, at the beginning of the twentieth century, would have been between about 60 and 64 years of age. Only 10 per cent of this cohort was found to be free of chronic disease conditions.

By contrast, survey data from 1994 indicated that 25 per cent of white males of the same age group were free of such conditions. Similar evidence indicates that the average age of onset for heart disease rose from 56 at the beginning of the twentieth century to 65 at the end of the century; for arthritis, the rise was from age 54 to age 65. Thus, the average delay in the onset of chronic conditions over the century was more than 10 years, whereas the average increase over the same period in male life expectancy at age 50 in the United States was about 6.6 years (Fogel, 2004). Significant factors underlying the declines in chronic disease observed during the twentieth century included reduced exposure to infectious diseases in childhood and young adulthood, occupational shifts leading to changes in the nature of work and working environments, and increases in average body size.

More recently, several health indicators designed to examine whether a compression of morbidity and related changes are taking place in a similar fashion in various populations have been proposed. Among these measures, a few variants under the rubric of "healthy life expectancy" are perhaps the most widely used. They measure how many years a person can expect to live in a healthy state, given current rates of mortality, morbidity and disability. Since, by definition, healthy life expectancy can be no greater than total life expectancy, a comparison of the two statistics provides an indication of the relative length of life spent in good as opposed to bad health. There are various definitions of "healthy"—it can mean living in the absence of all disease, or of severe disability, or of even mild disability—and thus healthy life expectancy can be computed in various ways. These computations have different names, including "active life expectancy", "disability-free life expectancy" and "health-adjusted life expectancy (HALE)". It should be noted that using these measures for comparing levels of healthy life expectancy across countries remains difficult, particularly because the resultant indicators are influenced by whether they are based on diagnosed conditions or self-reported health status, by the specific questions asked or the definitions applied to assess health and disability in surveys, and by cultural differences in the perceptions of health.

Despite these problems of comparability, a few general conclusions can be drawn from the available evidence. Most studies have found that women have longer life expectancy compared with men, but also spend a longer period of their life in poor health (Romero, da Costa Leite and Landmann, 2005). Another common finding in these studies was that people in developing countries are likely to spend a greater *fraction* of their total life spans in poor health. In developing countries, the onset of both fatal and non-fatal diseases tends to occur at younger ages than in developed countries. As a result, when developed and developing countries are compared using health-adjusted life expectancy by WHO, the estimated number of years spent with a disability is about the same in both groups of countries. Figure VI.2 presents the WHO estimates by sex of total and healthy life expectancy at birth and at age 60 for developed and developing regions. In the low-mortality countries, women typically live longer than men but spend a longer period—8.1 years for women as against 6.7 for men—in ill health at the end of their lives.

Figure VI.2.
Total and healthy life expectancy at birth and at age 60, by region and sex, 2002

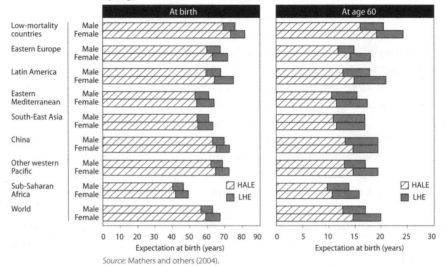

Source: Mathers and others (2004).

Note: HALE refers to health-adjusted life expectancy and LHE to the expectation of lost healthy years, that is to say, to the difference between total life expectancy and health-adjusted life expectancy.

It is difficult to go beyond these broad statements about differences in healthy life expectancy between men and women and between developed and developing countries, and draw firm conclusions about trends and differences in healthy lifespan around the globe and its relationship to total life expectancy. For example, in a recent study of trends in healthy life expectancy in countries of the European Union (European Health Expectancy Monitoring Unit (EHEMU), 2005), where one would expect comparable data to be most readily available, there were found wide variations in the estimated level of disability and different directions in trends. Although some countries showed evidence of a compression over time in the duration of morbidity across the age range, others showed evidence of an expansion. The study concluded that those conflicting results might have indicated that the estimates were still not comparable across countries, despite efforts to adjust and harmonize the data.

Another example of the difficulties of interpreting such information comes from a study in China (Qaio, 2005), which found that the active life expectancy of older persons—that is to say, the number of years of life spent disability-free—had declined between 1992 and 2000. This decline could have been due to a transition from a system of universal but often rudimentary Government-provided health care under the centrally planned economy to one characterized by an increased reliance on user fees and the privatization of many medical services, which might have been detrimental to the poor, especially in rural areas, with respect to coverage for their basic medical care. However, this conclusion constitutes only one possible interpretation of the data. Since the measure of active life expectancy was based on self-reported health in a series of surveys, it is unclear whether actual health had worsened over the study period or whether a negative reaction to changes in the health-care system and new expectations about medical care had led more people to report that they were unhealthy.

HEALTH DIFFERENTIALS AND THEIR
IMPLICATIONS FOR FUTURE TRENDS

Studies of older populations in developed countries have found consistent relationships between socio-economic status and levels of morbidity and mortality. In general, the more advantaged segments of those populations (comprising people with higher incomes, higher levels of education, higher perceived social status, etc.) tend to be healthier and to live longer than their less advantaged counterparts. Therefore, it is expected that future levels of health and disability will likely be influenced not only by changes in the general health environment and medical technology, but also by changes in the composition of the older population with respect to per capita income, educational levels, health status in early life and subsequent behaviour as adults.

Various studies have shown that lower levels of chronic disease and disability are experienced by those with higher levels of education. Experts have not yet reached an agreement on the exact mechanisms producing this link. Possible explanations include psychosocial effects on persons associated with different types of jobs and differential use of health knowledge and technology, and the high correlation between education and incomes and therefore the ability to pay for medical services (Cutler, Deaton and Lleras-Muney, 2005). As access to education, including higher education, is improving in most parts of the world, this should produce extra pressure for an expanded coverage and enhanced quality of health care. Moreover, the population cohorts moving into the older age range in the coming decades will be increasingly well educated, suggesting a possible beneficial effect on future trends in health and overall well-being for older persons and greater health-seeking activity by them. It should be stressed, though, that the strength of the relationship currently observed between education and health is not uniform across countries (Kinsella and Velkoff, 2001).

General living conditions at earlier ages, including nutritional status and exposure to communicable diseases, are known to have important impacts on health in later life. For example, exposure to the hepatitis B virus has been linked to later development of liver cancer, and acute rheumatic fever in childhood often leads to rheumatic heart disease, which is still a significant killer of adults in developing regions (Elo and Preston, 1992). Short stature, where it is an outcome of retarded growth due to nutritional deprivation and disease in childhood, has been associated in developed countries with higher risks of mortality at older ages, particularly from cardiovascular diseases (Aboderin and others, 2002; Elo and Preston, 1992; Fogel, 2004).

Nevertheless, there are still many unknowns with respect to the relationships between conditions in early life and health outcomes in later life. A WHO report concluded that it is still premature to recommend policy interventions in the early stages of life (for example, measures to increase birth weight) for the express purpose of influencing adult health, especially since evidence that these relationships hold in developing countries is still lacking (Aboderin and others, 2002).

More policy-relevant are trends in individual behaviour such as smoking, exercise and diet. For example, in 2000 an estimated 4.8 million adult deaths worldwide were attributable to smoking (Ezzati and Lopez, 2004). Compared with non-smokers, smokers are at extremely high risks for many diseases. The list includes but is not limited to lung cancer, cardiovascular disease and chronic obstructive pulmonary disease. This excess risk is reduced almost immediately by smoking cessation and continues to fall with increasing length of time after cessation.

Although smoking rates have been higher historically in developed countries, more than half of all deaths attributable to smoking now occur in developing countries. These countries are beginning to experience the impact of the accumulated hazards of the increase in smoking in recent decades. In Northern America, Japan and some Western European countries, smoking rates among men have declined in recent decades. However, over this same period, the prevalence of smoking among women in these regions has either continued to rise, stabilized at high levels or declined only slightly. Smoking rates vary widely among developing countries but are generally either rising or stable at high levels. In general, smoking is much more prevalent among men than among women in these countries.

The mortality burden from smoking in developing countries is concentrated in a relatively young age range compared with that in developed countries, reflecting a more recent widespread use of tobacco. However, given the population growth projected for developing countries, there will be an increasing burden of tobacco-related morbidity and mortality unless steps are taken soon to reduce rates of smoking in men and to prevent increases in those rates among women.

In developing countries, higher socio-economic status is sometimes associated with a higher prevalence of risk factors for cardiovascular disease, such as high blood pressure (Aboderin and others, 2002), since urban and other advantaged population segments are more likely to adopt "Western" lifestyles. However, as unhealthy behaviour patterns like smoking and overeating spread to larger segments of the population, it seems likely that socio-economic gradients in risk factors and non-communicable disease morbidity will come to resemble those in the developed countries, with worse outcomes among groups with lower socio-economic status.

Much of the preventable component of the non-communicable disease burden is linked to a number of risk factors that can be modified through individual behaviour. Risk factors with quantifiable causal effects on chronic diseases include high blood pressure, high cholesterol, overweight and obesity, low fruit and vegetable intake, physical inactivity, smoking and alcohol use (Ezzati and others, 2005).

ARE HEALTH-CARE SYSTEMS PREPARED FOR POPULATION AGEING?

Health resources and expenditures

The coverage and benefits provided by health-care systems to older persons vary considerably between developed and developing countries. The differences reflect not only the human and financial resources made available for older persons, but also societal values and views concerning the role and responsibilities of the public sector in caring for the general health of the public. Differences in the history and structure of overall social welfare programmes for income support and health care across countries therefore make it difficult to provide a general picture of the typical health-care system in developing countries (Ofstedal and Natividad, 2002).

The existing health systems in developing countries, particularly low-income ones, are still mainly geared towards providing care for acute episodic conditions and not towards chronic care needs and care specific to older persons. As noted above, however, evidence from developing countries shows a high prevalence of risk factors for chronic conditions, such as smoking, alcohol, diet and weight. The missed opportunity to prevent or deal earlier in life with age-related non-communicable diseases may lead to increases in their incidence, prevalence and complications later in life.

Overall, resources devoted to the health sector in developing regions are not up to the levels observed in the developed world (see table VI.1). For the most recent year in the period 1997-2004 for which data were available, African countries, for example, had 0.1 physicians per 1,000 residents, compared with 2.7 in developed countries and 3.5 in Eastern Europe and the Commonwealth of Independent States (CIS). Furthermore, the shortage of health workers is often associated with difficult working conditions—long hours, low pay and the shortage of adequate medical supplies, for example. While these differences in health-care inputs do not necessarily translate into similar differences in the general health status of populations, the lower availability of physicians and hospital beds no doubt do adversely affect health conditions. The World Health Organization (2006a) offers evidence that the number and the level of professional skill of health workers are positively correlated with the degree of immunization coverage and primary-care outreach, which in turn are important factors in infant, child and maternal survival.

Table VI.1.
Number of physicians and hospital beds, by region, 1997-2004

	Physicians per 1,000 residents (1997-2004[a])	Hospital beds per 1,000 residents (2000-2003[a])
Developed economies	2.7	6.3
Africa	0.1	1.2[b]
East Asia and the Pacific	1.3	2.4
South Asia	0.5	0.9
Western Asia	1.5	2.3
Latin America and the Caribbean	1.8	1.9
Economies in transition	3.5	8.5

Source: UN/DESA, based on World Bank, 06 World Development Indicators (Washington, D.C., World Bank, 2006), available from www.worldbank.org/data/onlinedatabases/onlinedatabases.html.
a   Data for most recent year available.
b   1990.

The emigration of health professionals (and home-care workers) from developing countries further aggravates the situation. This migration is a result of a shortage of nurses in many developed and some middle-income developing countries. Emigration of health workers from developing countries is further induced by the relatively low pay, unattractive working environment, and lack of investment in education and training in their own health sectors (World Health Organization, 2006a).

Medical care and delivery are indeed becoming more of a global industry, with doctors throughout the world learning of the latest techniques being practised in the countries with the most advanced medical research facilities. While this may be to the advantage of developing countries, the brain drain of health professionals is straining the required expansion of their health systems. According to one study, already 1 in 5 practising physicians in the United States is foreign trained and it has been estimated that by 2020 the United States could face a shortage of 800,000 nurses and 200,000 doctors (Garrett, 2007, p. 15). The same study argues that unless domestic training facilities and salaries of teachers expand sufficiently in the developed countries to be able to satisfy their expanding needs for medical personnel from their own populations, the result could be a further drain of medical personnel from developing countries. The brain drain phenomenon has been particularly noticeable in Africa: for example, Zimbabwe trained 1,200 doctors during the 1990s, but only 360 remain in the country today (ibid.). In 1980, the country had been able to fill 90 per cent of its nursing positions nationwide; today only 30 per cent are filled. In Zambia, only 50 of the 600 doctors trained over the last 40 years remain in the country today.

On the other hand, as the medical industry is a global industry, patients from developed countries are frequently visiting poorer countries to obtain at lower cost medical services that they would otherwise have received at home. This is especially the case for cosmetic and elective medicine that might not be covered by the insurance policy or health system at home. Similarly, in order to reduce their living costs—including medical and, in the case of a chronic illness, nursing costs—and perhaps in order to enjoy a healthier climate, richer older persons often choose to relocate to a poorer country. It could be the case that this extra demand for the medical services of poorer countries will help them to retain medical and nursing staff and to expand coverage to the overall population.

In general, however, developing countries, particularly low-income ones, tend to spend a much lower share of their national income on health care (see table VI.2). For example, per capita health expenditure in sub-Saharan Africa is over 50 times less than the average of such expenditure in the developed world.[5]

Table VI.2.
Total health expenditure, by region, 2000-2003

	Health expenditure as percentage of GDP				Health expenditure per capita (current United States dollars)			
	2000	2001	2002	2003	2000	2001	2002	2003
Developed countries	10.3	10.8	11.2	11.3	2 705	2 806	3 019	3 415
Developing country regions								
Africa	5.4	5.5	5.6	5.6	41	43	48	54
South and East Asia	4.3	4.5	4.6	4.6	38	38	38	43
Western Asia	6.3	6.9	6.6	6.6	257	242	251	288
Latin America and the Caribbean	6.9	7.0	6.6	6.6	268	260	215	221
Economies in transition	5.7	5.7	5.9	5.8	76	87	102	124

Source: UN/DESA, based on World Bank, World Development Indicators Online, available from www.worldbank.org/data/onlinedatabases/onlinedatabases.html.

The disparity in health-care services between rich and poor countries becomes even clearer when sources of health spending are examined (see table VI.3). Notably, the public share of total health spending tends to increase with per capita income, implying that individuals in developing countries are more likely to obtain health care through private schemes. In practice, most people pay for such services directly out of their own pocket, given the low coverage of private health insurance schemes in developing countries. What is more, the poorer the country, the larger the share of out-of-pocket expenses is likely to be. In 2003, the share of public spending in total health expenditures was 29 per cent in the low-income countries group, as defined by the World Bank, 44 per cent in lower middle income countries, and 58 per cent in upper middle income countries. In particular, the share of public spending in total health expenditure in South Asia as a whole in 2003 was 26.3 per cent, the lowest among the regions. Also within developing countries, it mostly holds that poorer people have a higher share of out-of-pocket expenses on health care than richer households (see World Bank, 2006b). The lower public share of total health spending not only implies a heavier financial burden at the personal level, but also reflects the relatively lower revenue-raising capacity of poor countries and the lower level of the Government's health interventions to mitigate market failures in health-care and health insurance markets (see Schieber and Maeda, 1999).

Table VI.3.
Share of public spending in total health expenditures, by region, 2000-2003

Percentage	2000	2001	2002	2003
Developed countries	59.8	59.6	59.4	60.0
(excluding United States)	76.6	76.9	76.7	76.5
Developing country regions				
Africa	44.3	44.3	43.4	42.8
South and East Asia	37.9	38.0	37.4	38.3
Western Asia	63.0	65.3	65.7	67.3
Latin America and the Caribbean	48.5	47.7	47.9	48.3
Economies in transition	58.9	60.4	60.8	61.3
Memorandum items:[a]				
Low-income countries	27.1[b]	25.0	27.8	29.1
Lower middle income countries	49.4[b]	46.6	45.5	43.7
Upper middle income countries	54.2[b]	57.8	57.6	57.9

Source: World Development Indicators Online.
a Country groupings as defined by the World Bank.
b Based on the latest data available before 2000.

Ageing and the need for reform of health-care systems

To meet the changes in health demands emanating from the unprecedented trend in population ageing, major adjustments will have to be made in every dimension of a health-care system. There will be important changes in the type of health-care services that are demanded, and in the required coverage of health insurance schemes, as well as in the direction of research agendas. The enhanced prevalence of chronic diseases and needs for long-term care will likely also have implications for the living arrangements of older persons and the relatives engaged in caring for them.

The fact that in developed countries population ageing has been accompanied by substantial increases in medical expenditures has led to the widely held perception that it is population ageing in particular that is driving up health costs and that these costs may become unsustainable. This perception is based on the following simple reasoning: Since older persons have a higher risk of being affected by disease and thus of requiring more medical attention than younger people, an increase in their share of the total population would be expected to drive up medical expenditures. Even though the United States lacks universal health coverage, unlike most other developed countries, health-care expenditure per capita (inflation-adjusted) has consistently outgrown gross national product (GNP) per capita since 1929, pushing that country's share in GNP from 3.5 per cent (Newhouse, 1992, table 1) to about 15 per cent at present. The trends have been similar in other countries that are members of the Organisation for Economic Co-operation and Development (OECD), although none has so far reached the level of health-care expenditure as a share of GNP or of health-care expenditure per capita attained by the United States. The question, however, is to what extent ageing has been a factor in these rising health costs. The answer to this question as supplied by the experience of the developed countries can help point the way for developing countries.

Some studies show that the relationship between population ageing and health expenditure is not as close as it is perceived to be. Based on age differentials in spending on health care, the demographic change in the United States for the period 1940-1990 can explain a mere 15 per cent of the total increase (Lloyd-Sherlock, 2000). Similarly, changes in demographic structure over the period from 1985-1987 to 1996-1999 were also estimated to be responsible for 6 per cent of the observed increases in health-care expenditure in Australia and for 14 per cent in Canada (Gray, 2005). Apparently, non-demographic factors explain most of the rise in health expenditures in these countries. In contrast, over the same period, the comparable figure for Japan was 56 per cent. The demographic structure of the country is becoming older at a faster pace than that of other developed countries, making population ageing a larger factor in explaining observed increases in health expenditures.

Cross-country comparisons also indicate significant disparities in health spending among OECD countries and show that population ageing is not the main explanation thereof (see figure VI.3A). While Turkey and, to a lesser extent, the United Kingdom have a younger age structure than that of Italy and Japan, the four countries spend similar shares of GDP on health care. Germany, in turn, has a share of older persons in the population similar to that of Japan and Italy but spends about 3 percentage points more of GDP on health care. Among the developed countries, the United States has a relatively young population but its health spending exceeds by far that of any other country. Also when looking at changes over time, no close correlation can be observed between population ageing and health-care spending in developed countries (see figure VI.3B and C).

A study on health expenditures for the period 1951-2000 in New Zealand (Bryant and Sonerson, 2006), points out two non-demographic mechanisms at work in affecting health expenditure: the level of general revenues of the Government and pressure from the salaries and wages of health workers. The demographic structure of the country has become steadily older since

Figure VI.3.

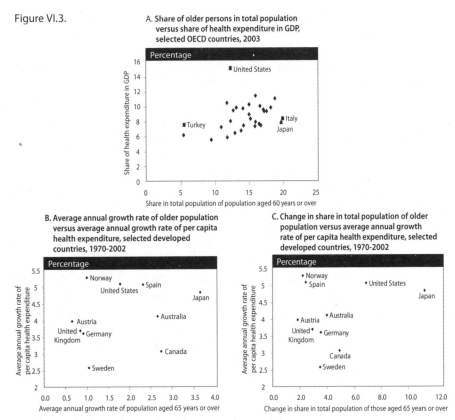

A. Share of older persons in total population versus share of health expenditure in GDP, selected OECD countries, 2003

B. Average annual growth rate of older population versus average annual growth rate of per capita health expenditure, selected developed countries, 1970-2002

C. Change in share in total population of older population versus average annual growth rate of per capita health expenditure, selected developed countries, 1970-2002

Source: UN/DESA, based on World Development Indicators Online.

1950 while health expenditures have experienced large fluctuations. The study shows that it was government revenues and salaries and wages of health workers, rather than demographic changes, that moved with health expenditures.

Technological progress (new scientific discoveries and new drugs and treatment) and changes in health policy have been other major drivers of health expenditures. Public and private health insurance schemes responded, in terms of the type and extent of coverage, to people's greater desire to use new health-care services, as incomes rose and technological advances were achieved; and technological advances have transformed the health-care system, including the intensity and coverage of health services. At the same time, the interaction among technology advance, policy change and demand for better health have often induced inflation of health-care services. A measure of technological advance is the fact that the majority of diagnostic capabilities, medical procedures, equipment and pharmaceuticals used today were developed in the past 50 years and can effectively deal with diseases that were not curable in the past.

Technological progress and health policy are closely related (Weisbrod, 1991). The pace and types of medical and pharmaceutical research and development are functions of expected monetary rewards for the pharmaceutical industry. These potential rewards are determined partly by the prevalence of diseases for which a cure or treatment is being sought, and partly by the possibility of reimbursement for research and development and product development which depends in turn on the comprehensiveness of public and private health insurance coverage and its accessibility by the general public. At the same time, the emergence of new technologies and medicine tends to place upward pressure on prices of health-care services and on the need for public or private health insurance. In other words, medical technologies and health-care expenditures are at least partly determined independent of population ageing.

The analysis thus far suggests that population ageing is not the dominant factor in rising health costs. This does not imply, however, that health costs will remain low and that their distribution over different age groups will remain stable in coming decades in developing countries. Population ageing will change the composition of overall health expenditures, as older persons—high-cost medical users—constitute a larger share of the population. Furthermore, rising income levels and increasing awareness by the public of the availability and effectiveness of new medical technologies and medicine will create greater demands for health-care services, irrespective of population ageing.

Table VI.4 demonstrates the extent to which older persons' expenditure on health care is different from that of younger persons by presenting information on per capita health expenditures in several age groups for selected countries.

Relative health spending differs strongly by age group in these selected countries. In general, though, health spending directed at meeting the needs of older persons tends to be higher. This is very pronounced for Canada, for example, although it also tends to be the case for other OECD countries.[6] In Canada, health expenditures are especially high for very old persons (aged 85 years or over). Similarly, in developing countries, the cost of health care for older persons seems to be relatively higher than for other age cohorts. This has been observed, for instance, in Brazil and the State of Punjab in India. In other countries and other States in India, however, per capita relative health expenditures on older persons are significantly lower than in Canada.

The different spending patterns reflect the types of health-care services provided at the end of life in developing and developed countries. While there

Table VI.4.
Distribution of total health-care expenditure, by age group, selected countries[a]

Brazil

Age group	Average	0-4	5-44	45-54	55-64	65-74	75+
Public expenditures[b]	100.0	165.7	55.2	129.0	193.1	292.0	415.5

Canada

Age group	Average	0-14	15-24	25-34	35-44	45-54	55-64	65-74	75-84	85+
Total expenditures	100.0	45.3	59.0	59.4	61.1	79.0	114.1	208.7	394.9	854.9

China

Age group	Average	0-4	5-9	10-14	15-19	20-24	25-29	30-34	35-39	40-44	45-49	50-54	55-59	60-64	64+
Total expenditures[c]	100.0	35.0	17.9	11.8	51.4	12.6	7.2	8.6	146.8	127.6	89.9	104.9	323.9	212.1	250.4

Egypt

Age group	Average	0-4	5-15	16-29	30-39	40-49	50-59	60-69	70-98
Total expenditures	100.0	73.0	61.6	78.1	123.5	167.5	203.7	209.1	177.7

India

Age group	Average	0-59	60+
Andhra Pradesh – Total expenditures	100.0	97.3	138.1
Karnataka – Total expenditures	100.0	89.7	237.7
Punjab – Total expenditures	100.0	89.9	374.0

Table VI.4 (cont'd)

Sri Lanka

Age group	Average	0-14	15-59	60-74	75+
Total expenditures	100.0	96.7	90.9	163.2	184.2

Uruguay[d]

Age group	Average	0-14	15-44	45-64	65-69	70-74	75-79	80+
Total expenditures	100.0	54.0	72.5	117.6	150.4	154.3	158.1	154.3

Source: UN/DESA, based on national sources.

a Index: average total health expenditure per capita for all age groups, set at 100.
b At hospitals only, not including birth-related health expenditures.
c Curative treatments only.
d Based on costs of hospital stays borne by the Uruguayan health-care organization Centro de Asistencia del Sindicato Medico del Uruguay (CASMU).

has been little research on health-care services at end of life in developing countries, it is still possible to make some inferences based on demographic and sociological circumstances. In developing countries, a far smaller proportion of those over age 60 live alone than in the developed countries (about 7 per cent as against 25 per cent), although in both groups of countries this proportion has tended to increase over time. Those living alone tend to have significantly lower levels of well-being than people who live with others and in the poorest countries older persons living alone tend to constitute an especially disadvantaged group. Surprisingly, perhaps, once controls for other variable have been put in place, the effects of urban or rural residence on older persons' living arrangements are not significant. In the developed countries, those living alone face an elevated likelihood of entry into long-term institutional care and this is especially the case for those who have no children, siblings or relatives who can be the main providers of informal support (United Nations, 2005b).

In Canada, the major portion of the health expenditures on those aged 85 years or over (about 75 per cent) is related to the costs of long stays in residential care facilities (for example, nursing homes) and the use of beds for palliative care in hospitals providing long-term care. Out of a total per capita health expenditure of Can$27,135 per year for those aged 85 years or over in 2000-2001, $10,401 was allocated to hospital care and $9,358 to long-term care provided by other institutions.[7] The high costs of health care are partly a result of the use of high-tech medical treatments and new drugs when the health status of a person deteriorates over an extended period of time owing to chronic illness (Mathiason, 2003).

However, over time, medical advances can help to contain costs. In Canada, the total health expenditures consumed by those aged 65 years or over had increased by 22 per cent between 1980-1981 and 2000-2001, during which period the population in this age group grew by 33 per cent. The replacement of surgical procedures with drug therapy, wider use of one-day surgery, reductions in the duration of hospital stays and the greater use of community and home-care services made it possible for the Government to decelerate the escalation of health costs during the mid-1990s (Health Policy and Communications Branch, Health Canada, 2001).

It should be noted that a person's "calendar age" is not necessarily a reliable indicator of health expenditures; instead, what determines in part the level of health needs and expenditures per person is proximity to death or (expected) remaining lifetime, according to various medical analyses conducted in several developed countries (Gray, 2005). This is largely because much of lifetime health-care expenditure is incurred during the last year of life regardless of a person's calendar age; in many cases, the patient stays, before dying, in high-cost facilities for a lengthy period of time. The concentration of medical expenditures at the end of life, independent of calendar age, is evident in some categories such as heart disease and cancer.

The experience of Medicare in the United States has been that medical expenditures in the last year of life *decrease* with age, particularly for those aged 85 years or over.[8] The pattern was found in different geographical areas (California and Massachusetts), for both sexes, for different races, irrespective of degree of co-morbidity, in hospices and hospitals, and regardless of cause or site of death. Moreover, the intensity of medical care in the last year of life decreases with increasing age:[9] expenditures for hospital services decline, with reduced intensity of care of the older groups during hospitalization. Recently, similar patterns were observed in two out of the three States investigated in India, namely, Karnataka and Punjab (see Mahal and Berman, 2006).

In summary, the evidence indicates that there does exist a relationship between ageing and health expenditures, but one that is weaker than is often thought. The pattern of end-of-life medical expenditures in many developing countries seems to differ from that in developed countries, owing to the lack of access to nursing and palliative care, and the lower intensity of medical interventions. As a result, the end of life may come with more suffering, but also more quickly. Low public-health coverage and relatively high out-of-pocket spending in many developing countries are likely to put such services as might prolong life in the developed countries out of reach of the majority of people in developing countries (Rannan-Eliya, Vidal and Nandakumar, 1998).

The challenge for health policies

Improvements in health conditions do not depend solely upon the delivery of health or medical services. They are also the result of such factors as improvements in nutrition from the earliest ages, and improvements in education and sanitation, the amount of exercise being undertaken and reduction of tobacco and alcohol consumption, and of the risks of contracting infectious diseases, including HIV/AIDS. At the Second World Assembly on Ageing held in Madrid in April 2002, WHO launched its life course approach to healthy ageing, which recommended that Governments address those factors that contributed to the onset of disease and disabilities (World Health Organization, 2002e). These factors will help determine the course—and costs—of the epidemiological transition.

Two different transition scenarios are usually considered: one is referred to as the conventional wisdom or "the failures of success", and the other as "the compression of morbidity".[10] Depending on which course prevails in the future, policymakers will face different sets of challenges.

The first scenario projects an extended period of life spent in a state of chronic illness, such as heart disease, stroke or dementia, or with one or more functional disabilities. Each of these sets of factors will require large shifts in health-care inputs and the acquisition by health-care workers of new skills. The country will have an ever-larger number of fragile persons and incur substantial increases in health expenditures, associated with new technologies and the need for new medical infrastructures. Care for older persons would be expanded as well. The increased expenses will have to be borne by private individuals and Governments. Healthy members of the society—young and old alike—will be required to make greater contributions. Insurance schemes and the securing of adequate public and private financing through tax increases in general and private financing supported by tax breaks for families caring for older persons, will be needed, entailing a wholesale rebuilding of the existing national health-care system. Because of this very success in achieving greater longevity, pressure on the health system becomes greater. Hence, the failures of success (Gnanasekaran, 2006).

The second scenario paints a brighter picture, in which increases in the age of onset of chronic disease or disability are greater than increases in life expectancy, and morbidity is thereby compressed into the very late stage of the life of individuals. For this to happen, the Government, communities, families and individuals—young and old—are required to take conscious and concerted actions, including various measures promoting health and healthier lifestyles at younger ages through proper nutrition, non-smoking, moderate alcohol consumption, regular exercise and education—the very factors that WHO is promoting for healthy ageing.

The health policy implications to be drawn from the two scenarios are not mutually exclusive. For many developing countries, providing care for acute episodic conditions or preventing infectious diseases are health policy priorities; at the same time, health education and promoting a healthier lifestyle can be seen as constituting a long-term health policy goal. Health policy derived from the first scenario, on the other hand, entails a warning to many Governments and the international community at large that, without a significant expansion and improvement of the existing health-care systems, developing countries will face large increases in health expenditures when they are still relatively poor.

As the relative importance of communicable diseases decreases and that of non-communicable diseases and disabilities increases, a larger pool of geriatric and gerontology specialists and health workers will be required. Because older persons tend to develop multiple medical conditions (co-morbidity), their symptoms are often different from those of younger persons. At the same time, the expansion of hospital facilities and beds and the introduction of modern innovations are necessary not only for an ageing population, but also for the improvement of the health of the general population which faces severe shortages of necessary medical treatment.

It is not unimaginable that an increase in disabled persons may also have a negative impact on the quality of life of "caregivers" who often provide unpaid care. Even in those countries where the Government has established formal arrangements for dependency care, the family and community are the main providers for older persons. However, when, as has historically been the case, the demographic transition is taking place in a period of accelerated economic growth, the combination can also induce unexpected changes in social values as they relate to care of aged parents and community members. For instance, a study on health care in Japan (Ogawa and others, 2006) showed a sudden shift in attitudes towards caring for elderly parents. In a series of nationwide surveys concerning family planning conducted since 1950, a dramatic decline was observed between 1986 and 1988—a period of two years—in the proportion of married female respondents under age 50 who believed that providing care for old-age parents was either a good custom or a child's natural duty (see figure VI.4). This drop has been part of an ongoing declining trend

Figure VI.4.
Trends in norms and expectations with respect to care for the elderly among married females under age 50, Japan, 1950-2004[a]

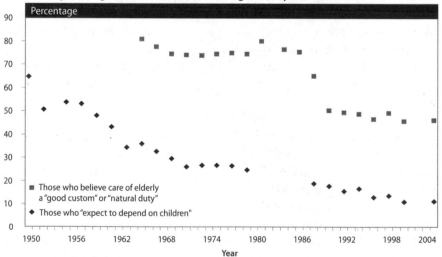

Source: Ogawa and others (2006).

a As determined by a series of nationwide surveys.

in perceived willingness to care for elderly parents; but according to the study, the indicated sudden decline in 1986-1988 "corresponds to the period when the government shifted more of the burden of care for the elderly from the state to families", to which "the middle-aged women responded negatively" (ibid., p. 16).

The traditional family structure and the role of women are thus changing or will change, sometimes drastically. It will become more difficult for many countries to maintain the current forms of traditional arrangements for long-term care. As will be discussed later, every society needs to introduce a formal system that may serve as a complement to, but not a substitute for, the traditional arrangements.

THE PROVISION OF LONG-TERM CARE

There is universal concern over how to provide long-term care for those whose health condition is irreversible. While most older persons remain active and relatively healthy, it is foreseen that there will be an increase in the need for long-term care, particularly for "persons needing help in daily living" (World Health Organization, 2002b)—a need to which every society should be able to respond in a manner that accords with its own traditions and the best interests of those needing such care.

In general, the growing concern reflects two trends, namely, the increase in the prevalence of long-term disability in the population and the change in the capacity of the institutional and informal systems to provide support (World Health Organization, 2002d). The rate of increase in the number of persons needing help in daily living and the rate of change of the institutional and informal capacity shape the framework of a nation's system of long-term care as a whole.

In developed countries, long-term care needs mainly results from population ageing, although the level and mix of services differ among them. On the whole, they are attempting to include home-based care service as part of a *continuum* of different types and levels of care, as called for by the Madrid International Plan of Action on Ageing (United Nations, 2002a). Many of these countries are thinking of ways to put greater emphasis on bringing home-care services to the appropriate level and to support and build the skills of family caregivers. Home-based health care is being encouraged through the provision of several financial incentives and various health-care and welfare services.

Experiences in developed countries with home-based care

Family caregiving and programmes for older persons have recently received much policy-related attention in many countries, owing to the recognition that most families around the world continue to provide some care in spite of changing living patterns. The "ageing in place" movement, designed to help older people stay at the family home or in a home-like environment, emphasizes the need for programmes that support family caregivers to help achieve this objective. In developed countries where formal care is in place, there is a growing emphasis on making it complementary to, rather than a substitute for, informal care.

In some developed countries, there has been a rapid expansion of policies and programmes designed to support family caregivers. In Sweden, for example, municipal governments give priority attention to caregiver support policies and programmes (Herlitz, 1997; Sundstrom, 1994). These policies and programmes can be classified within three major categories: job support, financial support, and social services. Job support policies are designed to help working caregivers. They include a caregiver insurance programme which provides paid leave when a worker cannot report to work because of caregiving responsibilities, a family leave policy which guarantees job security without pay, and employment-based eldercare, which allows flexible work schedules and includes provision of counselling and referral services, adult day care in or near the workplace and other employee assistance programmes.

Financial support policies encourage family caregivers to offer care at home. They take three forms: subsidies, salaries and tax credits. Subsidies that older persons receive from government can be used to pay family members who provide care for them at home. Salaries can also be paid by government directly to the family caregiver so that the person can afford to "work" at home full-time. Finally, tax credits or deductions to lower the tax burden can be given to family caregivers who may have to incur expenditures on items for home-based care.

Social services, which are designed to assist the caregiver and provide relief from caring, include housekeeping and home maintenance services and day-care and sitter services for older persons. More recently, Governments in Scandinavian countries have started offering services to caregivers, including counselling, caregiver support groups, and information and referral services. Training programmes are designed to prepare caregivers for both the practical tasks of caregiving and the physical and emotional stress associated with care at home. The combination of these policies and programmes offers a multidimensional framework of support for family members providing care (Hokenstad and Johansson, 1996).

Norway has historically placed more emphasis on a programme in which family members—usually daughters or daughters-in-law—are paid part-time salaries to provide home help services for an elderly and/or disabled relative. Some provide care for elders of other families and so become full-time home helpers. About 25 per cent of all home helpers in the country are relatives or neighbours of those for whom they provide care. From the perspective of the family, this programme provides additional income while allowing a family member to have a major caregiving role. This approach to government financial support of family caring is now being expanded to many countries as part of the "consumer choice" movement in eldercare. Consumer choice enables older people receiving long-term care in their homes to choose between receiving home care from government and private agencies and having family members subsidized to provide the care.

Developing country challenges

Caregivers in the developing world have less access to both economic and service support, but such programmes are growing. Social development programmes in a number of countries help provide a source of income for older women, many of whom have primary caregiving responsibilities. An example of this type of programme is the Samridhi day-care centre set up in rural India, which helps elderly women learn traditional crafts that can assist them in earning a living, thereby supplementing the family living. Samridhi also helps by providing the women with raw materials and the infrastructure needed to earn an income through craft-making.[11]

In general, however, population ageing in developing countries is but one of the factors underlying the need for long-term care. Infectious diseases and injuries caused by armed conflicts and traffic accidents, which affect all age cohorts, also require such care. Demand for long-term care resulting from ageing is strongly increasing with the speed of the demographic transition in these countries. The focus of the remainder of the present section will be on the provision of long-term care to older persons.

In many developing countries, institutionalized forms of long-term care services tend to be in poor supply. The extended family and networks of relatives, friends and neighbours remain the major sources of support and care. Even in cases where some forms of formal support are available, the health authorities often mainly concentrate on family guidance, counselling and education about health care. The care itself is then provided at home by family members.[12] Yet the declining importance of the extended family in many developing countries, as discussed in chapter III, is making it more and more difficult to rely exclusively on this form of informal care.

It is difficult, however, to draw an aggregate sketch of the coverage of long-term care because of widely differing country situations. Moreover, because the long-term care services are often provided not only to older persons, but also to the poor and the disabled within a single institutional or informal support system, separating the two components is not possible in many cases.[13] To achieve a better understanding of existing realities and to learn from what already existed in developing and transition countries in terms of care services available also for older persons, WHO (2002b; 2002c; 2002d) chose a case-study approach to the subject.

The WHO case studies show that developed countries typically offer a broad package of long-term services.[14] In contrast, publicly funded long-term care is not available in the majority of the 10 countries that were examined by WHO (2002c).[15] Of these, only richer countries, such as the Republic of Korea, as well as Lithuania and Ukraine, offer a wider range of long-term care services.

More generally, the sample countries with higher per capita income levels tend to provide a mixture of home-based long-term care services for those needing help for daily living, irrespective of age, and institutional long-term care. The broader package of services offered in Lithuania and Ukraine includes institutional care, home health care,[16] personal care at home and homemaking. In these countries, personal care at home and homemaking services are targeted at the poor in all age cohorts and at older persons without families. Publicly funded personal care services are not available to the non-poor population in these countries, but home health care is offered based on health conditions and disability, irrespective of their income levels.

In Lithuania, in 1998, there were found to be 90 institutional care facilities, 29 of which were operated by non-governmental organizations, including the Red Cross Society and faith-based organizations. Until 1990, the country had focused its social programmes on institutional care for older persons and the physically and mentally disabled. Since then, however, the number and variety of public institutions has grown, non-governmental organizations have become more active in providing long-term care for both older and younger persons, and the development of "non-institutional" (also called "community-based") forms of care have gained in importance (World Health Organization, 2002d). These government and non-government organizations offer a variety of types of care for disabled persons, both young and old, including personal care (grooming, bathing and provision of meals); household assistance (cleaning, laundry and shopping); remodelling of the home to meet the needs of disabled persons; provision of supplies, assistive devices, equipment and medicine; palliative care; and provision of information and guidance to the patient's family.

Non-governmental organizations in Lithuania were taking care of about 14 per cent of the total number of residents living in institutions in 1998, representing a doubling of the proportion in 1995. Health-care workers under the community-based form of programmes provide home-care nursing, but also other services such as shopping and housekeeping as mentioned above. In 1997, more than 2,200 workers and volunteers had been involved in care delivery, but WHO concluded that this number was insufficient to meet the current level of needs and also cautioned that the same conclusion applied to funding.

The other countries studied provide smaller ranges of care services for older persons. Yet, even if these services are available, the number of people covered is relatively small. In Thailand, for example, the Department of Public Welfare provides services for older persons, particularly those who are socially isolated and vulnerable, that include prevention of homelessness, abuse and family neglect through, inter alia, residential care, the creation of service centres, the dispatch of mobile units and the provision of emergency shelters. The private sector and non-governmental organizations also have programmes designed for older persons, including the provision of a monthly subsistence allowance and service centres located in temples. The number of older persons covered by such public and private programmes is not known. Given that the number of older persons in public institutions throughout the nation that provide for disabled residents who have been abandoned or neglected was 2,807 in 2000, it can be seen that the provision of public services is not yet satisfactory (World Health Organization, 2002d).

Many countries envisage taking measures to develop formal community health care. This approach seems compatible with the development of home-based long-term care. As noted previously, Lithuania and Ukraine, where long-term care has been institutionalized, are now making community-based care part of their formal health-care system. The Republic of Korea, where the formal system is still in its infancy, also emphasizes the importance of creating formal long-term care within the framework of community-based care in order to lower the rates of utilization by patients of more expensive hospital services.

The first and foremost challenge in home and long-term care for countries where large numbers of the populations are living in poverty, compared with the relatively rich countries considered above, is to provide, next to medical services, an adequate supply of food, decent housing, safe water and waste disposal, affordable soap and other basic supplies and medicines.

Meanwhile, the role of older persons in caregiving, to their children, grandchildren and to the community at large, should be stressed; and as called for in the Madrid International Plan of Action, provisions should be made to assist older persons in their caregiving role. This has been especially important in families where the parents of children have been lost to HIV/ AIDS and other diseases and grandparents are providing support. In more general terms, it would appear that the ageing of the population will be accompanied by the growth in the number of healthy older persons who will be willing and able to serve as professional caregivers or volunteers. In this respect, the importance of non-governmental organizations and volunteers in the delivery of long-term care has been recognized in many countries including China, Indonesia, Sri Lanka and Ukraine.

Those countries that attempt to maintain their existing home-based, informal care system could encounter difficulties in the future, largely because the traditional family structure and the role of women are changing, sometimes faster than anticipated, as examined in chapter III.

The case of Mexico illustrates how the traditional system of provision of home care by a family member, usually the daughter who works at home, is tending to break down (World Health Organization, 2002c). Over the past few decades, the country experienced an improvement in its educational performance, with higher enrolment ratios and higher average number of school years attended, and an increase in labour participation rates among working age groups. The economic crises that hit the country during this period may also have contributed to higher labour-force participation, with women, youth and children entering the labour market. This reduced the time that family members had available to care for young children, older persons and the sick (Knaul and others, 2002). Generally, long-term factors are making traditional care arrangements more difficult, including the increase in female labour-force participation, often associated with migration, and the greater importance of the nuclear household in urban areas. Some of these factors have been observed in other countries, such as China, where the massive migration of individuals from rural to urban areas has left behind older persons and disabled relatives for whom the migrants were formerly expected to care (Hua and Di, 2002).

Unfortunately, the extent of the provision by the State of alternative means of support, such as through social security institutions, has been insufficient to offset the effect of the diminishing role of the extended family. In the case of Mexico, for instance, about 45 per cent of the population over age 65, as well as many who suffer from a disability or a chronic disease, have no access to social security benefits. Moreover, the financial deficit of the social security system limits the level of the social benefits that can be paid out to those who are covered.

Data on disability rates and morbidity are limited in many developing countries and thus the future need for long-term care services is difficult to predict. Moreover, studies on long-term care systems—both institutional and informal—are in their infancy. Even where such studies exist, the impacts of various long-term care measures on the welfare of older persons are not yet clearly understood. There is thus an urgent need for more studies on long-term care in developing countries which could facilitate a better-informed dialogue within and among countries.

IMPLICATIONS FOR FUTURE HEALTH COSTS

The above analysis was necessary to place in context attempts to calculate the future public-health costs of an ageing population. Many of the private and public actions aimed at improving overall health involve expenditure and lifestyle choices by individuals—factors that are not included in existing future health cost projections but they could play a major role in determining levels of health expenditure.

The expected rise in expenditure on health and long-term care, while not necessarily a result of ageing per se, will put pressure on the national economy and government budgets in many developing countries, particularly if economic growth does not turn out to be as robust as expected. Pressing questions concern how much health and long-term care expenditure could grow as a result of the various factors examined previously and how such increases could be contained if the financial burden on the national economy and the government budget is forecast to be too great.

Projections of the impact of ageing on health expenditures

Projections of the impact of population ageing on future health-care costs are mostly available only for developed countries, owing not only to greater policy interest in the issue, but also to the wider availability of data. Developing countries, in general, have only limited health data, making it more difficult for researchers to make such projections for those countries.

Actuarial and epidemiological approaches have been developed to project future health expenditure depending on the research objectives and policy/planning goals (see box VI.1). As demonstrated above, the relationship between population ageing and health expenditures displays a complex pattern and understanding it requires identifying all the factors that influence health expenditures and building a framework that can capture the complexity of the underlying dynamics.

Box VI.1.
Projecting health-care expenditures into the future[a]

Growth in health expenditures since the last quarter of the twentieth century and, more recently, increasing awareness of the potential impacts of population ageing on fiscal balance and on national economic vitality have ignited considerable interest among policymakers and the general public in the possible future health "burden". Projecting health-care expenditures into the future is a useful tool in helping policymakers understand key factors that would influence expenditures and placing population ageing in a wider perspective. As analysed in the subsection of this chapter entitled "Ageing and the need for reform of health-care systems", the relationship between ageing and aggregate health expenditure is not straightforward. It is thus necessary for health authorities and experts to carefully analyse the existing relationship and to extrapolate it to the future.

Undertaking a projection requires a large amount of information on the factors that would influence total health spending at present and in the future. Typically, the information required includes current and projected data on demography, mortality, morbidity and costs per health-care intervention or series of treatments. If a model is to estimate the share of health-care expenditures in national income or the total government budget, the current and projected values of these variables must be at hand as well. At the same time, a projection should be able to attribute changes in future spending to the various factors considered, otherwise it will not service as a guideline for policymaking. Owing to the wider availability of data, as well as the greater amount of human and financial resources and the greater degree of policy interest in the issues, the majority of projections have been done for developed countries, although some have been attempted for a few middle-income developing countries.

There are four broad categories of projection methods: time-series analysis, economic equilibrium models, actuarial models and epidemiological models. Time-series analysis uses econometric methods to fit statistical models to time-series data on aggregate health expenditures and other socio-economic variables. The goal of economic equilibrium models is to investigate the interaction between the health sector and the rest of the economy by employing a two- or multisector approach. Demographic transition, including population ageing, enters the picture via the labour supply and the demand for health-care services. The two types of models have not yet been applied to developing countries.

In the actuarial methods, the population is divided into several age-sex groups. Aggregate personal health expenditures (that is to say, those for health services delivered to individuals) are calculated as the sum of the products of the number of people in each age-sex group and the average expenditure for health care per capita used by persons in the same group. Persons in older age groups are likely to use health-care services more often than their younger counterparts (although not necessarily) and when they use them, they are likely to require more resources. Similarly, older women are likely to use health services more than their male contemporaries. Population ageing, by this construction, leads to higher aggregate health expenditures. The per capita average health expenditure in each age group can further be decomposed into the age-sex-specific use of medical services per capita (the utilization component) and the unit costs or price of delivering medical services or pharmaceuticals (the price component). Public expenditures on preventive and

---

a   Based on Rannan-Eliya and Wijesinghe (2006) and Mahal and Berman (2001).

Box VI.1 (cont'd)

collective health, administrative costs and capital expenditures are added to the aggregate costs of services delivered to individuals.

The epidemiological methods, as the name indicates, are based on epidemiological trends. Utilization of and expenditure for health services are linked to specific diseases or morbidity conditions. Aggregate health expenditures are calculated as the sum of the products of the number of persons in each age-sex group, the incidence of disease or morbidity in each group, the average volume of health-care services per capita used by persons in the group with a specific disease or morbidity condition, and the average price of the services. To undertake projections, the diseases or morbidity patterns have to be predicted based on current trends, and future expenditures per person in a specific age-sex group with a particular disease or morbidity condition must be estimated. The major difference between this and the actuarial approach is the inclusion of the prevalences of diseases or morbidities as cost-drivers.

An advantage of the epidemiological method lies in its ability to project the incidence of diseases or morbidities and their associated expenditures. By knowing what types of diseases or morbidities are to prevail in the future, the health authorities will be able to arrange necessary health facilities and services in advance (treatments and necessary facilities for patients with dementia or diabetes, for example, are different from those for patients with ischaemic heart disease). Public campaigns for a healthy lifestyle—one that includes non-smoking, diet and moderate consumption of alcohol—can be cost-effective tools with which to reduce future costs if the incidence of such non-communicable diseases is projected to grow considerably. Information requirements for undertaking such an epidemiological approach are greater, however, than for an actuarial one, thus making the former a more difficult and expensive undertaking for developing countries. While in the actuarial approach in its calculations of per capita health spending is more likely to capture all the major cost elements, it is silent about the linkage between diseases/morbidity and age-sex-specific health costs. Because of the lesser information requirement, this approach has been widely applied in both developed and developing countries.

It is interesting to note that both methods are likely to reach similar conclusions, namely, that population ageing is an important influence on future health expenditures, but not a dominating one. Non-demographic factors, such as new technologies and pharmaceuticals, medical price inflation and productivity of the health sector as a whole, have impacts that are at least as significant as those of the demographic factor. In the past, they did contribute to the increase in health expenditures in many developed countries.

The non-demographic factors are also sources of the uncertainties of any projections. The pace of development of new medical technologies and pharmaceuticals may help reduce the disease burdens of many patients, but may also lead to medical price inflation (relative to economy-wide inflation rates). Another source of uncertainty is the fact that the health status of people may improve faster than past trends in disease/morbidity patterns would have indicated.

Among all these factors, perhaps two stand out as most influential: changes in health-seeking behaviours of people and changes in health policies. Changes in the coverage and rates of reimbursement affect aggregate expenditures significantly and the mechanism by

> **Box VI.1 (cont'd)**
>
> which doctors' fees and pharmaceutical prices are determined also influences expenditures. Improving access to quality public-health care services or new services (such as formal long-term care) may bring about a change in the public-private mix of health spending. Likewise, public actions affect people's behaviour: as the health system improves, utilization rates are likely to increase. Greater awareness of the causes of certain diseases—diabetes and ischaemic heart disease, for example—may lead to less cigarette smoking and to changes in diet, thereby reducing the incidence of these diseases from that projected.
>
> Finally, it should be noted that projections are not forecasts: they do not attempt to predict the actual future trends in health expenditures. They are produced in order to measure the impact of specific factors on aggregate expenditures. Forecasts, on the other hand, require taking into account possible changes in health polices and health-seeking behaviours in order to describe those trends.

In an actuarial framework, future expenditure requirements are calculated based on the existing age and sex profile of expenditure. Projected population changes and changes in projected per capita costs, which are often extrapolated from observed trends, can then produce estimates of future health expenditures. Implicitly, the projected per capita costs are assumed to include all growth factors and can be seen to constitute the composite effect of the non-demographic factors discussed above. A study on Sri Lanka (Rannan-Eliya, 2007) offers an insightful application of the actuarial framework for a developing country.

The actuarial approach applied to Sri Lanka

Although Sri Lanka is a low-income country, it has relatively good coverage of social services, which is also reflected in a relatively good performance in terms of human development indicators. The adult literacy rate is over 90 per cent and life expectancy at birth was 68.7 years for men and 76.8 years for women according to the standard projection in 2002-2006. The fertility rate in Sri Lanka is around replacement level, varying from 1.86 according to the low projection to 2.1 according to the high projection for 2002-2006. The country has an extensive network of health institutions, and it is estimated that no one has to travel further than 1.4 kilometres to reach a fixed health facility (Abeykoon, 2002). Sri Lanka thus shares many of the demographic and epidemiological characteristics of a developed country. Total expenditure on health in 2005 was 4.2 per cent of GDP and was split between the private sector (2.0 per cent of GDP) and the public sector (2.2 per cent).

The proportion of the total population over age 65 is projected to increase from 6.3 per cent in 2001 to between 23.5 and 29.7 per cent in 2101, by which time life expectancy is expected to have increased by about nine years. Because the available data for Sri Lanka indicate that morbidity compression is not taking place, the Sri Lankan study assumes that there would be no change in the age-sex-specific health status of the Sri Lankan population in future decades. This would put an upward bias in the projections if, in fact, the compression of morbidity does take place.

Health-seeking behaviour is one factor of importance in determining future health expenditure. Such behaviour refers to cases where individuals begin to visit the doctor or health facilities more often than before. The rate of outpatient visits is already relatively high in Sri Lanka (5.2 per capita per annum in 2005), and according to the different assumptions, this figure could increase slowly to 8.4 visits per capita per annum in 2101 or more rapidly to 13.5 visits in 2101 (compared with, for instance, 16 per capita per annum in Japan between 1993 and 1996). Little change is foreseen in the inpatient utilization rates over the period. In addition to the behavioural changes, productivity and price inflation are also expected to affect future expenditures on health-care services.[17]

Three scenarios for projected health-care expenditures by 2101 were analysed in the study of Sri Lanka. The baseline projection assumes that the cost-drivers follow historical trends and that there will be no change in the public-private mix of provision. In this case, total national health expenditure would increase from 4.2 per cent of GDP in 2005 to 11.1 per cent in 2101. The low-cost projection envisages the Government acting to increase its role in the health sector. There would be high productivity gains from the public sector, a shift in patients from the private to the public sector and controls on price escalation in the private sector. In this case, expenditures would rise to 6.7 per cent of GDP in 2101. In the high-cost projection, government policy would work to reduce the involvement of the Government in the health sector, encourage private sector responsibility, not actively seek to control prices in the private sector and invest less effort in achieving productivity gains in the public sector. In this scenario, total national health expenditures would rise to 13.2 per cent of GDP in 2050 and to 26.4 per cent of GDP in 2101. In that year, public expenditure on health would amount to 4.8 per cent of GDP and private expenditure to 21.6 per cent of GDP. Figure VI.5 shows the impact of some of the different factors that, according to the baseline scenario, will help increase health expenditure as a percentage of GDP between 2005 and 2101. Over the longer term, outpatient activity rates would play a more important role than demographic factors in driving up this proportion.

This variance in projected health spending under different cost assumptions is in itself much higher than the impact of ageing on future

Figure VI.5.
Range in impacts, under three different scenarios, of key cost drivers on national health-care expenditure in Sri Lanka in 2025 and 2101[a]

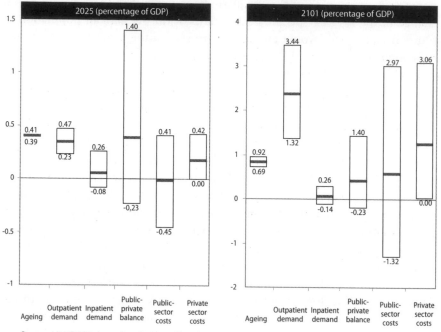

Source: UN/DESA, based on Rannan-Eliya (2007).

Note: The values in the top and bottom boxes represent the maximum and minimum; the middle bar represents the median.

a As measured by the change in health spending as a percentage of GDP from the level in 2005.

health costs under the three scenarios. In fact, the demographic factor would raise health expenditures by a mere 0.7 to 0.9 per cent of GDP by 2101. The conclusion therefore is that the key driver of increasing cost will in fact be not demographic change but the changing health awareness and increased propensity of Sri Lankans to use medical care when ill. According to Rannan-Eliya (2007, p.33): "It is possible to maintain current levels of provision, access and quality levels, with no substantial increase in national health spending as a proportion of GDP, that is to say, within the range of 5-7 per cent of GDP, if productivity improvements can keep pace with ageing."

Other actuarial health cost projections

A similar actuarial study for Hong Kong Special Administrative Region of China (SAR) also found that population ageing and growth per se, without taking into account related technological innovation for chronic conditions that particularly afflict older adults, contributed relatively little to projected future health costs. Under the given assumptions of the study,[18] total health spending is projected to increase to close to 10 per cent of GDP in 2033, up from 5.5 per cent of GDP in 2001-2002. According to the projections, the share of public-health spending would gradually decline from 57 per cent in 2001-2002 to somewhere between 46 and 49 per cent by 2033 (Leung, Tin and Chan, 2007, p. 1). The results were highly sensitive to the assumption about the expected future increase in unit costs for health-care delivery. The authors concluded that adaptation of new medical technology was the major long-term cost growth-driver and that, while measures of expenditure control could perhaps slow such growth in costs, in practice the imperative to innovate and deliver higher-quality care would almost always prevail over efforts to economize.

An OECD study (2006b), like the study on Sri Lanka, emphasizes the importance of the cost-push factors in health expenditures. In this study, changes in the cost of health and long-term care are determined as a result of technological progress and relative price movements in the supply of health-care services. Under a "cost pressure" scenario, health expenditures are assumed to grow at a rate that is 1 percentage point faster than the growth of mean incomes. For given trends in demographic change, this scenario projects that public-health and long-term care spending across OECD countries would almost double from close to 7 per cent of GDP in 2005 to about 13 per cent in 2050. Under a "cost containment" scenario, average expenditures would still reach 10 per cent of GDP, an increase of 3.5 percentage points (Organisation for Economic Co-operation and Development, 2006b, p.7). The study observes that non-demographic factors—the effects of technology and movements in relative prices—are important in determining the degree of upward pressure on long-term care expenditures and, indeed, constitute the most important driver of the projected increase in health-care expenditures.

The health status of older persons in future generations also affects the projected cost estimates of health-care delivery. According to the calculations of the European Commission, Directorate-General for Economic and Financial Affairs (2006), public health care expenditures would rise from 6.4 to 7.5 per cent of GDP between 2004 and 2030 and further to 8.2 per cent of GDP in 2050 in the case of the member countries of the European Union prior to 1 May 2004 (EU-15). The more recent member States, EU-10, which were poorer when entering EU and spent less on health, would have to increase health spending from 4.9 per cent of GDP in 2004 to 5.7 per cent in 2030 and to 6.1 per cent in 2050 (ibid., p. 9). The above figures are for the "pure ageing" scenario, under which age-related expenditure per capita on health care in the base year would remain constant over time. This assumes that there would be no compression of morbidity. An alternative set of projections assumed the presence of the compression of morbidity. In this scenario, the number of years spent in bad health during a lifetime in 2050 would be identical to that in 2004, even though people are expected to live longer. In this case, public spending on health would have to increase to 7.4 per cent of GDP in EU-15 by 2050 and to 5.5 per cent of GDP in EU-10. The projections therefore show that "if healthy life expectancy (falling morbidity rates) evolve broadly in line with change in age-specific life expectancy...then the expected increase in spending on health care due to ageing would be approximately halved" (ibid., p. 16).

The epidemiological approach applied to Australia

One weakness of the actuarial approach is that it does not take into account the disease profile of the country and its future evolution and the cost of treating each disease. The data required for this are very difficult to obtain even in developed countries, let alone developing ones. If such data were available, an alternative method could be used, namely, the epidemiological approach, whereby disease rates and the costs of treatment are projected into the future. A study for Australia (Vos and others, 2007) derived a consistent set of five epidemiological parameters for each disease, with those parameters being incidence, prevalence, remission (that is to say, cure), average duration and excess mortality. The study found that total health expenditure is expected to increase by 127 per cent in the period from 2002-2003 to 2032-2033 from A$71 billion to A$162 billion. The Australian Treasury forecasts that over the same period GDP in real terms would increase by 97 per cent (or 2.3 per cent per annum); as a result, health expenditure is projected to increase from 9.4 per cent of GDP in 2002-2003 to 10.8 per cent in 2032-2033. Of the total increase of $91 billion, about $17.7 billion would be on account of increased demand for residential long-term care (a cost increase of 242 per cent), with neurologic cases accounting for 47 per cent of long-term care expenditures in 2032-2033.

The projected cost increase is largest for diabetes (by 401 per cent), largely owing to expected growth in the prevalence of obesity, followed by that for neurologic disorders (280 per cent), musculoskeletal conditions (164 per cent) and dental services (144 per cent). Expenditures on preventing cardiovascular disease through blood pressure lowering drugs and lipid lowering drugs are projected to increase by 96 per cent, leading to an overall change in cardiovascular expenditure of 105 per cent. Increases in cancer (84 per cent), injuries (67 per cent) and maternal and neonatal services (41 and 42 per cent) would be comparatively low.

The study estimates that of the $91 billion growth in total health expenditure, $29 billion (32 per cent of the increase) will be due to the ageing of the population and $28 billion (31 per cent) to normal overall population growth (Australia's population is forecast to increase from 19.9 million in 2003 to 26.6 million in 2033) (see figure VI.6). Excess price inflation ($19 billion), changes in the number of health services provided per case ($14 billion) and, to a lesser extent, the proportion of cases treated ($1.3 billion) would account for smaller increases in overall expenditure. Projected health expenditures would be $1.3 billion higher if disease trends were ignored. Favourable trends in the disease rates of cardiovascular disease, chronic obstructive pulmonary disease, cancers and injuries over the period would lead to a reduction in expenditure of $5.5 billion, countered by the steep increase in the projected cases of diabetes and other diseases estimated, which would result in an expenditure increase of $4.0 billion (see figure VI.6).

The study concedes that "in most cases the changes into the future have been estimated according to what has happened with a particular disease in the past, but the future does not necessarily repeat the past. For instance, developments in health technologies and health service utilisation may drastically alter the outlook for some diseases" (Vos and others, 2007, p. 35). Given the forces driving medical research and advances in medical technologies referred to

Figure VI.6.
Australia: decomposition of projected change in health expenditure for all projected disease patterns between the base year of 2002-2003 and 2012-2013, 2022-2023 and 2032-2033

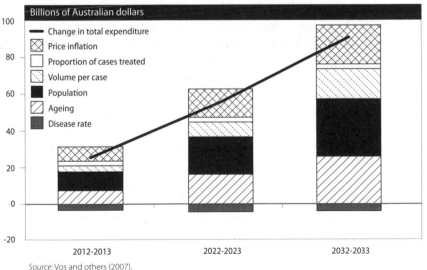

Source: Vos and others (2007).

earlier which now include considerable work on stem cells, it is highly likely that significant advances will be made over the next thirty years and that, indeed, the outlook for some diseases could be completely different. Nevertheless, an increase in overall expenditure on health of 1.4 percentage points of GDP (from 9.4 to 10.8) between 2002-2003 and 2032-2033, especially when the size of the economy is expected to double in the same period, would seem quite manageable for a wealthy country like Australia.

The epidemiological approach can help identify some areas where countries can make progress in combating disease. In Australia, almost all the gains in life expectancy in recent decades have occurred in just two areas: tobacco-related disease and cardiovascular health. Thus, measures to discourage tobacco use should be vigorously pursued in developing countries. In regard to cardiovascular health, the Disease Control Priorities Project in developing countries (see Jamison and others, 2006) indicated that in those countries the "poly-pill"—a combination of aspirin and blood pressure- and cholesterol-lowering agents produced cheaply as a generic drug—would be an affordable and cost-effective intervention with a sizeable impact on reducing the disease burden.

Projections of the impact of ageing on future expenditures on long-term care

In the developed countries, the obligation of the Government to contribute towards long-term care has budgetary implications; and attempts have been made, using the actuarial or the epidemiological approach, to provide estimates for the future share of GDP that will be absorbed by public long-term care costs. As shown previously, Canada, for example, allocated about 35 per cent of total per capita health expenditure for those aged 85 years or over in 2000-2001 for institutions other than hospitals. Whereas health-care services aim at changing a health-care condition, long-term care aims at making the current condition of ill health bearable and so is treated separately.

Vos and others (2007) project that for Australia health expenditure (excluding aged long-term care) will increase by 114 per cent between 2002-2003 and 2032-2033, while that for residential aged care will grow by 242 per cent during the same period. Neurologic-related expenditure associated with dementia is expected to dominate this large increase. In the EU-15 countries, it has been estimated that the costs of public long-term care will rise from 0.9 per cent of GDP in 2004 to 1.5 per cent in 2050. In EU-10, these costs are expected to increase from 0.2 to 0.5 per cent of GDP in the same period (European Commission, Directorate-General for Economic and Financial Affairs, 2006, p. 10). According to OECD estimates, these costs are expected to increase on average from 1.1 per cent of GDP in 2005 in member countries to between 1.9 and 3.9 per cent in 2050, depending on the assumptions made (Organisation for Economic Co-operation and Development, 2006b, pp. 65-72). The pure ageing effect is estimated to be 1.7 percentage points of GDP.

Public spending on long-term health care varies greatly across countries. The Scandinavian Governments are among the highest spenders. Public spending on long-term care in Denmark, for instance, was 2.6 per cent of GDP in 2005, well above the OECD average of 1.1 per cent (Organisation for Economic Co-operation and Development, 2006b, p. 65). This public spending priority is part of extended social welfare provisioning. This system is sustained by high tax rates and high labour-force participation, both for men and for women, a relatively late retirement age and a higher rate of employment for those over age 60 than the EU average. These high activity levels sustain the tax base, but also require high investment in services such as childcare and services for older persons. In a way, "the services support the employment which supports the services" (United Kingdom, 1999, Research Vol. 1, chapter 6, p. 178).

It should be noted that the Scandinavian countries are further into their demographic transition and thus the growth in demand for long-term care as a result of ageing between 2005 and 2050 is expected to be below the OECD average (Organisation for Economic Co-operation and Development, 2006b, p. 65). In the Republic of Korea, in contrast, rapid ageing is projected to lead to a rise in the costs of long-term care from 0.3 to 4.7 per cent of GDP between 2005 and 2050. For Mexico, where spending was 0.1 per cent of GDP in 2005, the pure ageing effect has been calculated as adding 2.6 per cent of GDP to public long-term care costs. These figures are illustrative of the magnitudes of changes in the public cost of the provision of long-term care brought about by ageing, but these costs could be offset over time by reductions in the need for such care as a result of healthy ageing and advances in preventive and rehabilitative medicine.

CONCLUSIONS

The demographic transition towards ageing societies is almost universally accompanied by an epidemiological transition from the predominance of infectious diseases to the predominance of chronic diseases. Both transitions have been well under way in developed countries and are now under way in developing ones. Increased longevity in developing countries is the result of improved nutrition, sanitation and hygiene and, more recently, the rapid spread of medical knowledge and its application in medical practices. In the developed countries, increased longevity has been accompanied by longer healthy life expectancy and the compression of morbidity. However, a positive correlation between longevity and healthy life expectancy is not so clear in developing countries, where people are more likely to spend a greater portion of their total—and shorter—life in poor health.

This chapter has demonstrated that population ageing challenges the existing national health systems in many parts of the world. Developed countries are concerned with the possibility of the future strain on national and budgetary resources as a consequence of increased demand for health- and long-term care services by an ageing population. The challenge for many developing countries is larger: they have not yet addressed adequately public-health goals such as sanitation, clean water, better nutrition, reproductive health education and mass vaccination whose achievement results, in particular, in the lowering of infant and maternal mortality rates and of the incidence of HIV/AIDS and tuberculosis. While grappling with these challenges, which largely impact upon the younger populations, developing countries are also confronting rapid population ageing, which is leading to greater demands for health-care services by older persons.

In examining such developments, this chapter has argued that the challenge they pose is large, but not insurmountable. It has shown that population ageing contributes to rising health-care spending, but is not necessarily the most significant cost-driver: By itself, its impact would be reflected in no more than a few percentage points of GDP. Indeed, the experience of many countries suggests that changes in health-seeking behaviour, in productivity in the health sector, in prices of pharmaceuticals and medical care services and in health policies are other significant cost-drivers. In the past, new drugs and treatments exerted, on the whole, an upward pressure on the prices of health-care services. Public and private health insurance has, in turn, become more comprehensive in covering such new items, in response to the desire of the public to have access to better health- and medical-care services. Yet, such increased coverage is pushing up insurance costs, and some countries are now introducing mandatory insurance to cover the cost of long-term care. Germany established a new system of statutory long-term care insurance in 1995-1996 (United Kingdom, 1999, Research Vol. 1, chapter 6, p. 182) and Singapore formulated a family-based savings account scheme, called Medisave, in1983 (Phua and Teng, 1998). The establishment of a medical savings account scheme to finance acute care for those over age 65 has been proposed in Hong Kong SAR (Leung, Tin and Chang, 2006, p. 3).

Despite the challenges, policymakers in developed and developing countries are finding that the existing health-care systems can be adapted to cope with population ageing. This chapter has cautioned that the increasing number of cases of chronic illness associated with ageing and disabilities will require significant changes in the composition of overall health expenditures and in the range of services provided. At the same time, rising income levels and increasing awareness by the public of the availability and effectiveness of new medical treatment and medicines will create greater demands for health-care services, particularly in developing countries, irrespective of population ageing. These factors are likely to push up medical expenditures.

This chapter, looking beyond cost considerations, has argued that population ageing is most likely to affect the health-care system in two ways. First, the increase in the total number of cases of chronic illness and the larger number of persons with disabilities will require large shifts in health-care inputs and the acquisition by health-care professionals and workers of new skills. As noted here, per capita health expenditures on older persons in developing countries are significantly lower than those in developed countries, partly reflecting the shortage of access to the nursing, palliative care and more intensive medical treatment that are widely available to older persons in developed countries. It is suggested that developing countries need to expand such health-care services for older persons and to expand access through a combination of new tax sources and public pensions so as to cover high medical costs at older ages.

Second, there is the concern over how to provide long-term care for those whose health conditions are irreversible. The challenge is to find solutions that preserve the dignity and independence of those who need care, while allowing them to maintain contact with a familiar environment and not to be fearful of the consequences of entering long-term care, such as the loss of their house or other assets. The traditional family structure and the role of women, who provided much informal care to older persons, especially family members, are changing and the number of children per family is declining in many parts of the world. It will thus become increasingly difficult for many developing countries to maintain the current forms of informal long-term care arrangements, which are mainly provided by the family or friends of older persons or by their community. While every society should build a long-term care system in a manner that accords with its own traditions and the best interests of those needing such care, the trend has been to seek to provide care to persons in their own home or community. Where home care is not possible, a home-like environment in which the number of residents is not so great as to break the personal bonds between caregivers and residents is considered to be desirable.

However, it is of interest to policymakers and the general public to know how much the costs of health and long-term care could grow as a result of the various factors examined above. Projections are based on, among other things, the recent trends of epidemiological patterns and per capita health-care costs by age and sex, together with information on health cost inflation, public expenditures on preventive care and collective health. Several studies show that non-demographic factors have at least as significant an impact on future health expenditure as the demographic factors. The non-demographic factors include medical price inflation, the productivity of the health sector as a whole and new technologies and pharmaceuticals. It has been noted above, however, that these non-demographic factors are also sources of uncertainties in all the projections.

Overall, these projections as well as the experience of many countries indicate that, although population ageing will definitely influence health-care expenditures, it need not consume an unsustainably large share of national income in the future. What the projections into the future and the recent trends show is that population ageing will not only alter the composition of health-care spending by age, but also require the health system to introduce or to strengthen, if they are already in place, certain types of medical and long-term care services so as to cope with the increasing number of cases of chronic illness and disabilities. Policymakers in developing countries need to upgrade the existing health-care systems to encompass preventive measures, such as those aimed at reducing smoking and excessive alcohol intake and encouraging exercise and rehabilitative regimens for chronic illness, as well as palliative treatment, while improving the provision of effective essential health care for all and of those public services that improve health and reduce infection.

The demographic and epidemiological transitions will pose challenges to health-care financing for developing countries which have to deal with the double burden of disease that is the need to combat communicable diseases while at the same time meeting the rising health demand associated with non-communicable diseases and population ageing. To meet these challenges, developing countries need to pool the financial risks associated with poor health or morbidity by adopting better-organized schemes, including insurance schemes. At the present time, private payments account for a major share of total health expenditure in developing countries. Because the scope for private insurance schemes is still limited in many developing countries, Governments should initiate risk-pooling mechanisms. In middle-income developing countries, there may be greater scope for combining social health insurance with private health insurance schemes to provide universal coverage for all, including older persons who have never been insured previously. For low-income developing countries, however, the expansion of health-care systems also needs a combination of different private and public mechanisms; but if financing this expansion risks crowding out other social goals, external financing could be needed for the formation of an ultimately self-sustaining health-care system.

With population ageing, the demand for medical practitioners in developed countries is set to rise. This demand must not be met through the brain drain of skilled medical staff from the developing countries. Developing countries need to strengthen their own health delivery systems, including a sufficient growth in the supply of qualified health-care personnel. This will require action in both the developed countries and the developing countries to increase the resources available for the training of medical personnel. The developed countries should expand their teaching facilities in order to train domestic medical students and also students from developing countries. They can also take steps like those taken by the United Kingdom through the 2002 Commonwealth Code of Practice for the International Recruitment of Health Workers to encourage increase domestic health-care training and eliminate recruitment in poor countries without the full approval of the host Government (Garrett, 2007, p. 31). The developing countries, too, need to expand their medical training programmes to meet present unmet needs and the new and rising demands that population ageing is already creating.

Notes to Chapter VI

1   Comprising all African countries except Egypt, Libyan Arab Jamahiriya, Morocco, Somalia, Sudan and Tunisia.

2   Comprising Bangladesh, Bhutan, Democratic People's Republic of Korea, India, Indonesia, Maldives, Myanmar, Nepal, Sri Lanka, Thailand and Timor-Leste.

3   Comprising Afghanistan, Bahrain, Djibouti, Egypt, Iran (Islamic Republic of), Iraq, Jordan, Kuwait, Lebanon, Libyan Arab Jamahiriya, Morocco, Oman, Pakistan, Qatar, Saudi Arabia, Somalia, Sudan, Syrian Arab Republic, Tunisia, United Arab Emirates and Yemen.

4   In fact, more than half of all deaths in this region have been due to cardiovascular disease. The region comprises all of the Commonwealth of Independent States (CIS), Europe (including Turkey) and Israel.

5   The difference is calculated using market exchange rates to convert costs to United States dollars; when purchasing power parity dollars are used, per capita health expenditure in sub-Saharan Africa is about 33 times less (see World Bank (2006b), table A1.1).

6   These data are not shown in the table but see, for instance, Organisation for Economic Co-operation and Development (2006b, figure 2.1).

7   The rest was spent on pharmaceuticals and health-care supplies.

8   See, for example, Levinsky and others (2001).

9   This is based on intensive care unit admission and the use of ventilators and pulmonary artery monitors and of cardiac catheterization and dialysis.

10   The analysis here is largely based on Fries (2005) and Gnanasekaran (2006).

11   Further information available from http://www.helpageindia.org/daycarecentres.php.

12   "Home care for the chronically ill" under the Mexican Institute for Social Security, the main social security institute in the country, is an example of such a strategy (see World Health Organization, 2002d).

13   Under the Mexican Institute for Social Security, only 8 per cent of total users were persons aged 65 years or over (World Health Organization, 2002d).

14   The countries examined were Austria, Canada, Germany, Israel, Italy, Japan, the Netherlands, Sweden and the United States (see World Health Organization, 2000; and Brodsky and others, 2002).

15   The countries examined were China, Costa Rica, Indonesia, Lebanon, Lithuania, Mexico, the Republic of Korea, Sri Lanka, Thailand and Ukraine.

16   Home health care refers to situations where doctors or nurses visit patients at home.

17   Productivity is measured by the non-quality-adjusted unit costs, that is to say, recurrent expenditures at the facility level divided by the volume of units of services for outpatient visits and inpatient admissions. A decline in unit costs is regarded as a productivity improvement.

18   These assumptions include, for the baseline scenario, increases in unit costs of health over and above average inflation of 0.8, 1.6, and 1.2 per cent per year for, respectively, public, private and other costs/charges. The baseline scenario further assumes a constant growth rate in the use of services of 0.2 per cent per annum.

STATISTICAL ANNEX

Contents

A. FIGURES

Figure A.1.
Trends in three types of dependency ratios for developing regions, 1950-2050

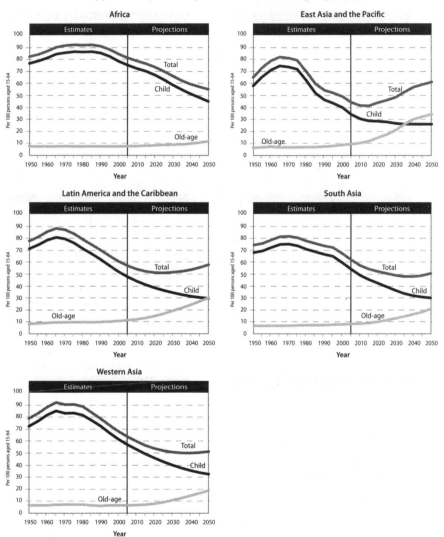

Source: United Nations (2005a).

Note:

(1) The graphs show estimates (until 2005) and medium-variant projections (after 2005).

(2) The total dependency ratio is defined as the ratio of the sum of the population aged 0-14 and the population aged 65 years or over to the population aged 15-64. The child dependency ratio is the ratio of the population aged 0-14 to that aged 15-64. The old-age dependency ratio is the ratio of the population aged 65 years or over to that aged 15-64.

Figure A.2.
Trends in three types of dependency ratios for developed countries and regions and for economies in transition, 1950-2050

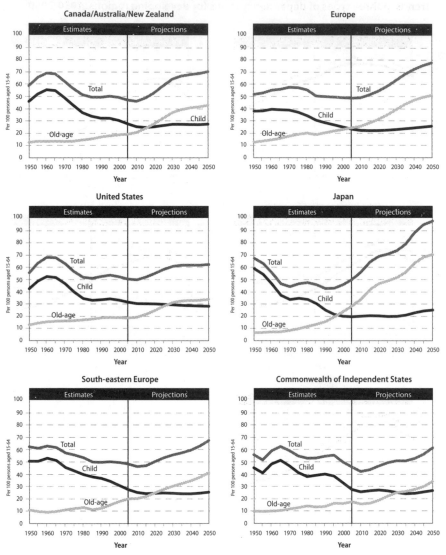

Source: United Nations (2005a).

Note:

(1) The graphs show estimates (until 2005) and medium-variant projections (after 2005).

(2) The total dependency ratio is defined as the ratio of the sum of the population aged 0-14 and the population aged 65 years or over to the population aged 15-64. The child dependency ratio is the ratio of the population aged 0-14 to that aged 15-64. The old-age dependency ratio is the ratio of the population aged 65 years or over to that aged 15-64.

Figure A.3.
Distribution of the working-age population by age group for developing regions, 1950-2050

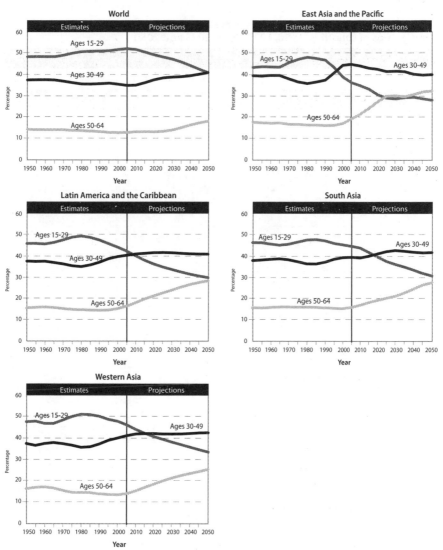

Source: United Nations (2005a).
Note: The graphs show estimates (until 2005) and medium-variant projections (after 2005).

B. TABLES

Table A.1.
Population by broad age group for selected countries and groups of countries, 1950, 1975, 2005, 2025 and 2050

Age group	Millions					Percentage				
	1950	1975	2005	2025	2050	1950	1975	2005	2025	2050
Developed countries										
Europe										
0-14	96	109	80	73	72	25.1	23.7	16.0	14.5	14.8
15-24	61	71	63	53	49	16.0	15.6	12.7	10.4	10.2
25-59	175	198	248	232	193	45.8	43.1	49.5	45.9	39.9
60+	50	81	110	148	170	13.1	17.6	21.9	29.2	35.1
Total	382	459	502	505	485	100.0	100.0	100.0	100.0	100.0
65+	34	57	84	112	139	8.9	12.5	16.6	22.2	28.7
80+	4	9	21	30	52	1.1	2.0	4.1	6.0	10.7
Japan										
0-14	30	27	18	16	15	35.4	24.3	14.0	12.5	13.4
15-24	16	17	14	12	10	19.6	15.4	11.0	9.4	9.1
25-59	31	54	62	54	40	37.2	48.6	48.6	42.9	35.8
60+	6	13	34	44	47	7.7	11.7	26.3	35.2	41.7
Total	84	112	128	125	112	100.0	100.0	100.0	100.0	100.0
65+	4	9	25	36	40	4.9	7.9	19.7	29.1	35.9
80+	0.4	1	6	13	17	0.4	1.1	4.8	10.6	15.3
United States of America										
0-14	43	55	62	65	68	27.0	25.2	20.8	18.6	17.3
15-24	23	41	42	46	48	14.9	18.7	14.2	13.1	12.1
25-59	72	91	144	156	175	45.6	41.3	48.3	44.5	44.2
60+	20	33	50	83	104	12.5	14.8	16.7	23.8	26.4
Total	158	220	298	350	395	100.0	100.0	100.0	100.0	100.0
65+	13	23	37	62	82	8.3	10.5	12.3	17.7	20.6
80+	2	5	11	14	29	1.1	2.1	3.6	4.1	7.3
Canada, Australia and New Zealand										
0-14	7	11	10	11	12	28.5	27.0	18.6	16.4	15.9
15-24	4	7	8	7	8	15.4	18.7	13.7	11.0	11.0
25-59	11	17	28	31	32	44.2	41.8	50.1	45.9	42.0
60+	3	5	10	18	23	11.9	12.5	17.6	26.8	31.0
Total	24	40	56	67	76	100.0	100.0	100.0	100.0	100.0
65+	2	3	7	13	19	7.9	8.6	12.9	20.1	24.8
80+	0.3	0.6	2	3	7	1.1	1.6	3.5	4.9	9.4

Table A.1 (cont'd)	Millions					Percentage				
Age group	1950	1975	2005	2025	2050	1950	1975	2005	2025	2050
Economies in transition										
Commonwealth of Independent States										
0-14	51	66	53	47	40	28.9	26.5	19.0	17.8	16.6
15-24	36	45	49	33	26	20.4	18.4	17.8	12.4	11.0
25-59	71	104	133	129	104	40.8	42.1	47.7	48.6	43.3
60+	17	32	43	56	70	10.0	12.9	15.5	21.2	29.1
Total	175	247	278	266	239	100.0	100.0	100.0	100.0	100.0
65+	12	21	34	40	51	6.7	8.6	12.2	15.0	21.1
80+	2	3	5	7	13	1.0	1.3	1.9	2.7	5.3
South-eastern Europe										
0-14	5	6	5	4	3	31.0	27.3	18.7	16.3	15.3
15-24	3	4	4	3	2	20.2	18.3	15.0	11.2	10.6
25-59	6	9	12	11	9	38.7	42.8	48.1	48.0	42.2
60+	2	2	4	6	7	10.2	11.6	18.2	24.5	31.8
Total	16	21	24	24	22	100.0	100.0	100.0	100.0	100.0
65+	1	2	3	4	5	7.1	8.2	13.7	18.2	24.6
80+	0.2	0.2	0.5	0.9	1	1.1	0.9	2.0	3.7	6.9
Developing countries										
Latin America and the Caribbean										
0-14	67	133	168	163	141	40.0	41.3	30.0	23.3	18.1
15-24	31	63	106	110	99	18.6	19.6	18.8	15.8	12.6.
25-59	59	105	238	323	354	35.4	32.6	42.4	46.4	45.2
60+	10	21	49	101	189	6.0	6.5	8.8	14.5	24.1
Total	167	322	561	697	783	100.0	100.0	100.0	100.0	100.0
65+	6	14	34	70	144	3.7	4.3	6.1	10.1	18.4
80+	0.7	2	7	15	40	0.4	0.6	1.2	2.1	5.2
East Asia and the Pacific										
0-14	270	525	466	428	369	35.1	40.1	23.8	19.3	16.4
15-24	142	253	339	286	253	18.5	19.3	17.3	12.9	11.3
25-59	302	447	958	1 104	983	39.3	34.1	48.8	49.8	43.8
60+	54	86	199	401	637	7.1	6.6	10.1	18.1	28.4
Total	768	1 311	1 961	2 217	2 242	100.0	100.0	100.0	100.0	100.0
65+	33	55	137	271	482	4.3	4.2	7.0	12.2	21.5
80+	2	6	20	43	137	0.3	0.5	1.0	2.0	6.1

Table A.1 (cont'd)	Millions					Percentage				
Age group	1950	1975	2005	2025	2050	1950	1975	2005	2025	2050
South Asia										
0-14	186	341	515	528	479	38.8	40.6	33.2	26.0	19.8
15-24	91	159	307	343	325	19.1	19.0	19.8	16.9	13.4
25-59	173	288	617	933	1 151	36.1	34.4	39.7	46.0	47.6
60+	29	51	114	224	465	6.0	6.0	7.4	11.1	19.2
Total	479	839	1 553	2 029	2 419	100.0	100.0	100.0	100.0	100.0
65+	17	31	76	149	329	3.6	3.7	4.9	7.3	13.6
80+	1	3	11	23	69	0.3	0.3	0.7	1.1	2.9
Western Asia										
0-14	17	38	69	79	79	40.4	43.7	34.8	28.1	21.4
15-24	8	17	38	49	53	19.4	19.3	19.4	17.5	14.5
25-59	15	27	79	127	172	34.2	31.2	39.8	45.0	46.8
60+	3	5	12	26	63	6.1	5.9	6.1	9.4	17.3
Total	43	87	198	282	367	100.0	100.0	100.0	100.0	100.0
65+	2	3	8	17	46	3.6	3.8	4.1	6.0	12.4
80+	0.1	0.3	1	2	9	0.3	0.3	0.5	0.8	2.4
Africa										
0-14	94	187	376	495	556	42.0	44.9	41.5	36.9	28.7
15-24	42	79	189	270	350	18.9	19.0	20.8	20.0	18.1
25-59	76	129	294	494	838	33.9	31.1	32.5	36.7	43.3
60+	12	21	47	86	193	5.3	5.0	5.2	6.4	10.0
Total	224	416	906	1 344	1 937	100.0	100.0	100.0	100.0	100.0
65+	7	13	31	57	129	3.2	3.1	3.4	4.2	6.7
80+	0.6	1	4	7	20	0.3	0.3	0.4	0.6	1.0

Source: United Nations (2005a).

Note: The table shows estimates (until 2005) and medium-variant projections (after 2005).

Table A.2.
Dependency ratios according to different projection variants for the world and groups of countries, 2025 and 2050

	Type of ratio	2005 estimates	2025			2050		
			Low	Medium	High	Low	Medium	High
World	Total	55	46	53	60	52	57	63
	Child	44	30	37	44	23	32	40
	Old-age	11	16	16	16	29	25	22
Developed countries	Total	49	53	59	65	71	72	75
	Child	26	19	25	31	19	27	35
	Old-age	23	34	34	34	52	45	40
Economies in transition	Total	46	42	49	56	59	61	66
	Child	28	19	26	33	18	27	36
	Old-age	18	23	23	22	41	34	29
Developing countries	Total	57	46	52	59	50	55	61
	Child	48	32	39	46	24	32	41
	Old-age	9	13	13	13	26	23	20

Source: United Nations (2005a).

Note: The total dependency ratio is defined as the ratio of the sum of the population aged 0-14 and that aged 65 years or over to the population aged 15-64. The child dependency ratio is the ratio of the population aged 0-14 to that aged 15-64. The old-age dependency ratio is the ratio of the population aged 65 years or over to that aged 15-64. The ratios presented in the table are multiplied by 100.

Table A.3.
Dependency ratios according to different definitions for the world and groups of countries, 1950, 1975, 2005, 2025 and 2050

Type of ratio	A. Old-age dependency threshold = 65+[a]					B. Old-age dependency threshold = 60+[b]				
	1950	1975	2005	2025	2050	1950	1975	2005	2025	2050
World										
Total	65	74	55	53	57	74	83	63	65	72
Child	57	64	44	37	32	60	67	46	40	35
Old-age	9	10	11	16	25	14	16	17	25	37
Developed countries										
Total	54	55	49	59	72	65	67	67	78	92
Child	42	38	26	25	27	45	41	41	28	30
Old-age	13	17	23	34	45	20	26	26	50	62
Economies in transition										
Total	56	54	46	49	61	64	65	53	64	84
Child	45	41	28	26	27	48	44	29	29	30
Old-age	11	13	18	23	34	16	21	24	35	54
Developing countries										
Total	71	82	57	52	55	79	90	64	63	69
Child	65	75	48	39	32	67	78	50	42	35
Old-age	7	7	9	13	23	11	12	13	21	34

Source: United Nations (2005a).

Note:

(1) The ratios presented in the table are multiplied by 100.

(2) The table shows estimates (until 2005) and medium-variant projections (after 2005).

a The total dependency ratio is defined as the ratio of the sum of the population aged 0-14 and that aged 65 years or over to the population aged 15-64. The child dependency ratio is the ratio of the population aged 0-14 to that aged 15-64. The old-age dependency ratio is the ratio of the population aged 65 years or over to that aged 15-64.

b The total dependency ratio is defined as the ratio of the sum of the population aged 0-14 and that aged 60 years or over to the population aged 15-59. The child dependency ratio is the ratio of the population aged 0-14 to that aged 15-59. The old-age dependency ratio is the ratio of the population aged 60 years or over to that aged 15-59.

Table A.4.
**Selected economies in transition and developing countries:
cost estimate of universal old-age pensions, 2005 and 2050**

Percentage of GDP					
Country	Cost of universal pension - 2005 (percentage of GDP)	Experiment I: Cost of universal pension at $1 per day - 2050 (percentage of GDP)	2005 GDP per capita ($PPP)	Universal pension ($1 per day) - share of 2005 GDP per capita	Average GDP PPP growth, 1990-2005[a]
Kuwait	0.07	0.18	16 903	2.16	3.94
Bahrain	0.08	0.11	19 477	1.87	4.23
Oman	0.10	0.16	14 541	2.51	3.98
Saudi Arabia	0.13	0.22	12 874	2.84	3.30
Singapore	0.17	0.07	26 730	1.37	5.95
Botswana	0.20	0.03	9 472	3.85	4.85
Israel	0.23	0.12	21 074	71.73	3.90
South Africa	0.23	0.17	10 809	3.38	2.15
Malaysia	0.25	0.13	10 203	3.58	5.70
Korea, Republic of	0.27	0.08	18 634	1.96	5.07
Namibia	0.28	0.13	7 029	5.19	3.93
Barbados	0.30	0.39	16 066	2.27	1.52
Trinidad and Tobago	0.31	0.15	12 632	2.89	4.02
Costa Rica	0.32	0.23	9 560	3.82	4.22
Mauritius	0.32	0.15	11 029	3.31	4.39
Mexico	0.32	0.48	8 952	4.08	2.46
Dominican Republic	0.33	0.22	6 898	5.29	4.48
Iran (Islamic Republic of)	0.33	0.31	7 186	5.08	4.12
Gabon	0.36	0.45	6 255	5.83	1.96
Algeria	0.37	0.64	6 419	5.69	2.64
Cape Verde	0.38	0.25	5 287	6.90	5.57
Chile	0.40	0.14	10 674	3.42	5.43
Argentina	0.41	0.22	12 494	2.92	3.33
Colombia	0.41	0.58	6 738	5.42	2.56
Turkey	0.41	0.33	7 108	5.14	3.60
Jordan	0.42	0.40	4 381	8.33	4.42
Kazakhstan	0.42	0.49	9 809	3.72	1.39
Brazil	0.43	0.54	7 494	4.87	2.53
Tunisia	0.43	0.27	7 362	4.96	4.36
Panama	0.47	0.27	6 775	5.39	4.52
Philippines	0.49	0.75	4 487	8.14	2.71
Paraguay	0.50	1.19	4 118	8.86	1.93
Thailand	0.50	0.23	7 681	4.75	4.25
Venezuela (Bolivarian Republic of)	0.50	0.96	5 507	6.63	1.99

Table A.4 (cont'd)

Country	Cost of universal pension - 2005 (percentage of GDP)	Experiment I: Cost of universal pension at $1 per day - 2050 (percentage of GDP)	2005 GDP per capita ($PPP)	Universal pension ($1 per day) - share of 2005 GDP per capita	Average GDP PPP growth, 1990-2005[a]
Syrian Arab Republic	0.51	0.62	3 368	10.84	4.23
Nicaragua	0.52	0.93	3 443	10.60	2.93
Peru	0.53	0.4	5 375	6.79	3.90
Guatemala	0.55	0.58	4 044	9.02	3.25
Angola	0.56	0.82	2 549	14.32	2.42
Belarus	0.61	0.43	11 089	3.29	1.49
China	0.63	0.21	6 385	5.72	9.01
Morocco	0.64	1.00	3 881	9.41	2.49
Papua New Guinea	0.64	0.59	2 261	16.14	4.05
Guyana	0.65	1.18	4 150	8.80	1.19
Lebanon	0.65	0.23	5 777	6.32	7.03
El Salvador	0.68	0.61	4 099	8.90	3.57
Egypt	0.71	0.60	3 684	9.91	3.77
Uruguay	0.72	0.49	8 849	4.12	2.15
Azerbaijan	0.74	0.27	4 572	7.98	5.87
Honduras	0.75	1.42	2 704	13.5	2.45
Ecuador	0.76	1.17	3 998	9.13	2.15
Indonesia	0.78	0.50	3 906	9.35	3.93
Romania	0.78	0.80	8 987	4.06	0.87
Uzbekistan	0.78	1.22	2 887	12.64	2.61
Croatia	0.85	0.88	9 435	3.87	0.53
Cameroon	0.87	1.21	2 357	15.49	1.91
Albania	0.89	0.75	4 931	7.40	2.38
Armenia	0.92	1.17	5 767	6.33	0.89
Djibouti	0.93	3.25	1 853	19.69	0.54
Ghana	0.93	0.66	2 230	16.37	4.16
Pakistan	0.93	0.71	2 286	15.97	4.29
Jamaica	0.95	1.39	3 901	9.36	0.98
India	0.96	0.40	3 029	12.05	5.37
Bolivia	0.98	1.01	2 503	14.58	3.18
Mauritania	1.00	0.52	1 932	18.89	4.89
Sudan	1.00	0.47	2 060	17.72	5.44
Viet Nam	1.01	0.53	2 696	13.54	6.51
Bulgaria	1.03	1.16	7 930	4.60	0.02
Uganda	1.03	0.66	1 356	26.91	5.75
Sri Lanka	1.04	0.49	3 732	9.78	4.28
Bangladesh	1.06	0.78	1 944	18.78	4.38
Lesotho	1.09	0.14	2 490	14.66	4.82
Bosnia and Herzegovina	1.1	0.18	6 368	5.73	12.34

Table A.4 (cont'd)					
Country	Cost of universal pension - 2005 (percentage of GDP)	Experiment I: Cost of universal pension at $1 per day - 2050 (percentage of GDP)	2005 GDP per capita ($PPP)	Universal pension ($1 per day) - share of 2005 GDP per capita	Average GDP ppp growth, 1990-2005[a]
Guinea	1.14	1.1	1 795	20.33	3.12
Senegal	1.14	1.37	1 558	23.42	3.21
Kenya	1.17	3.1	1 282	28.48	1.77
Rwanda	1.17	2.62	1 228	29.72	1.73
Comoros	1.21	4.06	1 292	28.26	1.47
Gambia	1.21	1.42	1 797	20.31	2.89
Chad	1.23	0.48	1 399	26.09	-6.61
Togo	1.36	2.65	1 301	28.06	2.10
Burkina Faso	1.39	1.11	1 106	32.99	4.03
Côte d'Ivoire	1.42	3.90	1 351	27.02	0.66
Nigeria	1.46	1.15	1 193	30.61	3.49
Mozambique	1.55	0.48	1 223	29.83	6.12
Yemen	1.59	1.21	840	43.44	5.73
Mali	1.61	1.00	958	38.09	4.54
Congo	1.62	1.95	1 017	35.91	2.74
Nepal	1.64	1.34	1 281	28.50	3.94
Niger	1.68	3.64	711	51.37	2.18
Benin	1.69	1.62	933	39.12	4.08
Eritrea	1.78	1.48	813	44.91	4.26
Zambia	2.05	2.41	829	44.05	1.86
Central African Republic	2.14	3.34	1 035	35.26	0.70
Madagascar	2.29	5.19	768	47.52	1.62
Ethiopia	2.35	2.58	723	50.46	2.95
Sierra Leone	2.52	0.87	796	45.84	0.48
Guinea-Bissau	2.71	6.86	640	57.05	0.82
Tanzania (United Republic of)	2.94	2.18	632	57.79	3.62
Malawi	3.08	2.43	552	66.10	2.92

Source: UN/DESA.

Total number of countries: 100.

a   Projection periods for the following countries vary from those for the rest owing to considerations of data availability:

Bahrain	1990-2004
Barbados	1990-1999
Bosnia and Herzegovina	1994-2005
Eritrea	1992-2005
Kuwait	1995-2004
Oman	1990-2004
Uzbekistan	1992-2005.

Table A.5.
Selected parameters for, and impact on poverty of, non-contributory social pensions, selected countries

Country	Age eligibility	Universal (U) or means-tested (M)	Amount paid monthly		Percentage of people over over 60 receiving a pension	Annual basic pension as percentage of income per capita (data year)	Percentage GDP cost of social pension (circa 2000-2002)	Impact on poverty, circa 2000-2006
Argentina	70+	M	US$ 88	273 pesos	6	22 (2000)	0.23	Incidence of poverty dropped 31 per cent in households receiving tax-financed pension, while incidence of extreme poverty dropped 67 per cent (1997 data)
Bangladesh	57+	M	US$ 2	165 taka	16[a]	7 (2003-2004)	0.03	Increased expenditure on food, health and microinvestments (HelpAge International/Asia Pacific Regional Development Centre (2006))
Bolivia[b]	65+	U	US$ 18	150 bolivianos	69	23 (2004)	1.3	Beneficiary households increased food consumption by 6.3 per cent, with positive effects in rural areas in food consumption, output increase, and children's schooling
Botswana	65+	U	US$ 27	166 pula	85	9 (1999/00)	0.4	
Brazil: *Benefício de Prestação Continuada*	67+	M	US$140	300 reais	5	33 (2003)	0.2	Reduced to18 per cent probability of poverty of household members and increased income of the poorest by 100 per cent and 5 per cent
Brazil: *Previdência Rural*	60+ men 55+ women	M	US$140	300 reais	27	33 (2003)	0.7	Increased school enrolment for girls aged 12-14
Costa Rica	65+	M	US$ 26	13 800 colones	20	10 (2000)	0.18	
India	65+	M	US$ 4	200 rupees	13	10 (1999)[c]	0.01	
Lesotho	70+	U[d]	US$ 21	150 maloti	53	..	1.43	Established in 2004 and data on impact not available yet; first evidence, however, indicates that 65 per cent of pension income was spent on children cared for by older persons (Samson, 2006)

Table A.5 (cont'd)

Country	Age eligibility	Universal (U) or means-tested (M)	Amount paid monthly		Percentage of people over over 60 receiving a pension	Annual basic pension as percentage of income per capita (data year)	Percentage GDP cost of social pension (circa 2000-2002)	Impact on poverty, circa 2000-2006
Mauritius	60+*	U	US$ 60	1 978 rupees	100	18 (1999/00)	2	Poverty rates for older persons (single and couples) were reduced by over 40 per cent
Moldova	62+ men 57+ women	M	US$ 5	63 lei	12	23.3 (1996)	0.08	
Namibia	60+	M	US$ 28	200 dollars	87	17 (1999/00)	0.8	Increased expenditures on food, health, grandchildren's education, agricultural technology, livestock and microenterprises
Nepal	75+	U	US$ 2	150 rupees	12	10 (2001/02)	0.1	
Samoa	65+	U	US$ 33	100 tala	100	22 (2003)	1.4	
South Africa	65+ men 60+ women	M	US$ 109	780 rand	60	32 (2003)	1.4	Reduced the probability that a household member would become poor by 12.5 per cent; and increased by 50 per cent the income of the poorest 5 per cent; and improved children's nutrition, health, education, fostered expansion of microenterprises, and stimulated intergenerational living arrangements
Tajikistan	63+ men 58+ women	M	US$ 4	12 somoni	..	..		
Thailand	60+	M	US$ 8	300 baht	16	15ᶠ	1.3ᶠ	
Uruguay	70+	M	US$ 100	2 499 pesos	10	24 (2001)	0.62	Incidence of poverty and extreme poverty among older persons 70+ has been low owing to pension coverage of 75 per cent of those in this age group
Viet Nam	60+	M	US$ 6	100 000 dong	2	5 (1998)	0.02	
Viet Nam	90+	U	US$ 6	100 000 dong	0.5	..	0.0005	

Table A.5 (cont'd)

Sources: UN/DESA estimations; HelpAge International (2006b); Willmore (2006, table 2); Palacios and Sluchynsky (2006, table 1); HelpAge International/Asia Pacific Regional Development Centre (2006); and Johnson and Williamson (2006).

a Percentage of people over age 57 receiving a pension.
b Paid annually.
c From Palacios and Sluchynsky (2006); Willmore (2006) shows a figure of 5 per cent for the year 2000.
d Universal with exceptions, namely, people who already receive a substantial government pension (4 per cent of those who would otherwise be eligible).
e Age eligibility has recently been changed to age 65+.
f Estimated by Palacios and Sluchynsky (2006).

References

Abeykoon, Palitha (2002). Case study: Sri Lanka. In *Long-Term Care in Developing Countries: Ten Case-Studies*, Jenny Brodsky, Jack Habib and Miriam Hirschfeld, eds. Geneva: World Health Organization.

Aboderin, Isabella, A. Kalache, Y. Ben-Shlomo, J.W. Lynch, C.S. Yajnik, D. Kuh and D. Yach (2001). *Life Course Perspectives on Coronary Heart Disease, Stroke and Diabetes: Key Issues and Implications for Policy and Research*. Geneva: World Health Organization.

Aboderin, Isabella (2004). Intergenerational family support and older age economic security in Ghana. In *Living Longer: Ageing, Development and Social Protection*, Peter Lloyd-Sherlock, ed. London: United Nations Research Institute for Social Development and Zed Books, part III, chap. 10.

Acuña, R., and A. Iglesias (2001). Chile's pension reform after 20 years. World Bank Social Protection Discussion Paper, No. 0129. December. Washington, D.C.: World Bank.

Ahearne, Alan G., William L. Griever and Francis E. Warnock (2004). Information costs and home bias: an analysis of U.S. holdings of foreign equities. *Journal of International Economics*, vol. 62, pp. 313-336.

Ando, Alberto, and Franco Modigliani (1963). The "life cycle" hypothesis of saving: aggregate implications and tests. *The American Economic Review*, vol. 53, No. 1, pp. 55-84.

Anetzberger, G.J. (1987). *The Etiology of Elder Abuse by Adult Offspring*. Springfield, Illinois: Charles C. Thomas.

Anetzberger, G.J., J.E. Korbin and C. Austin (1994). Alcoholism and elder abuse. *Journal of Interpersonal Violence*, vol. 9, No. 2, pp. 184-193.

Apt, Nana Araba (1999). Rapid urbanization and living arrangements of older persons in Africa. Centre for Social Policy Studies, University of Ghana, Legon. Available from http://www.un.org/esa/population/publications/bulletin42_43/apt.pdf.

Bank for International Settlements (2006). *BIS Quarterly Review: International Banking and Financial Market Developments*. Basel, Switzerland: Bank for International Settlements. 14 March.

Banks, James, Richard Blundell and Sarah Tanner (1998). Is there a retirement-savings puzzle? *American Economic Review*, vol. 88, No. 4, pp. 769-788.

Barr, Nicholas (2000). Reforming pensions myths, truths and policy choices. IMF Working Paper, No. 00/139. Washington, D.C.: International Monetary Fund. 1 August.

Barr, Nicholas (2006). Pensions: overview of the issues. *Oxford Review of Economic Policy*, vol. 22, No. 1, pp. 1-14.

Barr, Nicholas, and Peter Diamond (2006). The economics of pensions. *Oxford Review of Economic Policy,* vol. 22, No. 1, pp. 15-39.

Barrientos, Armando (2007). Livelihood sources of older people and their households in developing countries. Background paper prepared for *World Economic and Social Survey 2007.* January.

Benjamin, Kirsten, and Sally Wilson (2005). Facts and misconceptions about age, health status and employability. Report No. HSL/2005/20. Buxton, United Kingdom: Health and Safety Laboratory.

Bernheim, B. Douglas, Jonathan Skinner and Steven Weinberg (2001). What accounts for the variation in retirement wealth among U.S. households? *American Economic Review,* vol. 91, No. 4, pp. 832-857.

Black, Sandra E., and Lisa M. Lynch (2004). Workplace practices and the new economy. *FRBSF Economic Letter,* No. 10 (16 April). San Francisco, California: Federal Reserve Bank of San Francisco.

Duncan Boldy, Barbara Horner, Kathy Crouchley, Margaret Davey and Stephen Boylen (2005). Addressing elder abuse: Western Australian case study. *Australian Journal on Ageing,* vol. 24, No. 1, pp. 3-8.

Bongaarts, John, and Zachary Zimmer (2001). Living arrangements of older adults in the developing world: an analysis of DHS Household Surveys. Policy Research Division Working Paper, No. 148. New York: Population Council.

Börsch-Supan, Axel (2004). Global aging: issue, answers, more questions. Michigan Retirement Research Center Working Paper, No. 2004-084. Ann Arbor, Michigan: University of Michigan, Michigan Retirement Research Center. June.

Bosworth, Barry, and Gary Burtless (1998). Population aging and economic performance. In *Private Markets for Public Goods: The Global Dimension,* Barry Bosworth and Gary Burtless, eds. Washington, D.C.: The Brookings Institution Press.

Brodsky, Jenny, Jack Habib and Miriam J. Hirschfeld, eds. (2003). *Key Policy Issues in Long-Term Care.* Geneva: World Health Organization.

Brodsky, Jenny, J. Habib, M. Hirschfeld and B. Siegel (2002). Care of the frail elderly in developed and developing countries: the experience and challenges. *Aging Clinical and Experimental Research,* vol. 14, No. 4, pp. 279-286.

Brodsky, Jenny (2003). Choosing overall LTC strategies: a conceptual framework for policy development. In *Key Policy Issues in Long-Term Care,* J. Brodsky, J. Habib and M. Hirschfeld, eds. Geneva: World Health Organization.

Bryant, John, and Audrey Sonerson (2006). Gauging the cost of aging. *Finance & Development,* vol. 43, No. 3 (September).

Chan, A.C.M., D.R. Phillips and F.M.S. Fong (2003). An exploratory study of older persons' computer and internet usage in Hong Kong. Monograph Series, No. 3 (August). Hong Kong: Asia Pacific Institute of Ageing Studies, Lingnan University.

Chan, Angelique, Ann E. Biddlecom Mary Beth Ofstedal and Albert I. Hermalin (2003). The relations between formal and familial support of the elderly in Singapore and Taiwan. Asian MetaCentre Research Paper, No. 9. Asian MetaCentre for Population and Sustainable Development Analysis, Asia Research Institute, National University of Singapore. January.

Cheng, Sheung-Tak, Alfred C.M. Chan and David R. Phillips (2006). The aging situation in Asia and the Pacific: trends and priorities. Unpublished paper to be included in the World Ageing Situation Report 2007.

Cho, A.J., S.K. Kim and Y.K. Kim (2000). Study on the prevalence of elder abuse in Korea. Seoul: Korea Institute for Health and Social Affairs.

Coe, D., and E. Helpman (1995). International R&D spillovers. *European Economic Review*, vol. 39, No. 5, pp. 859-887.

Commission of the European Communities (2006). A year of delivery: The European Commission's 2006 annual progress report on growth and jobs. Available from http://ec.europa.eu/growthandjobs/annual-report-1206_en.htm (accessed 9 May 2007).

Compton, S.A., P. Flanagan and W. Gregg (1997). Elder abuse in people with dementia in Northern Ireland: prevalence and predictors in cases referred to a psychiatry of old age service. *International Journal of Geriatric Psychiatry*, vol. 12, No. 6, pp. 632-635.

Council of the European Union (2000). Establishing a general framework for equal treatment in employment and occupation. Council Directive 2000/78/EC of 27 November 2000. Official Journal of the European Communities, 303/16 (2 December), pp. 0016-0022.

Cowgill, D.O. (1972). A theory of aging in cross-cultural perspective. In *Aging and Modernization*, D. O. Cowgill and L. D. Holmes, eds. New York: Appleton-Century-Crofts.

Coyne, A.C., W.E. Reichman and L.J. Berbig (1993). The relationship between dementia and elder abuse. *American Journal of Psychiatry*, vol. 150, No. 4, pp. 643-646.

Cutler, David (2006). The determinants of mortality. *Journal of Economic Perspectives*, vol. 20, No. 3 (summer).

Cutler, David, Angus Deaton and Adriana Lleras-Muney (2005). The determinants of mortality. Center for Health and Wellbeing (Princeton University) Working Paper, No. 48. Available from http://www.princeton.edu/~rpds/downloads/cutler_deaton_lleras-muney_determinants_mortality_nberdec05.pdf (accessed 22 January 2007).

D'Arista, Jane (2006). The implications of aging for the structure and stability of financial markets. Background paper prepared for *World Economic and Social Survey 2007*. December.

Davis, E. Philip (2002). Pension fund management and international investment: a global perspective. *Pensions Institute Discussion Paper*, No. PI-026. London: The Pensions Institute, Birbeck College, University of London. May.

Davis, E. Philip (2003). Institutional investors, financial market efficiency and financial stability. *Pensions Institute Discussion Paper*, No. PI-0303. London: The Pensions Institute, Birbeck College, University of London. January.

Davis, E. Philip (2005). The role of pension funds as institutional investors in emerging markets. Paper presented at the Korean Development Institute conference "Population Aging in Korea: Economic Impacts and Policy Issues", Seoul, March 2005. April. Available from http://www.brunel.ac.uk/329/efwps/05-18.pdf (accessed 9 May 2007).

Deaton, Angus, S. (2005). Franco Modigliani and the life cycle theory of consumption. Paper presented at the Convegno Internazionale Franco Modigliani, Accademia Nazionale dei Lincei, Rome, 17 and 18 February. March.

Delgado, G.C., and J.C. Cardoso (2000). Principais resultados da pesquisa domiciliar sobre a previdência rural na região sul do Brasil. *Texto para Discussão*, No. 734. Rio de Janeiro: Instituto de Pesquisa Econômica Aplicada.

Demeny, Paul (2000). Policy interventions in response to below-replacement fertility. In *Population Bulletin of the United Nations: Below Replacement Fertility*. Special Issue, Ños. 40/41 (1999), pp. 183-193. Sales No. E.99.XIII.13. New York: United Nations.

de Mesa, Alberto Arenas, and Carmelo Mesa-Lago (2006). The structural pension reform in Chile: effects, comparisons with other Latin American reforms, and lessons. *Oxford Review of Economic Policy*, vol. 22, No. 1, pp. 149-167.

de Mesa, Alberto Arenas, David Bravo, Jere R. Behrman, Olivia S. Mitchell and Petra E. Todd (2006). The Chilean pension reform turns 25: lessons from the Social Protection Survey. Pension Research Council Working Paper PRC WP 2006-9. Philadelphia, Pennsylvania: Pension Research Council, The Wharton School, University of Pennsylvania.

Dercon, Stefan (1998). Wealth, risk and activity choice: cattle in Western Tanzania. *Journal of Development Economics,* vol. 55, No. 1 (February), pp. 1-42.

Diamond, Peter (1996). Government provision and regulation of economic support in old age. In *Annual World Bank Conference on Development Economics 1995*, Boris Pleskovic and Michael Bruno, eds. Washington, D.C.: World Bank.

Diamond, Peter (2004). Social security. *American Economic Review*, vol. 94, No. 1, pp. 1-24.

Dirección General de Estadística y Censos (1994). *Encuesta de Hogares de Propósitos Múltiples*. San José: Ministerio de Economía, Industria y Comercio.

Dorbritz, J., and K. Schwarz (1996). Kinderlosigkeit in Deutschland: ein Massenphänomen? *Zeitschrift für Bevölkerungswissenschaft*, vol. 21, No. 3, pp. 231-261.

Ebrahim, Shah (2002). Ageing, health and society. *International Journal of Epidemiology*, vol. 31, No. 4, pp. 715-718.

Economic and Social Commission for Western Asia (2002). The Arab Plan of Action on Ageing to the Year 2012, p. 7. Available from http://www.escwa.org.lb/divisions/sdd/activities/aging/poa.pdf (accessed 15 January 2007).

Economic Commission for Latin America and the Caribbean (2000). *Equidad, Desarrollo y Ciudadanía*. Sales No. S.00.II.G.81.

Economic Commission for Latin America and the Caribbean (2006). Shaping the future of social protection: access, financing and solidarity. LC/G.2294(SES.31/3). March.

Economic Policy Committee (2003). Budgetary challenges posed by ageing population: the impact on public spending on education. Brussels, 22 October. EPC/ECFIN/435/03 final. Available from http://ec.europa.eu/economy_finance/epc/documents/2003/awgeducation_en.pdf (accessed 5 March 2007).

Elo, I., and S. Preston (1992). Effects of early-life conditions on adult mortality: a review. *Population Index*, vol. 58, No. 2 (summer), pp. 186-212.

El-Safty, M. (2006). Economic and Social Commission for Western Asia regional contribution to the World Ageing Situation Report 2007. Unpublished paper.

Employment Benefit Research Institute (EBRI) (2006). IRA and KEOGH assets and contributions, and income of the elderly population, age 65 and over, 2004. *EBRI Notes* (Washington, D.C.), vol. 27, No. 1. January.

Engelhardt, Gary V., and Jonathan Gruber (2004). Social security and the evolution of elderly poverty. NBER Working Paper, No. 10466. Cambridge, Massachusetts: National Bureau of Economic Research. May.

European Commission (2001). Reforms of pension systems in the EU: an analysis of the policy options. *European Economy,* No. 73, pp. 171-222.

European Commission (2004). Increasing the employment of older workers and delaying exit from the labour market. Communication from the Commission of 3 March. COM (2004) 146.

European Commission (2005). The economic impact of ageing populations in the EU25 Member States. *Economic Paper*, No. 236. December. Available from http:// ec.europa.eu/economy_finance/publications/economic_papers/2005/ecp236en. pdf (accessed 30 April 2007).

European Commission, Directorate-General for Economic and Financial Affairs (2006). The impact of ageing on public expenditure: projections for the EU 25 Member States on pensions, health care, long-term care, education and unemployment transfers (2004-2005). *European Economy* (Brussels), special report No. 1/2006.

European Foundation for the Improvement of Living and Working Conditions (2006a). *Foundation Focus: Age and Employment*, issue 2 (September). Dublin: European Foundation for the Improvement of Living and Working Conditions.

European Foundation for the Improvement of Living and Working Conditions (2006b). *Age and Employment in the New Member States*. Luxemburg: Office for Official Publications of the European Communities.

European Health Expectancy Monitoring Unit (EHEMU) (2005). Are we living longer, healthier lives in the EU? EHEMU Technical report 2. Montpellier, France. Available from http://www.hs.le.ac.uk/reves/ehemutest/pdf/techrep20507.pdf (accessed 14 August 2006).

Ezzati, Majid and Alan D. Lopez, (2004). Smoking and oral tobacco use. In *Comparative Quantification of Health Risks: Global and Regional Burden of Disease Attributable to Selected Major Risk Factors*, Majid Ezzati, Alan D. Lopez, Anthony Rodgers and Christopher J.L. Murray, eds. Geneva: World Health Organization, pp. 883–956.

Ezzati, Majid, Stephen Vander Hoorn, Carlene M.M. Lawes, Rachel Leach, W. Philip T. James, Alan D. Lopez, Anthony Rodgers and Christopher J.L. Murray (2005). Rethinking the "disease of affluence" paradigm: global patterns of nutritional risks in relation to economic development. *PLoS Medicine*, vol. 2, No. 5 (May), e133. San Francisco, California: Public Library of Science.

Fitzgerald, J. (2005). Progress on the Lisbon Agenda. Paper submitted to the Brussels Economic Forum. 21 April. Dublin: Economic and Social Research Institute.

Fogel, Robert William (2004). Changes in the process of aging during the twentieth century: findings and procedures of the *Early Indicators* project. In *Aging,*

Health and Public Policy: Demographic and Economic Perspectives, Linda J. Waite, ed. Supplement to *Population and Development Review* (Population Council, New York), vol. 30, pp. 19-47.

Forrester Research (2002). 3.3 million US services jobs to go offshore. Forrester Research Brief. 11 November. Authors: John C. McCarthy, Amy Dash, Heather Liddell, Christine Ferrusi Ross and Bruce D. Temkin.

Förster, Michael, and Marco Mira d'Ercole (2005). Income distribution and poverty in OECD countries in the second half of the 1990s. OECD Social, Employment and Migration Working Paper, No. 22. DELSA/ELSA/ED/SEM (2005) 1. 10 March. Paris: Organisation for Economic Co-operation and Development.

Freeman, Richard B. (2006). Is a great labor shortage coming? replacement demand in the global economy. NBER Working Paper, No. 12541. September. Cambridge, Massachusetts: National Bureau of Economic Research. Available from http://www.nber.org/papers/w12541 (accessed on 27 April 2007).

Friedman, Milton (1957). *A Theory of the Consumption Function*. Princeton, New Jersey: Princeton University Press.

Fries, James F. (2005). Compression of morbidity: in retrospect and in prospect. International Longevity Center-USA Issue Brief, vol. 2, No. 2. New York: Mount Sinai School of Medicine.

Garrett, Laurie (2007). The challenge of global health. *Foreign Affairs*, vol. 86, No. 1 (January/February), pp. 14-38.

Gasparini, Leonardo C., Leopoldo Tornarolli, Sergio Olivieri, Francisco Haimovich and Javier Alejo (2007). Poverty among the elderly in Latin America and the Caribbean. Background paper prepared for *World Economic and Social Survey 2007*. January.

Gill, Indermit S., Truman Packard and Juan Yermo (2004). *Keeping the Promise of Social Security in Latin America*. Palo Alto, California, and Washington, D.C.: Stanford University Press and World Bank.

Global Action on Aging (2006a). Argentina: launch of campaign that promotes healthy images of old age. 8 November. Newsletter (December). Article in Spanish. Available from http://www.globalaging.org/elderrights/world/2006/vejezpositiva.htm (accessed 1 January 2007).

Global Action on Aging (2006b). Conference about the situation of older people in Europe: a bet and a change. The contribution of older people. 13 September. Newsletter (September). Available from http://www.globalaging.org/elderrights/world/2006/abetandachance.htm (accessed 31 December 2006).

Gnanasekaran, Kottai S. (2006). Population ageing in the twenty-first century and its implications for the health sector. Paper presented at the International Conference on Emerging Population Issues in the Asian Pacific Region: Challenges for the 21st Century, Mumbai, India, 10-13 December 2006.

Goergen, Thomas (2001). Stress, conflict, elder abuse and neglect in German nursing homes: a pilot study among professional caregivers. *Journal of Elder Abuse & Neglect*, vol. 13, No. 1, pp. 1-26.

Gomes da Conceição, Cristina, and Veronica Montes de Oca Zavala (2004). Ageing in Mexico: families, informal care and reciprocity. In *Living Longer: Ageing,*

Development and Social Protection, Peter Lloyd-Sherlock, ed. London: United Nations Research Institute for Social Development and Zed Books, part III, chap. 11.

Grafstrom, M., A. Nordberg and B. Winblad (1993). Abuse is in the eye of the beholder. *Scandinavian Journal of Social Medicine*, vol. 21, No. 4, pp. 247-253.

Gray, Alastair (2005). Population ageing and health care expenditure. *Ageing Horizons* (Oxford Institute of Ageing, Oxford, United Kingdom), No. 2 (spring-summer), pp. 15-20.

Gruber, Jonathan, and David A. Wise (2005). Social security programs and retirement around the world: fiscal implications: introduction and summary. *NBER Working Paper*, No. 11290. Cambridge, Massachusetts: National Bureau of Economic Research. April.

Hammond Care Group (2003). Community care. Available from http://www.hammond. com.au/communitycare/index.html (accessed 14 December 2006).

Harper, Sarah, and Sue Marcus (2006). Age-related capacity decline: a review of some workplace implications. *Ageing Horizons: Policies for Ageing Societies*, issue 5 (autumn-winter). Oxford, United Kingdom: Oxford Institute of Ageing.

Health Policy and Communications Branch, Health Canada (2001). *Health Expenditures in Canada by Age and Sex, 1980-81 to 2000-01*. August. Ottawa: Health Canada. Available from http://www.hc-sc.gc.ca.

Heinrich, Georges A. (2000). Affluence and poverty in old age: new evidence from the European Community Household Panel. September.

HelpAge International (2001). Talking point: understanding older people's experience. *Ageing and Development*, issue 8 (May).

HelpAge International (2002). *A Generation in Transition: Older People's Situation and Civil Society's Response in East and Central Europe*. London: HelpAge International. May.

HelpAge International (2006a). Surviving with little support. *Ageing and Development*, issue 19 (February), p. 9.

HelpAge International (2006b). Why social pensions are needed now. October. London: HelpAge Inter-national. Available from http://www.globalaging.org/pension/ world/2007/needed.pdf (accessed 15 January 2007).

HelpAge International/Asia Pacific Regional Development Centre (2006). Working draft for discussion: an overview of social pensions in Asia. London. December.

Herlitz, C. (1997). Distribution of informal and formal home help for elderly people in Sweden. *The Gerontologist*, vol. 37, No. 1 (February), pp. 117-123.

Hermalin, Albert I., ed. (2002). *The Well-Being of the Elderly in Asia: A Four-Country Comparative Study*. Ann Arbor, Michigan: University of Michigan Press.

Hinrichs, Karl, and Paula Aleksandrowicz (2005). Active ageing and European pension systems: synthesis report. Bremen, Germany: University of Bremen Centre for Social Policy Research.

Hirsch, Tad, Jodi Forlizzi, Elaine Hyder, Jennifer Goetz, Jacey Stroback and Chris Kurtz (2000). The ELDer project: social, emotional, and environmental factors in the design of eldercare technologies. In *Proceedings on the 2000 Conference on Universal Usability*. Conference held in Arlington, Virginia, 16 and 17 November 2000. New York: ACM Press.

Hirschfeld, Miriam J. (2007). Health and long-term care systems for ageing societies. Background paper prepared for *World Economic and Social Survey 2007*.

Hokenstad, M.C., and L. Johansson (1996). Eldercare in Sweden: issues in service provision and case management. *Journal of Case Study Management*, vol. 5, No. 4, pp. 137-141.

Holzmann, Robert (2005). Demographic alternatives for aging industrial countries: increased total fertility rate, labor force participation, or immigration. World Bank Social Protection Discussion Paper, No. 0540. December. Washington, D.C.: World Bank.

Holzmann, Robert, and Richard Hinz (2005). *Old-Age Income Support in the 21st Century: An International Perspective on Pension Systems and Reform*. Washington, D.C.: World Bank.

Homer, A.C., and C. Gilleard (1990). Abuse of elderly people by their caregivers. *British Medical Journal*, vol. 301, No. 6765, pp. 1359-1362.

Horioka C.Y. (1989). Why is Japan's private saving rate so high? In *Developments in Japanese Economics*, R. Sato and T. Negishi, eds. Tokyo: Academic Press.

Horizon Foundation (2005). Aging-in-place initiative. Available from http://www.thehorizon foundation.org/ht/d/sp/i/1398/pid/1398 (accessed 8 January 2007). Columbia, Maryland: Horizon Foundation.

Howse, Kenneth (2006). Pension reform and age of retirement rules. *Ageing Horizons: Policies for Ageing Societies*, issue 5 (autumn-winter). Oxford, United Kingdom: Oxford Institute of Ageing.

Hua, Fu, and Xue Di (2002). Case study: China. In *Long-Term Care in Developing Countries: Ten Case-Studies*, Jenny Brodsky, Jack Habib and Miriam Hirschfeld, eds. Geneva: World Health Organization.

Iecovich, E., M. Lankri and D. Drori (2005). Elder abuse and neglect: a pilot incidence study in Israel. *Journal of Elder Abuse & Neglect*, vol. 16, No. 3, pp. 45-63.

International Institute for Democracy and Electoral Assistance (2006a). Voter turnout by age. Available from http://www.idea.int/vt/by_age.cfm (accessed 19 March 2007).

International Institute for Democracy and Electoral Assistance (2006b). Voter turnout statistics by age from the National Elections Commission, Liberia. Available from http://www.idea.nt/vt/by_age.cfm (accessed 19 March 2007).

International Labour Office (2004a). *HIV/AIDS and Work: Global Estimates, Impact and Response*. Geneva: International Labour Organization, ILO Programme on HIV/AIDS and the world of work.

International Labour Office (2004b). Global employment trends for women 2004. March. Geneva.

International Labour Office (2004c). *World Employment Report: Employment, Productivity and Poverty Reduction*. Geneva: International Labour Organization.

International Labour Office (2005a). Global employment trends brief. February. Geneva.

International Labour Office (2005b). *Key Indicators of the Labour Market*, 4th ed. Geneva.

International Labour Office (2006). *Changing Patterns in the World of Work: Report of the Director-General*. International Labour Conference, 95th Session 2006: report I (c). Geneva.

International Labour Organization (1975). Recommendation Concerning Vocational Guidance and Vocational Training in the Development of Human Resources. (Human Resources Development Recommendation), No. 150, adopted 23 June 1975. In *International Labour Conventions and Recommendations, 1952-1976* (vol. II). Geneva: International Labour Office, sect. II, pp. 572-602.

International Labour Organization (2002). Facts on social security. Geneva: International Labour Office. Available from http://www.ilo.org/public/english/protection/secsoc/downloads/events/factsheet.pdf (accessed 4 May 2007).

International Longevity Center-USA (2006). Ageism in America. New York: Anti-Ageism Taskforce at the International Longevity Center.

International Monetary Fund (2003). *Global Financial Stability Report: Market Developments and Issues*, March 2003. Washington, D.C.: International Monetary Fund.

International Monetary Fund (2005). *Global Financial Stability Report: Market Developments and Issues*, September 2005. Washington, D.C.: International Monetary Fund.

Jamison, Dean T., Joel G. Breman, and Anthony R. Mesham (2006). *Disease Control Priorities in Developing Countries,* 2nd ed. Washington, D.C., and New York: World Bank and Oxford University Press. Also available from http://www.dcp2.org/page/main/ViewPublications.html.

Jensen, Per H. (2005). Reversing the trend from "early" to "late" exit: push, pull and jump revisited in the Danish context. *The Geneva Papers on Risk and Insurance: Issues and Practice,* vol. 30, No. 4 (October), pp.656-673.

Johnson, Jessica K.M., and John B. Williamson (2006). Do universal non-contributory old-age pensions make sense for rural areas in low-income countries? *International Social Security Review,* vol. 59, No. 4, pp. 47-65.

Kakwani, Nanak, and Kalanidhi Subbarao (2005). Ageing and poverty in Africa and the role of social pensions. *International Poverty Centre Working Paper*, No. 8. August. Brasília: United Nations Development Programme International Poverty Centre.

Kinsella, Kevin, and David R. Phillips (2005). Global aging: the challenge of success. *Population Bulletin* (Population Reference Bureau, Washington, D.C.), vol. 60, No. 1 (March).

Kinsella, Kevin, and Victoria A. Velkoff (2001). *An Aging World: 2001.* U.S. Census Bureau, Series p 95/01-1. Washington, D.C.: U.S. Government Printing Office.

Kivelä, Sirkka-Liisa, Päivi Köngäs-Saviaro, Erkki Kesti, Kimmo Pahkala and Maija-Liisa Ijäs (1992). Abuse in old age: epidemiological data from Finland. *Journal of Elder Abuse & Neglect*, vol. 4, No. 3, pp. 1-18.

Knaul, Felicia, Gustavo Nigenda, Miguel Angel Ramírez, Ana Cristina Torres, Ana Mylena Aguilar, Mariana Lopez Ortega and José Luis Torres (2002). Case study: Mexico. In *Long-Term Care in Developing Countries: Ten Case-Studies*, Jenny Brodksy, Jack Habib and Miriam Hirschfeld, eds. Geneva: World Health Organization.

Lee, Ronald, and Andrew Mason (2007). Population aging, wealth, and economic growth: demographic dividends and public policy. Background paper prepared for *World Economic and Social Survey 2007.*

Leeson, George (2006). The employment equality age regulations and beyond. *Ageing Horizons: Policies for Ageing Societies*, issue 5 (autumn-winter). Oxford, United Kingdom: Oxford Institute of Ageing.

Lehman, H. (1953). *Age and Achievement*. Princeton, New Jersey: Princeton University Press.

Leung, A., Y.H. Lui and I. Chi (2005). Later life learning experience among Chinese elderly in Hong Kong. *Gerontology and Geriatrics Education*, vol. 26, No. 2, pp.1-15.

Leung, Gabriel, Keith Tin and Wai-Sum Chan (2007). Hong Kong's health spending projections through 2033. *Health Policy*, vol. 81, No. 1 (April), pp.93-101.

Levinsky, Norman G., Wei Yu, Arlene Ash, Mark Moskowitz, Gail Gazelle, Olga Saynina and Ezekiel J. Emanuel (2001). Influence of age on Medicare expenditures and medical care in the last year of life. *Journal of the American Medical Association*, vol. 286, No. 11 (September), pp. 1349-1355.

Levy, B.R., M.D. Slade, S.R. Kunkel and S.V. Kasl (2002). Longevity increased by positive self-perceptions of aging. *Journal of Personality and Social Psychology*, vol. 83, No. 2, pp. 261-270.

Lichtenberg, F. (1992). R&D investment and international productivity differences. NBER Working Paper, No. 4161. Cambridge, Massachusetts: National Bureau of Economic Research.

Lieras-Muney, A. (2007). A surprising secret to long life: stay in school. *The New York Times*, 3 January.

Lloyd-Sherlock, Peter (2000). Population ageing in developed and developing regions: implications for health policy. *Social Science and Medicine*, vol. 51, No. 6 (15 September), pp. 887-895.

Lloyd-Sherlock, Peter (2004a). Ageing, development and social protection: generalizations, myths and stereotypes. In *Living Longer: Ageing, Development and Social Protection*, Peter Lloyd-Sherlock, ed. London: United Nations Research Institute for Social Development and Zed Books.

Lloyd-Sherlock, Peter, ed. (2004b). *Living Longer: Ageing, Development and Social Protection*. London: United Nations Research Institute for Social Development and Zed Books.

Lloyd-Sherlock, Peter (2006). Identifying vulnerable older people: insights from Thailand. *Ageing and Society*, vol. 26, No. 1, pp. 81-103.

Lührmann, Melanie (2005). Population ageing and the demand for goods and services. Mannheim Research Institute for the Economics of Ageing. Discussion Paper, No. 95-05. Mannheim, Germany: Department of Economics, Universität Mannheim.

Mahal, Ajay, and Peter Berman (2001). Health expenditures and the elderly: a survey of issues in forecasting, methods used, and relevance for developing countries. Center for Population and Development Studies, Harvard Burden of Disease Unit, Cambridge, Massachusetts. December. Unpublished.

Mahal, Ajay (2006). Health expenditures on the elderly in India and their financing: future prospects. May. Unpublished.

Mahoney, Melissa, William Milberg, Markus Schneider and Rudi von Arnim (2006). Spurring growth dynamics from services offshoring. Schwartz Center for Economic Policy and Analysis (SCEPA) policy note. February. New York: The New School. Available from http://newschool.edu/cepa/publications/index. htm#Policy Notes (accessed 24 April 2007).

Maitland, Alison (2007). Make ready for the mother of all job changes. *Financial Times*, 2 April.

Mankiw, N., D. Romer and D. Weil (1992). A contribution to the empirics of economic growth. *Quarterly Journal of Economics*, vol. 107, No. 2, pp. 407-437.

Mann, Catherine L. (2003). Globalization of IT services and white collar jobs: the next wave of productivity growth. International Economics Policy Briefs, No. PB03-11. December. Washington, D.C.: Peter G. Peterson Institute for International Economics, December.

Mathers, Colin D., and Dejan Loncar (2006). Projections of global mortality and burden of disease from 2002 to 2030. *PLoS Medicine*, vol. 3, No. 11 (28 November). San Francisco, California: Public Library of Science.

Mathers, C.D., K.M. Iburg, J.A. Salomon, A. Tandon, S. Chatterji, B. Ustün and C.J. Murray (2004). Global patterns of healthy life expectancy in the year 2002. *BMC Public Health*, vol. 4, No. 66.

Mathiason, John R. (2003). An international perspective on aging and the end of life. *Home Health Care Management and Practice*, vol. 15, No. 2 (February), pp. 100-104.

McKay, Stephen, and Sue Middleton (1998). *Characteristics of Older Workers: Secondary Analysis of the Family and Working Lives Survey.* Research Brief RB 45. Suffolk, United Kingdom: Department for Education and Employment.

Meyer, S., and H. Mollenkopf (2003). Home technology, smart homes, and the aging user. In *Aging Independently: Living Arrangements and Mobility*, K.Warner Schaie, Hans Werner-Wahl, Heidrum Mollenkopf, and Frank Oswald, eds., New York: Springer.

Miniaci, Raffaele, Chiara Monfardini and Gugliemo Weber (2003). Is there a retirement consumption puzzle in Italy? *IFS Working Paper*, No. 03/14. July. London: Institute for Fiscal Studies.

Modigliani, Franco, and Richard Brumberg (1954). Utility analysis and the consumption function: an interpretation of the cross-section data. In *Post-Keynesian Economics*, Kenneth K. Kurihara, ed. New Brunswick, New Jersey: Rutgers University Press, pp. 388-436.

Morgan, D.L., T.L. Schuster and E.W. Butler (1991). Role reversals in the exchange of social support. *Journal of Gerontology* (Washington, D.C.), vol. 46, No. 5, pp. 5278-5287.

Mosisa, Abraham, and Steven Hipple (2006). Trends in labor force participation in the United States. *Monthly Labor Review*, vol. 129, No. 6 (October).

Munnell, Alicia H. (2006). Policies to promote labour force participation of older people. Work Opportunities for Older Americans Series Working Paper, No. 2. CRR WP 2006-2. January. Chestnut Hill, Massachusetts: Center for Retirement Research at Boston College.

National Commission for Enterprises in the Unorganised Sector (2006). Report on social security for unorganised workers presented to the Prime Minister. New Delhi: Government of India. Available from http://nceus.gov.in/ (accessed 15 October 2006).

Newhouse, Joseph P. (1992). Medical care cost: how much welfare loss? *Journal of Economic Perspectives*, vol. 6, No. 3 (summer), pp. 3-21.

Nishimura, Kiyohiko G., Kazunori Minetaki, Masato Shirai and Futoshi Kur (2002). Effects of information technology and aging work force on labor demand and technological progress in Japanese industries: 1980-1998. Discussion paper CIRJE-F-145. January. Tokyo: Faculty of Economics, University of Tokyo.

Novelli, William D. (2005). From the CEO: nurturing communities. In Global report on aging (summer). Available from http://www.aarp.org/research/international/gra/gra_special_05/. Washington, D.C.: AARP.

Ocampo, José Antonio (2005). A broader view of macroeconomic stability. DESA Working Paper, No. 1. Department of Economic and Social Affairs of the United Nations Secretariat. October. Available from http://www.un.org/esa/desa/papers/2005/wpl_2005.pdf (accessed 14 May 2007).

Ocampo, José Antonio, and Rob Vos (2006) Policy space and the changing paradigm in conducting macroeconomic policies in developing countries, Paper presented at FONDAD-UN/DESA seminar on 'Policy Space for Developing Countries in a Globalized World, New York, 7-9 December.

Ocampo, José Antonio, and Rob Vos (2007) *Uneven Economic Development*, Hyderabad, London, New York: Orient Longman, Zed Books, TWN.

Ocampo, José Antonio, Jomo K.S., and Rob Vos (eds) (2007) *Growth Divergences: Explaining Differences in Economic Performance*, Hyderabad, London, New York: Orient Longman, Zed Books, TWN.

Office for an Ageing Australia (2004). Media resources: positive images gallery. Australian Government Department of Health and Ageing. Available from http://www.health.gov.au/internet/wcms/publishing.nsf/Content/ageing-ofoa-media_resources-gallery-index.htm (accessed 1 January 2007).

Ofstedal, Mary Beth, and Josefina N. Natividad (2002). Patterns of health care utilization. In *The Well-Being of the Elderly in Asia: A Four-Country Comparative Study*, Albert I. Hermalin, ed. Ann Arbor, Michigan: University of Michigan Press.

Ogawa, Naohiro, Robert Clark and Andrew Mason (2006). Population aging and health care spending in Japan: public- and private-sector responses. Mimeo. 12 December.

Ogg, J. (1993). Researching elder abuse in Britain. *Journal of Elder Abuse & Neglect*, vol. 5, No. 2, pp. 37-54.

Oppong, Christine (2006). Familial roles and social transformations: older men and women in sub-Saharan Africa. *Research on Ageing*, vol. 28, No. 6 (November).

Organisation for Economic Co-operation and Development (2005). Pension Markets in Focus (Newsletter), issue 2 (December). Paris: Organisation for Economic Co-operation and Development.

Organisation for Economic Co-operation and Development (2006a). *Live Longer, Work Longer*. Paris: Organisation for Economic Co-operation and Development.

Organisation for Economic Co-operation and Development (2006b). Projecting OECD health and long-term care expenditures: what are the main drivers? Economics Department Working Paper No. 477. ECO/WKP(2006)5. Paris: Organisation for Economic Co-operation and Development.

Organisation for Economic Co-operation and Development (2007). Social Expenditure Database (SOCX). Available from http://ww.oecd.org/els/social/expenditure.

Paes de Barros, Ricardo, Rosane Mendonça and Daniel Santos (1999). Incidência e natureza da pobreza entre idosos no Brasil. *IPEA Texto para Discussão*, No. 686 (Dezembro). Rio de Janeiro: Instituto de Pesquisa Economica Aplicada.

Palacios, Roberto, and Oleksiy Sluchnysky (2006). Social pensions part I: their role in the overall pension system. *World Bank Social Protection Discussion Paper*, No. 601. Washington, D.C.: World Bank.

Palacios, Roberto, and Montserrat Pallarès-Miralles (2000). International patterns of pension provision. *World Bank Social Protection Discussion Paper*, No. 9. Washington, D.C.: World Bank.

Paveza, G.J., D. Cohen, C. Eisdorfer, S. Freels, T. Semla, J.W. Ashford, P. Gorelick, R. Hirschman, D. Luchins and P. Levy (1992). Severe family violence and Alzheimer's disease: prevalence and risk factors. *The Gerontologist*, vol. 32, No. 4, pp. 493-497.

Pelaez, M. (2006). Well-being and health in Latin America and the Caribbean: policy priorities for the implementation of the International Plan of Action on Ageing. Unpublished paper.

Peterson, Peter G. (2002). The challenge of global ageing. *Les Cahiers de la FIAPA: Action Research on Ageing*, No. 2 (December): *Grey Power?* vol. 1, *Political Power and Influence*, pp. 16-26.

Phillips, L.R. (1983). Abuse and neglect of the frail elderly at home: an exploration of theoretical relationships. *Journal of Advanced Nursing*, vol. 8, No. 5 (September), pp. 379-392.

Phua, Kai Hong and Yap Mui Teng (1998). Financing health care in old age: a case study of Singapore. In *Choices in Financing Health Care and Old Age Security: Proceedings of a Conference Sponsored by the Institute of Policy Studies, Singapore, and the World Bank, November 8, 1997*, Nicholas Prescott, ed. *World Bank Discussion Paper*, No. 392. Washington, D.C.: World Bank.

Pillemer, K., and J.J. Suitor (1992). Violence and violent feelings: what causes them among family caregivers? *Journal of Gerontology*, vol. 47, No. 4 (July), pp. S165-S172.

Podnieks, E. (1992). National survey on abuse of the elderly in Canada. *Journal of Elder Abuse & Neglect*, vol. 4 (1/2), pp. 5-58.

Podnieks, E., G. Anetzberger, and P. B. Teaster (2006). International Network for the Prevention of Elder Abuse: preliminary findings from a worldwide environment scan. Paper presented at the Annual Scientific Meeting of the Gerontological Society of America, Dallas, Texas.

Productivity Commission, Government of Australia (2005). *Economic Implications of an Ageing Australia*. Research Report. Canberra. 24 March.

Prskawetz, A., T. Fent and R. Guest (2005). Workforce aging and labor productivity: the role of supply and demand Purdie, Nola, and Gillian Boulton-Lewis (2003).

The learning needs of older adults. *Educational Gerontology*, vol. 29, No. 2 (February), pp. 129-149.

Qaio, X. (2005). Changes in the perceived health expectancy of the elderly in China, from 1992 to 2000. Paper presented at the seventeenth meeting of the International Network on Health Expectancy (REVES), Beijing, 18-20 May 2005.

RAND (2005). Population implosion? low fertility and policy responses in the European Union. RAND Corporation research brief series. Cambridge, United Kingdom: RAND Europe.

Rannan-Eliya, Ravi P. (2007). Population ageing and health expenditure: Sri Lanka 2001-2101. Institute for Health Policy, Colombo. Background paper prepared for *World Economic and Social Survey 2007*. February.

Rannan-Eliya, Claudia Blanco-Vidal and A. K. Nandakumar (1998). The distribution of health care resources in Egypt: implications for equity: an analysis using a national health accounts framework. Available from http://www.hsph.harvard.edu/ihsg/publications/pdf/No-81.PDF (accessed 3 November 2006).

Rannan-Eliya, and Ruki Wijesinghe (2006). Global review of projecting health expenditures for older persons in developing countries. Institute for Health Policy, Colombo. 25 August. Monograph prepared for WHO Kobe Centre, Kobe Japan.

Reay, A.M., and K.D. Browne (2001). Risk factors for caregivers who physically abuse or neglect their elderly dependents. *Aging and Mental Health*, vol. 5, No. 1, pp. 56-62.

Reis, M., and D. Nahmiash, (1998). Validation of the indicators of abuse (IOA) screen. *The Gerontologist*, vol. 38, No. 4 (August), pp. 471-480.

Rofman, Rafael (2005). Social security coverage in Latin America. May. Washington, D.C.: World Bank, Social Protection Unit, Human Development Network.

Romer, P. (1986). Increasing returns and long-run growth. *Journal of Political Economy*, vol. 94, No. 5, pp. 1002-1037.

Romero, Dalia Elena, Iúri da Costa Leite and Célia Landmann Szwarcwald (2005). Healthy life expectancy in Brazil: applying the Sullivan method. *Cadernos de Saúde Pública* (Rio de Janeiro), vol. 21, Supplement 1, pp. S7-S18.

Saad, Paulo M. (2001). Support transfers between elderly parents and adult children in two Brazilian settings (CD-ROM). Paper presented at the Twenty-fourth IUSSP General Population Conference, Salvador de Bahia, Brazil, 18-24 August 2001. Paris: International Union for the Scientific Study of Population.

Samson, Michael (2006). Tackling poverty with social transfers to vulnerable groups: evidence from Africa. International Forum on the Eradication of Poverty: UNICEF session on "Children and poverty", New York City, 15 and 16 November 2006.

Schaffnit-Chatterjee, Claire (2007). How will senior Germans spend their money? the interplay of demography, growth and changing preference. *Deutsche Bank Research*. 27 March. Frankfurt au Main, Germany: Deutsche Bank AG.

Schieber, George, and Akiko Maeda (1999). Health care financing and delivery in developing countries. *Health Affairs*, vol. 18, No. 3 (May/June), pp. 193-205.

Schwarz, Anita and Asli Demirguç-Kunt (1999). Taking stock of pension reforms around the world. World Bank Social Protection Discussion Paper, No. 9917. Washington, D.C.: World Bank.

Sengupta, Arjun (2007). A socially secure unorganized worker. Background paper prepared for *World Economic and Social Survey 2007*. January.

Shah, Ajay (2005). A sustainable and scalable approach in Indian pension reform. Available from http://www.mayin.org/ajayshah/pensions.html (accessed 5 November 2006).

Skirbekk, Vegard (2003). Age and individual productivity: a literature survey. MPIDR Working Paper WP 2003-028. August. Rostock, Germany: Max Planck Institute for Demographic Research.

Smith, Sarah (2004). Can the retirement consumption puzzle be resolved? Evidence from UK panel data. *IFS Working Paper*, No. WP04/07. London: Institute for Fiscal Studies.

Social Security Administration (2006). Income of the aged chartbook, 2004. SSA Publication No. 13-11727. Washington, D.C. September.

Sperling, G. (2004). The effects of offshoring. Progressive Politics, vol. 3, No. 2. June. Available from http://www.americanprogress.org/site/pp.asp?bijrj8ovf&b=105690.

Sundstrom, G. (1994). Care by families: an overview of trends. In *Caring for Frail Elderly People*. Social Policy Studies, New Directions in Care, No. 14. Paris: Organisation for Economic Co-operation and Development.

Sweden, Ministry of Health and Social Affairs (2005). Policy for the elderly. Fact sheet No. 14 (May). Stockholm.

Taeuber, Cynthia. M. (1992). Sixty-five plus in America. Current Population Reports, Special Studies, P23-178. Washington, D. C.: United States Bureau of the Census.

Thompson, L.H. (2001). Operation of pension systems: public or private? In *Social Protection in Asia and the Pacific*, Isabel D. Ortiz, ed. Manila: Asian Development Bank.

Thursz, Daniel, Charlotte Nusberg and Johnnie Prater (1995). *Empowering Older People: An International Approach*. Westport, Connecticut: Auburn House.

Tornstam, L. (1989). Abuse of the elderly in Denmark and Sweden: results from a population study. *Journal of Elder Abuse & Neglect*, vol. 1, No. 1, pp. 35-44.

Turner, Adair (2003). The macro-economics of pensions. Lecture to the Actuarial Profession at Staple Inn Hall, London, on 2 September 2003.

UNAIDS (2006). 2006 report on the global AIDS epidemic. Geneva: Joint United Nations programme on HIV/AIDS.

UNAIDS, and World Health Organization (2006). *AIDS Epidemic Update: December 2006*. Geneva: Joint United Nations Programme on HIV/AIDS and World Health Organization.

United Kingdom (1999). *With Respect to Old Age: Long Term Care – Rights and Responsibilities*. A Report by the Royal Commission on Long Term Care, Chairman Professor Sir Stewart Sutherland. Cm 4192-I. March. London: The Stationery Office.

United Nations (1982). *Report of the World Assembly on Ageing, Vienna, 26 July to 6 August 1982.* Sales No. E.82.I.16, chap. VI, sect. A. Also available from http://www.un.org/esa/socdev/ageing/ageing/ageipaa.htm.

United Nations (1997a). *Older Persons in Countries with Economies in Transition: Designing a Policy Response. Guidelines for Practical Strategies.* Sales No. E.96.IV.12.

United Nations (1997b). *Report on the World Social Situation.* Sales No. E.97.IV.1 and corrigenda.

United Nations (1998). *World Population Monitoring 1997: International Migration and Development.* Sales No. E.98.XIII.4.

United Nations (1999). *World Population Prospects: The 1998 Revision,* vol. I, *Comprehensive Tables,* and vol. II, *Sex and Age.* Sales Nos. E.99.XIII.9 and E.99.XIII.8.

United Nations (2000). *The World's Women 2000: Trends and Statistics.* Social Statistics and Indicators, No. 16. Sales No. E.00.XVII.14.

United Nations (2001). *Replacement Migration: Is It a Solution to Declining and Ageing Populations?* Sales No. E.01.XIII.19.

United Nations (2002a). *Report of the Second World Assembly on Ageing, Madrid, 8-12 April 2002.* Sales No. E.02.IV.4, chap. I, resolution 1, annexes I and II.

United Nations (2002b). *World Population Ageing 1950-2050.* Sales No. E.02.XIII.3.

United Nations (2003). *Major Trends Affecting Families: A Background Document.* Sales No. E.06.IV.4.

United Nations (2004a). *World Population to 2300.* Sales No. E.04.XIII.11.

United Nations (2004b). *Population Bulletin of the United Nations: Policy Responses to Population Decline and Ageing.* Special Issue, Nos. 44/45 (2002). Sales No. E.02.XIII.4.

United Nations (2005a). *World Population Prospects: The 2004 Revision,* vol. I, *Comprehensive Tables,* and vol. II, *Sex and Age Distribution of the World Population.* Sales Nos. E.05.XIII.5 and E.05.XIII.6.

United Nations (2005b). *Living Arrangements of Older Persons Around the World.* Sales No. E.05.XIII.9.

United Nations (2005c). Background note for the International Technical Workshop on Indigenous Traditional Knowledge, Panama City, 21-23 September 2005, prepared by the secretariat of the Permanent Forum on Indigenous Issues, Division for Social Policy and Development, Department of Economic and Social Affairs. PFII/2005/WS/TK.

United Nations (2005d). *World Economic and Social Survey 2005: Financing for Development.* Sales No. E.05.II.C.1

United Nations (2006a). *World Economic and Social Survey 2006: Diverging Growth and Development.* Sales No. E.06.II.C.1

United Nations (2006b). *World Population Prospects: The 2004 Revision,* vol. III, *Analytical Report.* Sales No. E.05.XIII.7.

United Nations Centre for Human Settlements (Habitat) (1999). *Living Conditions of Low-income Older Persons in Human Settlements.* HS/758/05E.

United Nations Development Programme and United Nations Population Fund (2005). The great generation of Kazakhstan: insight into the future. National Human Development Report for 2005. Almaty.

United Nations Population Fund (2006). Population ageing in Thailand: prognosis and policy response. October. Bangkok: UNFPA, Thailand.

U.S. Census Bureau (1992). An aging world II. International Population Reports, P95/92-3. Washington, D.C.: United States Government Printing Office.

U.S. Census Bureau (2005). Current Population Survey 1968 to 2004. Table A.9: Reported voting rates in presidential election years, by selected characteristics: November 1964 to 2004. Available from http://www.census.gov/population/socdemo/voting/tabA-9.xls (accessed 19 March 2007). Internet release date 26 May 2005.

U.S. Census Bureau (2006). Current Population Reports, P60-231, *Income, Poverty, and Health Insurance Coverage in the United States: 2005*. Authors: Carmen DeNavas-Walt, Bernadette D. Proctor and Cheryl Hill Lee. August. Washington, D.C.: U.S. Government Printing Office.

van der Gaag, Jacques, and Alexander Preker (1998). Health care for aging populations: issues and options. In *Choices in Financing Health Care and Old Age Security: Proceedings of a Conference Sponsored by the Institute of Policy Studies, Singapore, and the World Bank, November 8, 1997*, Nicholas Prescott, ed. *World Bank Discussion Paper*, No. 392. Washington, D.C.: World Bank.

Van Nieuwerburgh, Stijn, and Laura Veldkamp (2006). Inside information and the own company stock puzzle. *Journal of the European Economic Association*, vol. 4, Nos. 2-3 (April-May), pp. 623-633.

Victor, C.R. (1994). *Old Age in Modern Society: A Textbook of Social Gerontology*. London: Chapman & Hall.

Vittas, D. (1995). Pension funds and capital markets. Mimeo. Washington, D.C.: World Bank.

Vladeck, Fredda (2004). *A Good Place to Grow Old: New York's Model for NORC Supportive Service Programs*. New York: United Hospital Fund.

Vos, Theo, John Goss, Stephen Begg, and Nicholas Mann (2007). Projection of health care expenditure by disease: a case study from Australia. Background paper prepared for *World Economic and Social Survey 2007*. January.

Weil, David N. (1994). The saving of the elderly in micro and macro data. *Quarterly Journal of Economics*, vol. 109, No. 1 (February), pp. 55-81.

Weisbrod, Burton A. (1991). The health care quadrilemma: an essay on technological change, insurance, quality of care, and cost containment. *Journal of Economic Literature*, vol. 29, No. 2 (June), pp. 523-552.

Whitehouse, Edward (2000). How poor are the old? a survey of evidence from 44 countries. World Bank Social Protection Discussion Paper Series, No. 0017. June. Washington, D.C.: Social Protection Unit, Human Development Network, World Bank.

Willmore, Larry, (2006). Universal pensions for developing countries. May. Laxenburg, Austria: International Institute for Applied Systems Analysis. Available from http://www.geocities.com/larrywillmore/UniversalWD.pdf (accessed 15 January 2007).

Wolf, Rosalie S., Michael A. Godkin, and Karl A. Pillemer (1984). Elder abuse and neglect: final report from three model projects. Worcester, Massachusetts: University of Massachusetts Medical Center, University Center on Aging.

World Bank (1994). *Averting the Old Age Crisis: Policies to Protect the Old and Promote Growth*. New York: Oxford University Press.

World Bank (2005). *2005 World Development Indicators*. Washington, D.C.: World Bank.

World Bank (2006a). *2006 World Development Indicators*. Washington, D.C.: World Bank.

World Bank (2006b). *Health Financing Revisited: A Practitioner's Guide*. Authored by Pablo Gottret and George Schieber. Washington, D.C.: World Bank.

World Health Organization (2000). Long-term care laws in five developed countries: a review. WHO/NMH/CCL/00.2. September.

World Health Organization (2002a). *World Report on Violence and Health*, Etienne G. Krug, LindaL. Dahlberg, James A. Mercy, Anthony B. Zwiand and Rafael Lozano. Geneva: World Health Organization.

World Health Organization (2002b). Current and future long-term care needs: an analysis based on the 1990 WHO study the Global Burden of Disease and the International Classification of Functioning, Disability and Health. WHO/NMH/CCL/02.2.

World Health Organization (2002c). *Long-Term Care in Developing Countries: Ten Case-Studies*, Jenny Brodsky, Jack Habib and Miriam Hirschfeld, eds. The World Health Organization Collection on Long-Term Care. Geneva: World Health Organization.

World Health Organization (2002d). *Community Home-based Care in Resource-Limited Settings: A Framework for Action*. Collaboration of the Cross Cluster Initiative on Home-Based Long-Term Care, Non-Communicable Diseases and Mental Health; and the Department of HIV/AIDS, Family and Community Health. Geneva: World Health Organization.

World Health Organization (2002e). Active ageing: a policy framework. WHO/NMH/NPH/02.8.

World Health Organization (2005). *Preventing Chronic Disease: A Vital Investment*. Geneva: World Health Organization.

World Health Organization (2006a). *World Health Report 2006: Working Together for Health*. Geneva: World Health Organization.

World Health Organization (2006b). Projections of mortality and burden of disease to 2030 (data file). Available fromhttp://www.who.int/entity/healthinfo/statistics/bod_deathbyincome.xls (accessed 5 January 2007).

Zaidi, Asghar (2006). Pension policy in EU25 and its possible impact on elderly poverty. European Centre for Social Welfare Policy and Research Policy Brief. September. Vienna.

Zimmer, Zachary, and Julia Dayton (2003). The living arrangements of older adults in sub-Saharan Africa in a time of HIV/AIDS. Policy Research Division Working Paper, No. 169. New York: Population Council.

Index